Contemporary Issues in Finance, Investment and Banking in Malaysia

Zulkefly Abdul Karim · Ruzita Abdul Rahim ·
Wai Yan Wong · Siti Farah Dilla Zakaria
Editors

Contemporary Issues in Finance, Investment and Banking in Malaysia

Springer

Editors
Zulkefly Abdul Karim
Faculty of Economics and Management
Universiti Kebangsaan Malaysia
Bangi, Selangor, Malaysia

Ruzita Abdul Rahim
Faculty of Economics and Management
Universiti Kebangsaan Malaysia
Bangi, Selangor, Malaysia

Wai Yan Wong
Faculty of Economics and Management
Universiti Kebangsaan Malaysia
Bangi, Selangor, Malaysia

Siti Farah Dilla Zakaria
Faculty of Economics and Management
Universiti Kebangsaan Malaysia
Bangi, Selangor, Malaysia

ISBN 978-981-99-5446-9 ISBN 978-981-99-5447-6 (eBook)
https://doi.org/10.1007/978-981-99-5447-6

This Springer imprint is published by the registered company Springer Nature Singapore Pte Ltd.
The registered company address is: 152 Beach Road, #21-01/04 Gateway East, Singapore 189721, Singapore

Foreword

It is with great pleasure that I introduce this collection of articles, a collaborative effort by researchers from leading institutions in Malaysia. This anthology delves into the contemporary issues in capital investments, investment in equities and cryptocurrencies and Islamic banking, with a special focus on the Malaysian market and the influence of recent technological advancements and disruptive forces.

The collection begins with a systematic review of the literature on the role of technological revolution in corporate governance, emphasising the use of blockchain and smart contracts to mitigate information asymmetry and enhance governance practices.

A series of articles provide empirical observations on investments in Malaysian companies. One study highlights the positive relationship between market sentiment and capital investments, where optimistic market sentiment fosters optimism among firms, and increased long-term investments, while periods of pessimism lead to decreased capital expenditure. Another article examines the cross-section of returns in the Malaysian stock market, revealing significant positive size and dividend premia. Additionally, the impact of the COVID-19 pandemic on returns on the aggregate Malaysian stock market and its sectoral indices are investigated.

Subsequent articles analyse the volatile cryptocurrency market. The first of these introduces a comparative analysis of cryptocurrencies and stocks, offering foundational perspectives for beginners navigating these alternative investment choices. Additional articles explore the impact of the COVID-19 pandemic on the performance of cryptocurrencies and examine the interaction of Bitcoin with interest rates and exchange rate movements in countries, including United States, China and Malaysia.

In the realm of Islamic banking, the anthology explores the evolving landscape of fintech and its behavioural impact. One article presents a systematic overview on the effect of Fintech and financial literacy on the adoption of Islamic banking products and services. The collection also probes more specialised topics such as online investment adoption, financial literacy within Islamic banking and the ethical banking behaviour of millennials and Generation Z in Malaysia.

Throughout the collection, the authors provide extensive discussion of the literature and employ various research methodologies, including systematic literature reviews and empirical models, to ensure rigorous analyses. These chapters offer insights into the Malaysian equity market, cryptocurrencies and the changing landscape of financial services industry, elucidating their implications for market players. They demonstrate the growing expertise within the Malaysian research community.

I envision the collection to be beneficial to students and researchers interested in investments and Islamic banking, particularly those focusing on the Malaysian context. I commend the authors and editors for their dedication in assembling this timely and useful anthology. It is a testament to their commitment to advancing knowledge in these critical areas.

Allaudeen Hameed
Tan Peng Yue Professor of Finance
National University of Singapore
Singapore
Chairholder of Tun Ismail Mohamed
Ali Distinguished Chair (YTI-UKM)
2022–2023, Universiti Kebangsaan
Malaysia, Bangi, Selangor, Malaysia

Preface

This book is a collection of the works that have been conducted by experienced researchers at Universiti Kebangsaan Malaysia (UKM), Universiti Sains Malaysia (USM), Universiti Malaysia Sarawak (UNIMAS), Universiti Malaysia Terengganu (UMT), Universiti Malaya (UM), Universiti Putra Malaysia (UPM), Ministry of Finance Malaysia (MoF), and Hong Leong Bank Berhad. The main idea is started based on the collaboration between the Faculty of Economics and Management, Universiti Kebangsaan Malaysia and Tun Ismail Mohamed Ali Distinguished Chair (YTI-UKM). The main ideas of this book tackle the contemporary issues on finance, investment and banking. The first two chapters focus on the issues of corporate finance which examine the information asymmetric and corporate governance during the era of Industrial Revolution (IR) 4.0 and the impact of market sentiment on business fixed investment (capital expenditure). The subsequent five chapters cover issues on investment and stock market which include the comparison of cryptocurrency and stock as the investment tool and how the COVID-19 pandemic affected the stock market and cryptocurrency. The final three chapters delve into the banking and investment behaviour in the banking industry amidst the disruption of financial technology (fintech) and fintech start-ups. Various methodologies are used in this book such as systematic literature review (SLR) and empirical modelling that can be beneficial for policymakers and relevant agencies. The editors would like to express their gratitude to all the contributing authors for their great efforts and full dedication in preparing the manuscripts for the book. We would like to thank all reviewers for reviewing all manuscripts and providing very constructive feedback. This research book is also funded by various research grants such as YTI Industrial Grant (code project: EP-2020-005, EP-2020-003), Ministry of Higher Education Malaysia (code project: FRGS/1/2018/SS01/UKM/02/2, FRGS/1/2021/SS01/UKM/02/4) and Faculty of Economics and Management, UKM research grant (code project: EP-2020-061, EP-2020-007). This book is suitable for postgraduate students, researchers as well as other social scientists who are working in the area of finance, investment and banking. Any feedback can be directed to the editors.

Bangi, Malaysia
January 2024

Zulkefly Abdul Karim
Ruzita Abdul Rahim
Wai Yan Wong
Siti Farah Dilla Zakaria

Contents

Editors and Contributors

About the Editors

Zulkefly Abdul Karim (Ph.D.) currently is a Professor at the Centre for Sustainable and Inclusive Development Studies (SID), Faculty of Economics and Management, Universiti Kebangsaan Malaysia (UKM), Bangi, Selangor, Malaysia. His research interest has focused on monetary and financial economics, international finance, applied econometrics and public policy. He has an outstanding record in publications that have been published in various journals indexed in Web of Science (WoS) and SCOPUS. He also holds an administration post at university level as Chair of Social and Economic Transformation Research Cluster, Centre for IDEA-UKM, and also as Editor and Associate Editor for several journals.

Ruzita Binti Abdul Rahim (Ph.D.) is a Professor in Corporate Finance at the Centre for Global Business and Digital Economy Studies (GloBDE), Faculty of Economics and Management, Universiti Kebangsaan Malaysia (UKM), Bangi, Selangor, Malaysia. Her research interests are investments, corporate finance, international finance, financial economics, financial technology (fintech) and digital securities.

Wai-Yan Wong (Ph.D.) is a Senior Lecturer at the Centre for Global Business and Digital Economy Studies (GloBDE), Faculty of Economics and Management, Universiti Kebangsaan Malaysia, Bangi, Selangor, Malaysia. Her research interest is in the field of corporate finance, corporate governance and corporate political connection. She has published in Finance Research Letters, Pacific-Basin Finance Journal, Development Policy Review, and International Journal of Managerial Finance.

Siti Farah Dilla Zakaria is a senior researcher affiliated at Tun Ismail Mohamed Ali Distinguished Chair (YTI-UKM), Universiti Kebangsaan Malaysia, Bangi, Selangor, Malaysia. She has graduated with a Master of Business Administration (M.B.A.) specialising in Human Resource Management from the Graduate School of Business, Universiti Kebangsaan Malaysia (UKM-GSB).

Contributors

Aisyah Abdul-Rahman Faculty of Economics and Management, Universiti Kebangsaan Malaysia, Bangi, Selangor, Malaysia

Syahida Zainal Abidin Faculty of Economics and Management, Universiti Kebangsaan Malaysia, Bangi, Selangor, Malaysia

Norazlan Alias Centre for Governance Resilience and Accountability Studies (GRACE), Faculty Economics and Management, Universiti Kebangsaan Malaysia, Bangi, Selangor, Malaysia

Suhaili Alma'amun Faculty of Economics and Management, Universiti Kebangsaan Malaysia, Bangi, Selangor, Malaysia

Syajarul Imna Mohd Amin Faculty of Economics and Management, Universiti Kebangsaan Malaysia, Bangi, Selangor, Malaysia

Mohd Mursyid Arshad Faculty of Educational Studies, Universiti Putra Malaysia, Serdang, Selangor, Malaysia

Noor Azryani Auzairy Faculty of Economics and Management, Universiti Kebangsaan Malaysia, Bangi, Selangor, Malaysia

Nurul Murshida Benjamin Faculty of Economics and Management, Universiti Kebangsaan Malaysia, Bangi, Selangor, Malaysia

Phui-Chee Chong Faculty of Economics and Management, Universiti Kebangsaan Malaysia, Bangi, Selangor, Malaysia

Shu-Fen Chuah Faculty of Business, Economics and Social Development, Universiti Malaysia Terengganu, Kuala Terengganu, Terengganu, Malaysia

Ahmad Ibn Ibrahimy Faculty of Business and Economics, Universiti Malaya, Kuala Lumpur, Malaysia

Bakri Abdul Karim Faculty of Business and Economics, Universiti Malaysia Sarawak, Kota Samarahan, Sarawak, Malaysia

Zulkefly Abdul Karim Faculty of Economics and Management, Universiti Kebangsaan Malaysia, Bangi, Selangor, Malaysia

Norlin Khalid Faculty of Economics and Management, Universiti Kebangsaan Malaysia, Bangi, Selangor, Malaysia

Ai-Xin Lee School of Management, Universiti Sains Malaysia, Penang, Malaysia

Nur Arissa Maisarah Nadhri Faculty of Economics and Management, Universiti Kebangsaan Malaysia, Bangi, Selangor, Malaysia

Ruzita Abdul Rahim Faculty of Economics and Management, Universiti Kebangsaan Malaysia, Bangi, Selangor, Malaysia

Shahida Shahimi Faculty of Economics and Management, Universiti Kebangsaan Malaysia, Bangi, Selangor, Malaysia

Siti Aisyah Shari Faculty of Economics and Management, Universiti Kebangsaan Malaysia, Bangi, Selangor, Malaysia

Ng Suat Thing Faculty Economics and Management, Universiti Kebangsaan Malaysia, Bangi, Selangor, Malaysia

Wai-Yan Wong Faculty of Economics and Management, Universiti Kebangsaan Malaysia, Bangi, Selangor, Malaysia

Mohd Hasimi Yaacob Centre for Governance Resilience and Accountability Studies (GRACE), Faculty Economics and Management, Universiti Kebangsaan Malaysia, Bangi, Selangor, Malaysia

Lay Qin Yi Hong Leong Bank Berhad, Kuala Lumpur, Malaysia

Ahmad Yusmadi Yusoff Ministry of Finance Malaysia, Putrajaya, Malaysia

Siti Aisyah Zahari Faculty of Economics and Management, Universiti Kebangsaan Malaysia, Bangi, Selangor, Malaysia

Siti Farah Dilla Zakaria Tun Ismail Ali Distinguished Chair (YTI-UKM), Universiti Kebangsaan Malaysia, Bangi, Selangor, Malaysia

Bridging the Gap Between Information Asymmetry and IR4.0: A Systematic Literature Review

Mohd Hasimi Yaacob, Ng Suat Thing, and Norazlan Alias

Abstract With the growing literature on information asymmetry and industry 4.0 (IR4.0), a systematic review of the application of IR4 on mitigating information asymmetry is inevitable. Most of the existing literature focuses on management and computer science, and limited study links the analysis directly to the impact of technology on mitigating information asymmetry in corporate governance. Therefore, this study aims to fill in the literature gaps by refining and identifying the linkage between adoption IR4.0 or enabling technologies of IR4.0 (Blockchain, Cyber-Physical System (CPS), Internet of Things (IoT) and Cloud Computing) related to mitigating information asymmetry. Firstly, the systematic review found 521 research articles from Scopus and Web of Science database and analysed nine articles based on inclusion and exclusion criteria. The review analysis found that blockchain technology plays a vital contribution in representing the enabling technologies of IR4.0. Most of the review analysis discussed blockchain technology on mitigating information asymmetry in corporate governance. Only one review article discussed widely with enabling technologies of IR4.0 on mitigating information asymmetry. However, the management field report was discussed too widely with theory and concepts related to computer science literature. Therefore, this study will focus on the discussion of blockchain technology on mitigating information asymmetry. The findings conclude that the enabling technologies of IR4.0 will mitigate information asymmetry in corporate governance in the form of enabling open information transactions, decentralised governance, representing faithfulness of financial reporting, promote smart contracts, and enhance market competitiveness and social welfare. Finally, this study emphasised a framework based on the systematic literature review which suggested that IR4.0 will be a new mechanism to mitigate information

M. H. Yaacob (✉) · N. Alias
Centre for Governance Resilience and Accountability Studies (GRACE), Faculty Economics and Management, Universiti Kebangsaan Malaysia, Bangi, Selangor, Malaysia
e-mail: mhasimi@ukm.edu.my

N. S. Thing
Faculty Economics and Management, Universiti Kebangsaan Malaysia, Bangi, Selangor, Malaysia

Z. Abdul Karim et al. (eds.), *Contemporary Issues in Finance, Investment and Banking in Malaysia*,
https://doi.org/10.1007/978-981-99-5447-6_1

asymmetry in the corporate governance, which will directly influence the intention of the corporate governance players to mitigate information asymmetry.

Keywords Information asymmetry · Industry 4.0 · Blockchain · Corporate governance

1 Introduction

This study examines the impact of the adoption industry 4.0 on mitigating information asymmetry in corporate governance. This article also tries to identify the linkage between the adoption industry 4.0 and the effects on mitigating information asymmetry. Based on our knowledge, this issue had not been addressed yet in the systematic literature review. Since twentieth century, information asymmetry remains an unresolvable problem in corporate governance. Major prior studies determined that an individual tends to be involved in information asymmetry for the sake of their benefits or relies on the organisation's objective (e.g., Connelly et al., 2011; Hagedoorn, 2006; Zaheer & Soda, 2009). For instance, management manipulating accruals, constructing transactions, and disclosing false information to mislead information users (Healy & Palepu, 2001; Lie, 2005). The issue of information asymmetry brings negative consequences to corporate governance, such as impacts on decision-making and business growth. Hence, organisations have to find solutions to mitigate information asymmetry. The organisation had mitigating information by adopting a rewarding system, monitoring system, etc. However, information asymmetry still being unresolvable. Therefore, there are necessities to adopt disruptive technology to improve the resolutions of mitigating information asymmetry. By adopting industry 4.0, this will impact on the traditional methods of industrial production, corporate governance, and business regulations. Therefore, it will further improve corporate performance and leads the organisation into the new edge.

The terms of industry 4.0 or the fourth industrial revolution are based on integrating the systems through big data, the emergence of analytics and business-intelligence capabilities, generating new forms of human–machine interaction, and improvements in the transferring digital instructions to the physical world. Thus, brings a new value chain and management level across the products' life cycle (Baur & Kagermann, 2013; Wee, 2015). Many prior studies examined that adopting industry 4.0 will decentralise corporate governance, and the disclosed information would be high transparency, traceable, and tamperproof (e.g., Yu et al., 2019). However, a question of whether the adoption industry 4.0 will mitigate the problem of information asymmetry is unclear.

Notwithstanding its benefits, when we look into the literature of information asymmetry and industry 4.0 itself, there are limited study links between the management literature and computer science literature. From the perspective of management literature, prior studies have focused on studying the antecedent conditions that will lead information asymmetry, the motivation, resolutions on mitigating information asymmetry, and the impacts of information asymmetry towards the organisations. However, the literature of adoption disruptive technology on mitigating information asymmetry is limited in the management literature. On the other hand, from the viewpoint of industry 4.0 literature, most of the prior studies mainly focus on introducing, technology applied, research and development (R&D), opportunities and challenges on IR4 (e.g. Ghobakhloo, 2018; Moktadir et al., 2018; Zhou et al., 2015). While most of the existing literature focuses on computer science, limited study links the analysis directly to technology's impact on mitigating information asymmetry in corporate governance. Therefore, a systematic literature review on adoption industry 4.0 related to mitigating information asymmetry is necessary. The discussion in the article can improve our understanding of the linkage between industry 4.0 on mitigating information asymmetry in corporate governance.

The remainder of the article is structured as follows. Section 2 presents the literature review of information asymmetry and industry 4.0. Section 3 discusses the methodology. Section 4 discusses the linkage between the adoption industry 4.0 on mitigating information asymmetry. Section 5 concludes.

2 Literature Review

2.1 Information Asymmetry

Information asymmetry is defined as a condition wherein there is an imbalance of information between two parties in a relationship (Akerlof, 1970). Information asymmetry exists in all exchange relationship, including commerce relationship (Hambrick & Manson, 1984). Previous studies have explored information asymmetry in various ways with different theories. Bacharach (1989) examined that information asymmetry plays a mechanism role in Bacharach's theoretical models, which will impact the flow of independent to dependent variables. Stinglitz (2002) depicted information asymmetry as a condition wherein different party gains different information towards a thing.

Moreover, Connelly et al. (2011) further explained that information asymmetry is a type of private information, in which information-rich actors tend to involve in self-interest activity. Therefore, prior studies examined that information asymmetry is a mechanism that can be arbitrarily used by actors to pursue self-interest. Despite the dynamic research on information asymmetry theory, extensive research studies towards information asymmetry are sufficient to prove that information asymmetry is a severe problem in corporate governance. For instance, Healy and Palepu (2001) reported that capital markets and organisations encounter losses consequences of corporate disclosure related to information asymmetry. Bergh et al. (2019) justified that information asymmetry made a severe risk to the organisation.

Information asymmetry became a severe problem in corporate governance, particularly from the aspect of agency theory. Therefore, numerous researchers have identified various solutions on solving information asymmetry. According to Bergh et al. (2019), the answers of organisations' information asymmetry can be classified into two: (i) reduce information asymmetry and (ii) increase information asymmetry for the sake of self-benefits. Eisenhardt (1989) and Jensen (1983) explained that outcome-based incentives could reduce information asymmetry. Gomez-Mejia and Balkin (1992) supported it by explaining that monitoring systems are considered a costly and challenging system, which some agent has high autonomy, independence, and highly specialised information. However, Abrahamson and Park (1994) argued that agent would be unable to deceive their principal, which will directly reduce information asymmetry problem by monitoring the agent's behaviour. Moreover, some authors argue that information asymmetry can be reduced by using incentives to gather and disclose information (e.g., Heeley et al., 2007; Madhok & Tallman, 1998). Furthermore, according to Bovivie et al. (2016), information asymmetry occurs as a result of information concealing behaviours. The above argument shows that solution for information asymmetry remains unclear and needs further investigation. The answer could lie in the adoption of a new technology mechanism to reduce information asymmetry while minimising unanticipated cost and risk. This study aims to better understand the adoption of this new technology mechanism in solving the issue of information asymmetry.

2.2 Industry 4.0 and Its Enabling Technologies

The concept of industry 4.0 (IR4.0) was manifested at the Germany Hanover Fair in 2011 then officially declared as Germany National Strategy in 2013. IR4.0 is also called an industrial revolution, smart manufacturing, industrial internet, and smart product. Prior studies like Kagermann et al. (2013) claimed that the world started to aggressively engage in research and funding programs towards IR4.0 in order to take a pioneering role in the manufacturing industries. Although there is still no unanimous agreement in adopting the definition of IR4.0, Baur and Wee (2015) describe IR4.0 or the fourth stage of industrialisation as "the next phase in the digitisation of the manufacturing sector, driven by four disruptions: the astonishing rise in data volumes, computational power, and connectivity, especially new low-power wide-area networks; the emergence of analytics and business-intelligence capabilities; new forms of human–machine interaction such as touch interfaces and augmented-reality systems; and improvements in transferring digital instructions to the physical world, such as advanced robotic and 3-D printing." Moreover, Zhou et al. (2015) depicted that the integrations of IR4.0, horizontal integration, vertical integration, and end-to-end integration will bring interconnection with man-to-man to machine, machine-to-machine, or service-to-service. Therefore, IR4.0 will influence the traditional methods of industrial production and corporate governance business regulations.

There are numerous methods to apply technologies in the implementation of IR4.0. These technologies include the cyber-physical system (CPS), Internet of Things (IoT), cloud computing, blockchain, and other related technologies (Gobakhloo, 2018; Xu et al., 2018). Xu et al. (2018) explored that IR4.0 is mainly dependent on the use of CPS, IoT and cloud computing. Meanwhile, Viyasitavat et al. (2018) explained that blockchain is one of the core technologies applied in IR4.0. In this study, we will only examine a few core technologies that are particularly significant, such as IR4.0, CPS, IoT, cloud computing, and blockchain. In the context of IR4.0, IoT usually refers to the Industrial Internet of Things (IIoT) (Wang et al., 2016). The function is similar to IoT, enabling physical objects to communicate with each other and further share information and coordinate decisions (Ashton, 2009). CPS is defined as a collection of transformative technologies that enables the connection between the operations of physical assets and computational capabilities (e.g., Lee et al., 2015; Mladineo et al., 2017; Varghese & Tandur, 2014).

Moreover, the implementation of cloud computing allows all data to be stored in a private and public cloud server. Viryasitavat et al. (2018) further explained that blockchain provides a solution which can build trust, reduce costs, and accelerate transactions in business process management (BPM) framework for service composition in IR4.0. Prior studies show an in-depth explanation of what enables the technologies of IR4.0. However, there is a gap in the literature in explaining how these enabling technologies in IR4.0 can solve the issues of corporate governance, in particular, information asymmetry. Therefore, this study aims to understand better how these enabling technologies can help to solve information asymmetry.

3 Methodology

All studies involving information asymmetry and the applied technology of industry 4.0 were identified via two world-renowned indexed electronic databases: Web of Science (WoS) and Scopus, using the following search strings: ("information asymmetry") AND ("industry 4.0" OR "industrial revolution" OR "smart manufacturing" OR "industrial internet" OR "smart product") OR ("cyber-physical system" OR "CPS*" OR "internet of things" OR "IoT*" OR "cloud computing" OR "blockchain"). A research article was considered eligible for inclusion if: (1) it is in the Finance area; (2) technology of industry 4.0 was applied to study the information asymmetry issue; and (3) it is a peer-reviewed article. These types of articles are only limited to those written in English. Initial searches were conducted in August 2019 and then updated in September 2019 to ensure that all 1990 to September 2019 papers were included.

In phase 1, a total of 521 peer-reviewed research articles were retrieved at this stage. Restricting the search to WoS and SCOPUS means our review is not exhaustive and provides only a sample of the literature on information asymmetry in the finance area and in IR4.0. In phase 2, we scanned titles and abstracts to select articles with clear relevance to information asymmetry issues and the implied use of industry 4.0

technique. Twenty-two papers were retained and went through full-text review, of which, nine articles fulfilled the inclusion criteria. Seven articles were retrieved from Web of Science and two journal articles from SCOPUS, of which, no papers were common to the two databases as shown in Fig. 1.

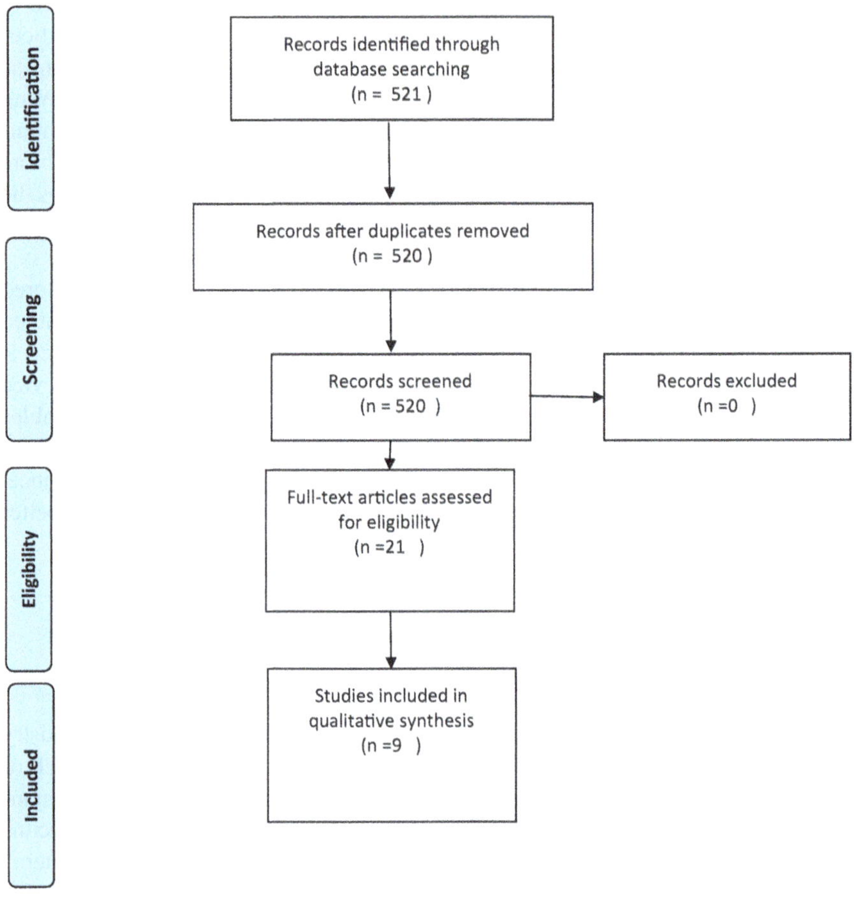

Fig. 1 Research framework

4 The Role of IR 4.0 Technology in Mitigating Information Asymmetry

From the systematic literature review, most of the articles discussed the blockchain technology—one of the enabling technologies in IR 4.0. This section explains the integration of blockchain to mitigate information asymmetry in corporate governance.

4.1 Open Information Transactions

Blockchain potentially mitigates the traditional information transaction asymmetries. Prior studies emphasised that blockchain systems play a significant role in accounting and supply chain transactions. The transaction information of accounting and supply chain would be visible to all blockchain participants kept in public ledgers or consortium-based quasi-public ledgers. In general, the peer-to-peer public blockchain system is fully decentralised. Anyone has the authority to access and view the transactions to ensure the availability of information is authentic. Therefore, all transaction information would be publicly exposed and solves the information transaction asymmetries. On the other hand, according to New Institutional Economics (NIE), blockchain technology enables anyone to share information in a transparent manner without the need for a centralised clearinghouse. Hence, with the exception of the accounting and supply chain systems, some organisations have applied blockchain in their governance aid system to reduce information asymmetry and increase effectiveness (O'Leary, 2017, 2018; Reinsberg, 2018).

4.2 Decentralised Governance

Blockchain and smart contracts can disrupt the traditional organisational governance structures. Conventional corporate governance systems tend to be centralised, with different hierarchical top-down command and degrees of rule-setting decision-making. Agent tends to be involved in self-beneficial activities by using their authority, and ignoring the instruction from the principal. The blockchain system introduces a decentralised and spontaneous coordination with resolving the problem of traditional centralised governance, known as the principal-agent dilemma (information asymmetry). In a simple form, blockchain enables a database system in which decentralised agents or institutions can record information and maintain it. For instance, the Schelling points (a kind of blockchain solution) allow people to converge on a mutually consistent decision framework, in the absence of direct communication and centralised coordination. Moreover, blockchain technology enhances a responsible and accurate record keeper, reducing the problem of manipulation and tampering. Hence, blockchain and smart contracts might exterminate information asymmetry by introducing new ways of coordinating activities. The activities such as task allocation, coordination, and supervision of a group of people who share common economic interests are geographically distributed, without the necessity of a centrally managed organisation (Cong & He, 2019; Eling & Lehmann, 2018; O'Leary, 2017; Shermin, 2017).

4.3 Representational Faithfulness of Financial Reporting

Stakeholders find it challenging to establish whether financial reporting information represents what it purports due to information asymmetry and agency problems. In theory, insiders use to mislead outside capital providers about the entity's financial positions and operating performance to obtain more capital or out of personal interests of insiders. Thus, the emergence and development of financial accounting and independent auditing to solve information asymmetry. However, it cannot wholly solve due to conflicting interests between insiders and outsiders, the denseness of accounting and auditing, and non-independence of the auditing, financial accounting, and external auditing. Blockchain technology creates a new Accounting Information System (AIS), which can address the information asymmetry and agency problems inherent in financial reporting and audit. These systems will enhance the representational faithfulness of financial reporting. The blockchain records and validates the information in a decentralised way. The entire process does not require any authority intermediaries, and the blockchain technology guarantees the information to be transparent, secure, tamperproof, and reliable. As a result, the application of blockchain technology in financial accounting can make firm's accounting process transparent, improve the quality of external reporting information, and effectively reduce the information asymmetry between firms and outside investors. In the short run, the blockchain technology could be used as a platform for firms to voluntarily disclose information, which is high-quality signalling that enables firms to solve the trust problem with investors. In the long run, the application will impact financial accounting, effectively reducing the errors in disclosure, increasing the quality of accounting information, and mitigating information asymmetry. In sum, this concept will reduce the agency problems and costs inherent in financial reporting and audit and enhance the financial reporting system's credibility and transparency (McCallig et al., 2019; Yu et al., 2019).

4.4 Smart Contracts

The problem of incomplete contracts is one of the challenges of governance as they cannot specify all contingencies such as information asymmetry and agency slack. Blockchain technology enables smart contract with some codes that run on top of a blockchain (Diedrich, 2016). In theory, smart contracts can bind parties effectively to mitigate uncertainty in relational contracting. In smart contracts, the parties will lose their stake resources if they did not behave compliant with not following through on its promise to provide an incentive or information. Moreover, the smart contracts will evaluate and verify whether a party complies with the terms and regulations. Once the smart contract has been set up, this immutable transaction record between the involved parties is verifiable and traceable. Hence, blockchain, notably smart contracts, mainly provides a mechanism for bringing trusted data which can reduce uncertainty around contract enforcement, while also decreasing information asymmetry by providing an impeachable record of transactions (Reinsberg, 2018; Yu et al., 2019).

4.5 Enhance Market Competitiveness and Social Welfare

Blockchain enables a decentralised record-keeper to decrease manipulation and misreport with allowing better and efficient information aggregation. This information distribution process changes the information environment and the economic behaviours of blockchain participants. Blockchain technologies will mitigate information asymmetry as a barrier to entering the market and greater the competition while enhancing the welfare and consumer surplus. In the traditional world, market players are not able to observe about their competitive business activities. In contrast, blockchain enables the market players to infer the aggregate business condition by serving as record-keepers (a system in the blockchain) and detecting deviations in any collusion equilibrium because the information is open and transparent. The market players (blockchain node) can observe all trade information in the exchange and all incoming exchange transactions. With this information, the market player can exploit the information asymmetry between what they can see and other market players, then enhance market competitiveness. However, even though the blockchain can mitigate information asymmetry barrier and encouraging entry for market players, it can also lead to greater collusive behaviour (Cong & He, 2019; Freund & Stanko, 2018).

5 Discussions

As mentioned, the issue of information asymmetry is common but its impact on corporate governance is not well researched. This is a significant problem for both shareholders and stakeholders. Information asymmetry commonly related to an individual tends to involve information asymmetry for the sake of own benefits or to realise organisation's goals (e.g., Connelly et al., 2011; Hagedoorn, 2006; Zaheer & Soda, 2009). The loopholes in management had created various opportunities for corporate governance player to be involved in information asymmetry. Thus, the

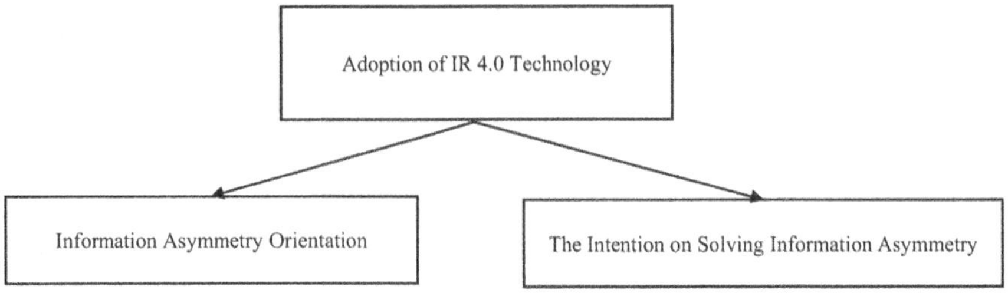

Fig. 2 Proposed framework

corporate governance players tend to lack initiative on mitigating information asymmetry due to their benefits. Hence, information asymmetry is still unresolvable and has negative consequences even though prior studies try to minimise information asymmetry. However, earlier studies argue that there are necessities to adopt technology in this technology era, thereby mitigating information asymmetry. Therefore, this study fills the research gaps and answers whether adoption IR4.0 will mitigate the problem of information asymmetry. This study concludes and suggests that IR4.0 will be a new mechanism to alleviate information asymmetry in corporate governance. The adoption of IR4.0 will increase corporate governance players' intention to mitigate information asymmetry by enabling open information transaction, decentralised governance, representing faithfulness of financial reporting, and promoting smart contracts. Hence, without the necessity of a centrally managed organisation, the corporate governance players have no opportunity to involve in information asymmetry activity for the sake of self-benefits or the organisation. On the other hand, blockchain technology's role enables the corporate transaction to be transparent, improves information quality, and effectively reduces information asymmetry between insider and outsider. Therefore, we suggest that the adoption of IR4.0 in corporate governance will boost the intention of solving information asymmetry and mitigate information asymmetry. The framework below shows that the adoption of IR4.0 technology will mitigate information asymmetry and increase their intention of solving information asymmetry (Fig. 2).

6 Summary and Conclusion

This study applied a systematic literature review to present the influence of IR4.0 in corporate governance and provided a set of empirical research related to the resolutions of information asymmetry in the area of corporate governance. Most of the prior studies focus IR4.0 on the area of computer science. There is limited study that links the analysis directly to the impact of technology on solving information asymmetry in corporate governance. However, some of the previous studies have emphasised how the influences of enabling technologies in corporate governance do not entirely focus on information asymmetry issues. Hence, prior studies have rarely addressed qualitative and systematic preferences. Notably, the literature does not have systematic study-related integration of IR4.0 on mitigating information asymmetry in corporate governance. Therefore, this study integrated all related articles to address those dilemmas from prior studies.

The findings conclude that enabling technologies of IR4.0 will mitigate information asymmetry of corporate governance in the form of enabling open information transactions, decentralised governance, representing faithfulness of financial reporting, promoting smart contracts, and enhancing market competitiveness and social welfare. The enabling technologies of IR4.0 will decentralise governance. Hence, this decentralised and spontaneous coordination will resolve the problem of information asymmetry. Also, IR4.0 enables open information transactions that anyone can share, access, and amend information in a fully transparent manner without centralised clearinghouse, meanwhile providing a representational faithfulness of financial reporting. Moreover, the decentralised record-keeper encourages entry for market players, and improves social welfare. Smart contracts, known as one of the enabling technologies of IR4.0, provide a mechanism for bringing trusted data which can reduce uncertainty around contract enforcement. Specifically, this study emphasised a framework based on a systematic literature review. The framework suggested that IR4.0 will be a new mechanism to mitigate information asymmetry in corporate governance. It will directly influence the intention of corporate governance players to mitigate information asymmetry.

Acknowledgements This research project was funded by the YTI-UKM Distinguish Chair (EP-2020-007) Universiti Kebangsaan Malaysia.

References

Abrahamson, E., & Park, C. (1994). Concealment of negative organisational outcomes: An agency theory perspective. *Academy of Management Journal, 37*(5), 1302–1334.

Akerlof, G. A. (1970). The market for "lemons": Quality uncertainty and the market mechanism. *The Quarterly Journal of Economics, 84*(3), 488–500.

Ashton, K. (2009). That "Internet of Things" thing. *RFiD Journal, 22*, 97–114.

Bacharach, S. B. (1989). Organisational theories: Some criteria for evaluation. *Academy of Management Review, 14*(4), 496–515.

Baur, C., & Wee, D. (2015, June). Manufacturing's next act. *McKinsey Quarterly*. https://timereaction.com/papers/manufacturing_next_act.pdf

Bergh, D. D., Ketchen, D. J., Jr., Orlandi, I., Heugens, P. P., & Boyd, B. K. (2019). Information asymmetry in management research: Past accomplishments and future opportunities. *Journal of Management, 45*(1), 122–158.

Boivie, S., Graffin, S. D., Oliver, A. G., & Withers, M. C. (2016). Come aboard! Exploring the effects of directorships in the executive labor market. *Academy of Management Journal, 59*(5), 1681–1706.

Cong, L. W., & He, Z. (2019). Blockchain disruption and smart contracts. *The Review of Financial Studies, 32*(5), 1754–1797.

Connelly, B. L., Certo, S. T., Ireland, R. D., & Reutzel, C. R. (2011). Signalling theory: A review and assessment. *Journal of Management, 37*(1), 39–67.

Diedrich, H. (2016). *Ethereum: Blockchains, digital assets, smart contracts, decentralized autonomous organizations*. Wildfire Publishing.

Eisenhardt, K. M. (1989). Agency theory: An assessment and review. *Academy of Management Review, 14*(1), 57–74.

Eling, M., & Lehmann, M. (2018). The impact of digitalisation on the insurance value chain and the insurability of risks. *The Geneva Papers on Risk and Insurance-Issues and Practice, 43*(3), 359–396.

Freund, A., & Stanko, D. (2018). The wolf and the caribou: Coexistence of decentralised economies and competitive markets. *Journal of Risk and Financial Management, 11*(2), 26.

Ghobakhloo, M. (2018). The future of manufacturing industry: A strategic roadmap toward Industry 4.0. *Journal of Manufacturing Technology Management, 29*(6), 910–936.

Gomez-Mejia, L. R., & Balkin, D. B. (1992). Determinants of faculty pay: An agency theory perspective. *Academy of Management Journal, 35*(5), 921–955.

Hagedoorn, J. (2006). Understanding the cross-level embeddedness of interfirm partnership formation. *Academy of Management Review, 31*(3), 670–680.

Hambrick, D. C., & Mason, P. A. (1984). Upper echelons: The organisation as a reflection of its top managers. *Academy of Management Review, 9*(2), 193–206.

Healy, P. M., & Palepu, K. G. (2001). Information asymmetry, corporate disclosure, and the capital markets: A review of the empirical disclosure literature. *Journal of Accounting and Economics, 31*(1–3), 405–440.

Heeley, M. B., Matusik, S. F., & Jain, N. (2007). Innovation, appropriability, and the underpricing of initial public offerings. *Academy of Management Journal, 50*(1), 209–225.

Jensen, M. C. (1983). Organisation theory and methodology. *Accounting Review, 50*, 319–339.

Kagermann, H. (2013). Change through digitisation—Value creation in the age of Industry 4.0. In *Management of permanent change* (pp. 23–45). Springer Gabler.

Kagermann, H., Helbig, J., Hellinger, A., & Wahlster, W. (2013). Recommendations for implementing the strategic initiative INDUSTRIE 4.0: Securing the future of German manufacturing industry; final report of the Industrie 4.0 Working Group. Forschungsunion.

Lee, J., Bagheri, B., & Kao, H. A. (2015). A cyber-physical systems architecture for industry 4.0-based manufacturing systems. *Manufacturing Letters, 3*, 18–23.

Lie, E. (2005). On the timing of CEO stock option awards. *Management Science, 51*(5), 802–812.

Madhok, A., & Tallman, S. B. (1998). Resources, transactions and rents: Managing value through interfirm collaborative relationships. *Organisation Science, 9*(3), 326–339.

McCallig, J., Robb, A., & Rohde, F. (2019). Establishing the representational faithfulness of financial accounting information using multiparty security, network analysis and a blockchain. *International Journal of Accounting Information Systems.*

Mladineo, M., Veza, I., & Gjeldum, N. (2017). Solving partner selection problem in cyber-physical production networks using the HUMANT algorithm. *International Journal of Production Research, 55*(9), 2506–2521.

Moktadir, M. A., Ali, S. M., Kusi-Sarpong, S., & Shaikh, M. A. A. (2018). Assessing challenges for implementing Industry 4.0: Implications for process safety and environmental protection. *Process Safety and Environmental Protection, 117*, 730–741.

O'Leary, D. E. (2017). Configuring blockchain architectures for transaction information in blockchain consortiums: The case of accounting and supply chainsystems. *Intelligent Systems in Accounting, Finance and Management, 24*(4), 138–147.

O'Leary, D. E. (2018). Open information enterprise transactions: Business intelligence and wash and spoof transactions in blockchain and social commerce. *Intelligent Systems in Accounting, Finance and Management, 25*(3), 148–158.

Reinsberg, B. (2018). Blockchain technology and the governance of foreign aid. *Journal of Institutional Economics, 15*(3), 413–429.

Shermin, V. (2017). Disrupting governance with blockchains and smart contracts. *Strategic Change, 26*(5), 499–509.

Stiglitz, J. E. (2002). Information and the change in the paradigm in economics. *The American Economic Review, 92*, 460–501.

Varghese, A., & Tandur, D. (2014, November). Wireless requirements and challenges in Industry 4.0. In *2014 International Conference on Contemporary Computing and Informatics (IC3I)* (pp. 634–638). IEEE.

Viriyasitavat, W., Da Xu, L., Bi, Z., & Sapsomboon, A. (2018). Blockchain-based businessprocess management (BPM) framework for service composition in industry 4.0. *Journal of Intelligent Manufacturing*, 1–12.

Wang, S., Wan, J., Zhang, D., Li, D., & Zhang, C. (2016). Towards smart factory for industry 4.0: A self-organised multi-agent system with big data-based feedback and coordination. *Computer Networks, 101*, 158–168.

Xu, L. D., Xu, E. L., & Li, L. (2018). Industry 4.0: State of the art and future trends. *International Journal of Production Research, 56*(8), 2941–2962.

Yu, T., Lin, Z., & Tang, Q. (2019). Blockchain: The introduction and its application in financial accounting. *Journal of Corporate Accounting & Finance, 29*(4), 37–47.

Zaheer, A., & Soda, G. (2009). Network evolution: The origins of structural holes. *Administrative Science Quarterly, 54*(1), 1–31.

Zhou, K., Liu, T., & Zhou, L. (2015, August). Industry 4.0: Towards future industrial opportunities and challenges. In *2015 12th International Conference on Fuzzy Systems and Knowledge Discovery (FSKD)* (pp. 2147–2152). IEEE.

The Impact of Market Sentiment on Business Fixed Investment in Malaysia

Zulkefly Abdul Karim, Ahmad Yusmadi Yusoff, Bakri Abdul Karim, and Norlin Khalid

Abstract Understanding how market sentiment reflects the firm investment decision (capital expenditure) is crucial for businesses to make a proper investment strategy. This is because investor sentiment and firms' investment decision-making lie behind the reasoning that a firm's investment selection forms the most crucial part of its overall business decisions. Thus, this study examines how market sentiment, measured by Business Condition Index (BCI) and Consumer Sentiment Index (CSI), reflects Malaysian firms' investment from 2000 to 2018. This study applies a system generalised method of moment (GMM) technique with 673 firms' unbalanced panel data. Due to global uncertainty and market downturn, an investor's confidence level can change from optimism to infectious pessimism. When the market is pessimistic, investors' confidence becomes negative, leading to a decline in capital expenditure (CAPEX). The findings show that both market sentiment indicators significantly influence private firms' investment. Higher market sentiment indices create optimism for firms and increase business fixed investment.

Keywords Market sentiment · Firm investment · Systematic GMM · Tobin Q · Investment

Z. A. Karim (✉) · N. Khalid
Faculty of Economics and Management, Universiti Kebangsaan Malaysia, Bangi, Selangor, Malaysia
e-mail: zak1972@ukm.edu.my

A. Y. Yusoff
Ministry of Finance Malaysia, Putrajaya, Malaysia

B. A. Karim
Faculty of Business and Economics, Universiti Malaysia Sarawak, Kota Samarahan, Sarawak, Malaysia

Z. Abdul Karim et al. (eds.), *Contemporary Issues in Finance, Investment and Banking in Malaysia*,
https://doi.org/10.1007/978-981-99-5447-6_2

1 Introduction

Market sentiment, which portrays investors' irrational expectations towards investment performance, has been a central focus of the economic research, as it holds the key to making sound investment decisions (Cuomo et al., 2018; Haritha & Rishad, 2020; Moseki & Rao, 2018). The financial market's uncertainties and complexities have influenced how investors perceive an investment instrument's future profitability, affecting its price, hence overall performance. Understanding how investors feel about any investment equity is crucial to help them seize better opportunities since such information can expose investors' investment preferences (Kenneth & Statman, 2000). For that reason, scholars have been exploring the correlation between market sentiment and investment returns, intending to find the empirical evidence of market sentiment's impact on the financial market; the significance of market sentiment in the investment performance; and the best indices to capture the market sentiment (Chen et al., 2020; Chowdhury et al., 2021; Danso et al., 2019).

However, as much as scholars want to unlock insights into how market sentiment plays a role in yielding investment performance, market sentiment analysis is certainly not an easy task. The intangibility of investors' feelings or beliefs towards the stock market makes it challenging to precisely measure the investors' confidence in a particular asset or the stock market. Moreover, the financial market is a complex system of key players and investors whose mindsets are influenced by numerous factors, including price history, economic reports, and other external factors, adding more to quantifying the market sentiment (Stauffer & Sornette, 1999). Past studies have used different indicators to represent market sentiment in their empirical analyses. Some examples are; Consumer Confidence Index (Schmeling, 2009; Wang, 2018), Conference Board's Consumer Confidence Index (CCI) (Ho & Hung, 2009), market liquidity (Baker & Stein, 2004), and Baker and Wurgler's index (Yu & Yuan, 2011). Creating an investment sentiment index by exacting principal components from several proxy variables suggested, is often associated with choosing suitable proxies (Baker & Wurgler, 2006). Meanwhile, some countries require other proxies of market sentiment depending on their actual market conditions and rules (Chen et al., 2020). A study by Chaiyuth et al. (2019) revealed that investor sentiment proxy by trading volume also plays an essential role in stock market activities. However, the relationships between investor sentiment and stock market activities are different between developed and developing markets. Interestingly, the developed stock markets over-react more to the search volume than developing markets.

The growing importance of understanding the relationship between investor sentiment and firms' investment decision-making lies behind the reasoning that a firm's investment selection forms the most crucial part of its overall business decisions. Hence, it is only relevant to identify the investor sentiment's direct impact on firms' investment decisions. Good market sentiment will encourage the managers to reinvest and encourage the participation of new investor in the market due to the positive expectation of the future profit. Meanwhile, the Malaysian financial market has not been excluded from the effect of market sentiment. The investment-sentiment literature for the Malaysian case has shown that investors' confidence in the stock market significantly influences stock market returns (Tuyon et al., 2016; Zainudin et al., 2019). Furthermore, scholars have extended market sentiment by investigating how such a sentiment drives firm investment decisions (Dang & Xu, 2018; Danso et al., 2019; Du & Hu, 2020; Zhaohui & Wensheng, 2013; Zhu et al., 2017). Nevertheless, despite the proliferation of market sentiment and firm investment studies as seen in the literature, there has been minimal research on such studies for Malaysia's case. Jiun Chia et al. (2020) have examined COVID-19 and Movement Control Order (MCO) on Malaysian equity return.

In the Malaysian context, private sector investment is more volatile than other aggregate demand components. The ratio of private sector investment as a percentage of GDP was higher at 27% in 2000. However, the rate dropped in 2009 to 18%, the lowest level due to the 2007/2008 Global Financial Crisis (GFC). Capital expenditure was up and down, recorded at 26% in 2016 before falling below 24% in 2018. Both market sentiment indicators fell below 100 points in 2008/2009 due to the GFC but showed a positive momentum after 2010 to rise above 100 points. Thus, examining how the movement in BCI and CSI has been reflected in the capital investment (firm-level) is crucial to understand further how the firm investment responds to market sentiment. Thus, given this background, the main objectives of this study are three-folds. First, it examines the determinants of Malaysian listed firms' investment decisions by focusing on the role of market sentiment indicators. Second, it examines how small and big firms' investment decisions behave differently in response to market sentiment and other firm-specific variables. Third, it analyses the long-run response of the firms-level investment spending to market sentiment and other variables.

This study contributes to potential stakeholders and the literature in the following ways. First, it shall have implications for investors and traders in planning their investment decisions prudently and for policymakers' relevance to precisely implementing a monetary policy to stabilise the market sentiment. Firms need to invest in proper capital investment strategies because its decision will affect their future performance. In contrast, stabilising the market sentiment is crucial for the monetary authority to minimise the fluctuation of the capital investment and stabilise the aggregate expenditure and domestic price level. Second, to the literature, this study extends the Malaysian market sentiment by focusing on the impact of market sentiment proxied by BCI and CSI on capital expenditure (CAPEX) of Malaysia's publicly listed firms, relying on a recent dataset (2000 to 2018) and an extensive sample of publicly listed firms (673 firms). This study also augments the Tobin-Q investment model by controlling firm characteristics such as size, asset tangibility, growth, and cash flow. Third, this study employs a recent dynamic panel GMM model to capture short-run and long-run relationships among variables. The dynamic panel technique can illustrate the dependent variable's lagged effect or temporal dependency on the explanatory variables, which indicates that its past realisations determine the dependent variable.

The remaining of this chapter is organised as follows. Section 2 summarises the related theory on investment and organised the literature debates regarding the determinants of firm-level investment. Section 3 focuses on the research methodology and econometric specification, whereas Sect. 4 summarises the main empirical findings using dynamic panel data. Section 5 concludes and discusses some policy implications of the new findings.

2 Market Sentiment and Investment Decision

2.1 *Theoretical Perspective*

The theory of market sentiment affecting investment decisions has been explored by a few researchers, such as Barberis et al. (1998), Daniel et al. (1998), Hong and Stein (1999), and Chari et al. (2017). Based on their studies, investors tend to overreact or underreact to the news prevailing in the stock market. Optimistic news can drive investors to an exaggerated optimism about the future; therefore, their overreaction can lead to increased stock prices. Contrariwise, when news announcements are likely to contradict optimism, it may lead to lower returns (Barberis et al., 1998). Markets become more dynamic as many investors enter them; therefore, intuition alone in making a decision will cause errors and losses in some cases (Hirshleifer, 2015; Norman et al., 2017). The decision maker's emotions drove the firm investment decision depending on the situation or event (Hribar et al., 2017).

Gao and Suess (2012) constructed their sentiment index based on six proxies: changes in implied volatility and skewness, first differences in Chicago Board Options Exchange Volatility Index (CBOE's VIX) and Chicago Board Options Exchange Skewness indexes (CBOE's SKEW), changes in closed-end fund discounts, first-day returns of IPOs, changes in trading volume, and changes in the dividend premium. Meanwhile, Baker and Wurgler (2007) formed a composite index of sentiment based on the common variation in six underlying proxies for sentiment: the closed-end fund discount, New York Stock Exchange (NYSE) share turnover, the number and average first-day returns on Initial Public Offering (IPOs), the equity share in new issues, and the dividend premium. Ishijima et al. (2015) built an index of the Nikkei market sentiment, a popular newspaper in Japan. Zhou (2018) reviewed various investor sentiment measures and applications based on market data, surveys, text, and news media. He concluded that there is a need to produce more accurate sentiment measures that yield a systematic sentiment factor explaining the cross-section of asset returns. This approach is vital to understanding how sentiment has been used in practice and affects prices, enhances the economic value of sentiment information, and understands the corresponding risk premium. Thus, investor sentiment shall not be taken lightly; it must be analysed and evaluated to consider the information forecasted before making an investment decision.

Investor sentiment reveals the movements in financial markets dictated by the psychological perception of operations or trades (Concetto and Ravazzolo, 2019). Extensive studies have been done on market sentiment, but most studies are on the relationship or effect of market sentiment on other important financial and economic variables. The market sentiment influences a foreign investor before deciding whether to proceed with an investment. Hassan et al. (2016) examined investor sentiment toward Foreign Direct Investment (FDI). They found that investor sentiment has a positive bidirectional relationship with FDI, surpassing all other macroeconomic variables regarding the impact on FDI. Malaysia must create good market sentiment conditions to attract more foreign sources as an emerging economy. Consistent with our argument, Hassan et al. (2016) suggested that Malaysia must positively impact the local and regional economy and financial development as an impetus for foreign investors to invest in Malaysia as an emerging country. The high and low market sentiment are essential indicators for an emerging market since market sentiment has a positive relationship with firms' investment and affects countries' performance in attracting FDI.

2.2 *Previous Empirical Evidence*

The sentiment is one of the essential behavioural risks reflected in the stock market (Tuyon et al., 2016). Market sentiment affects various areas of finance and the economy as it is responsible for the volatility of stock prices in the market, which may include macroeconomic factors such as inflation, FDI, unemployment, and income (Raza, 2015; Raza & Jawaid, 2014; Raza et al., 2015). These sentiments do not follow the necessary knowledge or statistics; they rely on general market information or particular market trends (Raza et al., 2019). Zhu et al. (2017) found that market sentiment affects firm investment through top management decisions. For example, top management teams' irrational investment decisions cater to investor sentiment and ignore the feasibility of companies' projects and conditions. Overconfident managers believe that they can generate greater profit from their investment ventures. This overconfidence often leads to overinvestment (Ben-David et al., 2013; Campbell et al., 2011; Goel & Thakor, 2008; Graham et al., 2013; Malmendier & Tate, 2008; Pikulina et al., 2017). As a result, they overvalue their investment ventures and incorrectly interpret negative net present value (NPV) projects as value-creating (Kim et al., 2016). Therefore, the companies' stock prices collapse due to continuously undertaking negative NPV projects, which leads to the company's bad performance. Besides, the manager's overconfidence may affect the crash risk if the manager is more dominant in the top management team, mainly if there are more significant differences in the investor.

On the other hand, Tuyon et al. (2016) found that sentiment captures price overreaction, which is corrected in the short-run as in two-sized portfolios. Besides, Jiang et al. (2018) stated that market sentiment affects firms' top management's investment decisions. Danso et al. (2019) found that market sentiment and firm investment positively correlate using alternative investment measures. They also observed that the sentiment-investment relationship is significant and positive across all models, even after dealing with possible endogeneity issues. Research on market sentiment supports the role of psychological and cognitive biases in influencing firms' corporate decisions. Top management teams are not rational; they may make investment decisions that cater to investor sentiment and ignore the feasibility of projects and companies' conditions to some extent (Danso et al., 2019; Zhu et al., 2017).

Zhou (2018) argued that investor sentiment shows the gap between the asset's valuation and its economic bases, which can be measured from various sources such as market surveys and official documentation. Mushinada and Veluri (2018) found that the post-investment analysis is necessary for the investment to correct the errors from previous behavioural estimates. Market participants' behaviour is heterogeneous due to the assumptions regarding risks and returns and induces market noise. The findings contradict the idea that efficient markets will make the information sufficient if the investor behaves rationally. Meanwhile, Dang and Xu (2018) further found that market sentiment affects R&D investments through its influence on manager sentiment. Market sentiment is imperative to firms' investment levels. The effect of market sentiment on firm investment is amplified when there is an influx of free cash flow and unused debt capacity. Besides, Danso et al. (2019) found that excess cash flow reinforces the sentiment-investment relationship, intensifying the manager's choice to invest more during high sentiment periods. Otherwise, market sentiment can be valuable in driving firms' investment decisions. Researchers also found evidence of the relationship between investors' sentiment and firm investment even for IPO performance (Danso et al., 2019; Giannini et al., 2017; Zalina et al., 2019; Zhu et al., 2017). Market sentiment undoubtedly affects firm managers' decisions to invest. Increases in market sentiment may cause investors to increase their investments in higher-risk fund categories and reduce their investments in safer funds (Hilliard et al., 2019). Human factors such as judgement and behaviour (optimism or pessimism) hold an essential position in a firm. Even with information in hand, managers responsible for investing in the future face an absolute risk that must be dealt with.

In the Malaysian context, studies relating to firm investment determinants highly concentrate on capital structure and financial constraints (Abdulazeez et al., 2020; Ismail et al., 2016; Ramli et al., 2019). Malaysia and the investors have unique features such as culture and government institutions comparable to other developing and developing countries in the market (Vuong & Suzuki, 2020). Furthermore, well-developed and functioning bonds in Malaysia are compatible with developing an equity market (Matemilola et al., 2018). Ramli et al. (2019) suggested that capital structure is vital in managerial decisions. The study about market sentiment which affects firm investment in Malaysia is relatively understudied. Zainudin et al. (2019) focus on Malaysian IPO firms, while Tuyon et al. (2016) have studied the role of investor sentiment in the Malaysian stock market. Their principal findings revealed a positive long-term and short-term relationship, which is more pronounced in a big company and cyclical industry in the market. The sentiment data from news prevailing in the market is considered reliable information to the investor (Kuan et al., 2017). Besides, Zainudin et al. (2019) support the notion of investor sentiment and timing theory as a valid phenomenon in Malaysia.

Given this background, this present study differs from the previous studies, particularly in the Malaysian context, in the following ways. First, compared with the previous study that has concentrated on the impact of market sentiment on stock return, this study extends the literature by focusing on market sentiment (BCI and CSI) on firm-level investment spending. Second, although Karim and Azman-Saini (2013) have modelled the determinants of firm-level investment in Malaysia, their study has not considered the role of both market sentiments, namely, BCI and CSI. Third, this present study has used more recent data (up to 2018) and large firm size (673 firms) to better understand how market sentiment reflects the investment decision by controlling firm-specific variables.

3 Research Methodology

According to Toit and Moolman (2003), there are four main investment models: the accelerator model, cash-flow model, neoclassical model, and Tobin's Q model. However, the most widely used investment model is Tobin's Q model (Harrison et al., 2004; Laeven, 2002) and is also commonly used in empirical studies (Bharadwaj et al., 1999). One of Tobin's Q model advantages is that it can calculate the firm's past and expected future performance. Tobin's Q is calculated as the ratio of market value to the book value of total assets. This ratio shows the importance of investments in a firm. Tobin's Q above 1 indicates that the firm has expanded in value and managed accurately. It means higher economic performance (Copeland & Weston, 1988). An essential strength of Tobin's Q model is that it shows the present value of expected future profits. For this reason, the study employs the Q investment model in investigating the relationship between market sentiment and firm capital investment in Malaysia. The baseline model used in this study can be represented as follows:

$$Investment_{i,t} = \propto + \beta_1 TobinQ_{i,t} + \beta_2 Sentiment_{i,t} + \beta_3 X_{i,t} + \omega_i + \mu_t + \varepsilon_{i,t} \quad (1)$$

In Eq. (1), i denotes the ith firm, and t represents the fiscal year. Investment as the dependent variable is firm capital expenditure (CAPEX). The use of CAPEX to proxy the firm's investment is in line with many previous studies, for example, Chirinko et al. (1999), Bhagat et al. (2005), Karim and Azman-Saini (2013), and Ismail and Yunus (2015). The market performance indicator Tobin's Q measures firm performance in the stock market (Koo & Maeng, 2005). Singhal et al. (2016) found that higher Tobin's Q ratios are related to firms' higher future operating performance. The sentiment variable was based on the Malaysian Institute of Economic Research (MIER), Business Sentiment Index (BSI), and Customer Sentiment Index (CSI) and counted as a yearly average of the past four quarters of data. X is the vector of the control variables employed in the analysis, α and β are parameters, ω_i is a firm-fixed effect, and μ_t is a year-fixed effect, and $\varepsilon_{i,t}$ is the errors term. All continuous variables are tested using Cook distance to mitigate outliers' effect (Cook, 2000). Finally, to deal with potential reverse causality between dependent and independent variables, this study follows existing literature (e.g. Danso et al., 2019) by considering the lagged dependent variables by one period ($INV_{i,t-1}$). Thus, the baseline model in Eq. (1) can be rewritten as follows:

$$INV_{i,t} = \propto INV_{i,t-1} + \beta_1 Q_{i,t} + \beta_2 Sentiment_{i,t} + \beta_3 GROW_{i,t} + \beta_4 CF_{i,t} + \beta_5 TANG_{i,t} + \omega_i + \mu_t + \varepsilon_{i,t} \tag{2}$$

In Eq. (2), INV refers to CAPEX as a percentage of the previous capital stock (PPE), Q refers to the firm performance measured by Tobin's Q, GROW is the one-year growth rate of sales, CF is the cash flow, which is defined as operating income plus depreciation, and TANG is asset tangibility, which is the ratio of property, plant, and equipment to the value of total assets.

3.1 Data and Variables

This study used the sample of companies listed on the Main Market of Bursa Malaysia (Malaysian Bourse) from 2000 to 2018. The financial data have been collected from Thompson Reuters Datastream, and the sentiment index is obtained from the MIER survey. The data for a listed firm represents various sub-sectors of the economy, such as construction, food production, industrial, household goods and home construction, general industry and retail, technical hardware and equipment, software and computer services, finance, support services, travel, and leisure, personal goods, oil equipment services, oil and gas production, REIT and services, and a few other sectors. The raw data went through a refining process. First, financial firms were excluded because they are high in cash flow but low in capital expenditure (Karim & Azman-Saini, 2013); therefore, only non-financial firms were considered. Second, only firms consecutively present for at least five years (2014–2018) were considered to ensure that a sufficient number of lags was available for the explanatory variables. This selection is also essential to avoid data reduction because of the data transformation process and the selection of the instrument choice for the dynamic panel data. Third, firms with many missing values were deleted as it can cause discontinuities if not dropped. Fourth, the Cook's distance outlier test (Cook, 2000) was used to detect outliers influencing the estimation results. After refining the data, the data became an unbalanced panel, representing 673 firms or 7595 firm-year observations.

3.2 Variables Measurement

In line with Danso et al. (2019), this study also uses several control variables likely to affect firm investment, such as firm size, asset tangibility, growth, and cash flow.

3.2.1 Splitting the Sample

To further explore the heterogeneous effects of market sentiment on firm investment, the sample is divided into two size categories: small and medium and large firms. There are a few ways that firms can be segmented. Laeven (2002) and Rungsomboon (2005) segmented firms according to their total assets, while Zainudin et al. (2019) and Danso et al. (2019) measured firm size as the natural log of total sales, and Gupta et al. (2017) controlled firm size using the natural logarithm of market value. This study divides the firms using their index size classification based on the definition used by Tuyon et al. (2016), Baker and Wurgler (2007), and Bursa Malaysia. The firms are segregated into small and medium capital firms and large capital firms. The small and medium cap category refers to firms with a market capitalisation of up to RM2 billion, while large-cap firms have above RM2 billion. Segmenting the firms according to their market capitalisation resulted in 60 large-cap firms and 613 small and medium-cap firms.

3.2.2 Variable Definitions

a. Investment ($INV_{i,t}$)

This section briefly explains the definitions of variables used in this study.

Capital expenditure is measured in domestic currency (Malaysian Ringgit) at current market prices following extant literature (e.g., Chirinko et al. (1999), Bhagat et al. (2005), and Karim and Azman-Saini (2013). The dependent variable was measured as the current-period investment spending for a firm i at time t, which included the capital expenditure (CAPEX) on property, plant, and equipment (PPE) for the current year as a percentage of the previous PPE. Thus, the ratio of investment as a percentage of previous capital stock can be rewritten as follows:

$$INV_{i,t} = \frac{CAPEX}{l.PPE} \tag{3}$$

b. Tobin's-Q ($Q_{i,t}$)

The independent variable for firm performance at the beginning of period t, Q is measured by dividing total debt and market capitalisation by total firm assets. This definition of Q is used in Koo and Maeng (2005). Singhal et al. (2016) found that higher Tobin's Q ratios are related to firms' higher future operating performance.

$$Q_{i,t} = \frac{(tdebt + mcap)}{tasset} \tag{4}$$

c. Market sentiment

Business Sentiment Index (BSI).

The BSI is constructed from surveys conducted on over 350 manufacturing businesses incorporated locally and foreign manufacturers operating in Malaysia, covering 11 industries. The BSI index gives advanced information that permits inferences drawn regarding emerging economic trends. The quarterly data are taken from the Malaysian Institute of Economic Research (MIER). However, for this study, we average the figure yearly.

d. Customer Sentiment Index (CSI)

The CSI is a series of surveys conducted quarterly on a sample of over 1200 households in peninsular Malaysia to gauge consumer spending trends and sentiments. Consumer behaviour reflects the income level and general economic conditions. Respondents are asked about perceptions of their household's current and expected financial positions and their employment outlook. The survey also seeks to uncover general economic conditions such as inflation from the consumers' perspective. The quarterly data are taken from the MIER. However, for this study, we average the figure yearly.

e. Growth (GROW)

Firm growth (GROW) refers to the one-year growth rate of sales, that is sales or revenue of the current period divided by revenue of the previous period (t–1). This calculation follows extant literature such as Zhu et al. (2017) and Danso et al. (2019).

$$GROW_{i,t} = \left(\frac{salesv_t}{salesv_{t-1}}\right) - 1 \tag{5}$$

Tangibility (TANG): Asset tangibility is the ratio of PPE to the book value of total assets (tasset) (see Zainudin et al. 2019), as follows:

$$TANG_{i,t} = \frac{PPE}{tasset} \tag{6}$$

Cash flow (CF): Cash flow is defined as operating income plus depreciation (OPRM) calculated at the beginning of period t as a percentage of the previous PPE. Depreciation includes total depreciation, amortisation, and depletion. This variable is used to measure the degree of market imperfections caused by financial constraints and is measured in Malaysian Ringgit. The calculation follows extant literature such as Karim and Azman-Saini (2013).

$$CF_{i,t} = \frac{(OPRM + Dep)}{l.PPE} \tag{7}$$

3.3 GMM Estimation

Panel data estimation has been increasingly used in economic and other social studies (Gujarati, 2003). Hsiao (2006) found that this development is partly contributed by the availability of panel data sets and partly by the individual researcher's rapid growth in computational power. Law (2018) indicates that panel data are (i) able to control for individual heterogeneity; (ii) allow more information on data sets; (iii) suitable for studying the dynamics of the adjustment process; and (iv) identification of parameters. Using a dynamics model is crucial for recovering consistent estimates of other parameters. Thus, this study employs a dynamic panel data estimation to examine the relationship among interest variables. According to Nickell (1982), correlation creates a large sample bias in estimating a lagged dependent variable coefficient that is not mitigated with increasing N (number of individual units). An OLS estimator will result in upward bias since correlation does not increase with increasing N, producing biased results due to the endogeneity problem.

Endogeneity is a problem when there is a correlation between the X variable and the model's error term. It may arise due to the omission of explanatory variables from the regression. This issue will result in the error term being correlated with the explanatory variables, violating a fundamental assumption behind ordinary least squares (OLS) regression analysis. Endogeneity bias can cause inconsistent estimates and incorrect inferences, contributing to misleading conclusions and inappropriate theoretical interpretations. Blundell and Bond (1998) suggested a system estimation of the generalised method of moments (system GMM). This model solves all three endogeneity types: omitted variables, simultaneity, and selection bias. The fixed effects estimator will result in a downward bias where the tendency which decreases with larger t would yield consistent coefficients in the absence of serial correlation. Using the unbiased estimator GMM technique provides an excellent solution to the problem. Specifically, the GMM uses all the linear moment conditions specified by the model. The GMM estimators are robust concerning the non-normality of the dependent variable (Blundell & Bond, 1998).

Choosing the optimal instrument set may lead to several instruments that are more than the number of observations. Therefore, this study applies the J-test of over-identifying restrictions to evaluate the validity of instruments used in estimation. The validity of instruments can be assured if the residuals do not exhibit second-order serial correlation. This property can be achieved by testing the second-order autocorrelation (AR(2)) using the Arellano-Bond (1991) tests. Another test is Sargan's over-identifying restrictions, which tests the validity of the moment conditions imposed in the GMM (Blundell et al., 2000). The null hypotheses of these tests indicate the validity of the models. Therefore, if the nulls failed to be rejected at least at the 10% significance level, though the nulls are true, the instrument variables are considered valid. For removing firm-specific effects in Eq. (1), Arellano and Bover (1995) proposed a forward orthogonal deviation transformation or a forward Helmert's procedure. This transformation subtracts the mean of future observations in the sample from the first T–1 observation. This procedure will remove the firm-specific effect. Its main advantage is to preserve sample size in panels with gaps.

Roodman (2009) stated that the system GMM could generate instrument proliferation effectively. Too many GMM system instruments can overfit an endogenous variable and weaken the Hansen test for the joint instrument validity. Therefore, to deal with instrument overfit, this study uses two techniques to lessen the number of instruments. First, only certain lags are used as instruments rather than all the available lags. Second, the instruments are combined into smaller sets by collapsing the block of the instruments' matrix. This technique was used by previous studies such as Karim and Azman-Saini (2013) and Roodman (2009).

4 The Impact of Market Sentiments on Firms-Level Investment

Table 1 reports the short-run coefficients of firm-level investment spending determinants using the one-step system GMM estimation for the whole sample period. The results show that the business sentiment index's coefficient is statistically significant at the 5% level. The coefficient of 0.0147 indicates that a 1% increase in the business sentiment index (BSI) causes the firms' investment spending to increase by 0.0147%. The consumer sentiment index's (CSI) coefficient has also been statistically significant at 5%. The coefficient of 0.0146 indicates that a 1% increase in the consumer sentiment index causes firm investment spending to increase by 0.0146%. Thus, the significant and positive effect of both the business sentiment index and the consumer sentiment index on firms' investment in Malaysia supports the notion that the sentiment index influences firms' investment decisions.

The significant and positive effects of both market sentiment indicators, BCI and CSI, provide some implications for the economic and financial aspects of the firms. First, in terms of the economic aspect, the significant effects of BCI and CSI on capital expenditure (INV) provide the investor and the policymakers some insight to ensure that the capital expenditure is not volatile according to the changes in market sentiment. This conjecture is because capital expenditure is more volatile than other aggregate demand components, in which market conditions influence investment decisions. Thus, policymakers should prioritise ensuring a good business environment and consumer sentiment in stabilising the firm capital expenditure. Second, in terms of the financial aspect, stability in BCI and CSI is very important for the firm's top management in planning their sources of capital expenditure, whether from internal financing (cash flow) or external financing (borrowing). This finding is because both sources of funding have a different financial risk to the firm, thus needing the top management to choose the fund accordingly to expand their business.

Meanwhile, the Q ratio is also statistically significant at the 5% significance level, positive for both market sentiment indicators. The results show that a 1% increase in the Q ratio leads to a rise in firm investment spending by 0.0486%. Thus,

Table 1 System GMM estimation for the whole sample

Independent variables	Business sentiment index (BSI)			Consumer sentiment index (CSI)		
	Coef	S.E	*p*-value	Coef	S.E	*p*-value
Lagged INV	0.179	(0.111)	0.107	0.179	(0.111)	0.107
Q	0.0486***	(0.0162)	0.003	0.0486***	(0.0162)	0.003
BSI, log	0.0147**	(0.00590)	0.013			
CF	–0.00382	(0.00440)	0.385	–0.00382	(0.00440)	0.385
GROW	0.0281	(0.0263)	0.286	0.0281	(0.0263)	0.286
TANG	–0.102**	(0.0493)	0.040	–0.102**	(0.0493)	0.040
CSI, log				0.0146**	(0.00585)	0.013
Year Dummies		Yes				
Number of observations		7465			7465	
Number of groups		673			673	
Observations per group avg		11.09			11.09	
Number of instruments		76			76	
Number of firms		673			673	
AR(2): *p*-value		0.132			0.135	
Hansen test: *p*-value		0.111			0.103	

Notes Robust standard (S.E) errors in parentheses. Asterisks ***, **, and * indicates significant at 1%, 5%, and 10%, respectively

these findings indicate the importance of the q ratio in influencing firms' investment spending. Asset tangibility is also statistically significant at the 5% significance level but with a negative sign, in which a 1% increase leads to a decrease in firm investment spending by 0.102%. These findings indicate that higher asset tangibility reduces the firms' investment spending. The full sample results in Table 1 suggest that the business sentiment index, consumer sentiment index, q ratio, and asset tangibility are essential in influencing firm-level investment spending.

Table 2 provides the short-run coefficients of the determinants of firm-level investment spending for large sample firms. From the table, the results also show that both the business sentiment index and consumer sentiment index are statistically significant at a 5% significance level. Both coefficients are positive, indicating that the good market sentiment (optimist sentiment) leads the higher firms' investment. Simultaneously, the effect of asset tangibility on firms' investment spending is also statistically significant at a 5% significance level for both models but negatively. This result means that the higher asset tangibility, the lower firms' capital investment. The results also show a positive and significant lag dependent on firms' investment, indicating that the previous year's investment significantly influences the current year's investment. However, the results show that the q factor is insignificant for both models for large sample firms.

Table 3 reports the short-run coefficients of firms' investment spending determinants for small and medium sample firms. Results in Table 2 are consistent with

Table 2 System GMM estimation for the large cap firm sample

Independent variables	Business sentiment index (BSI)			Consumer sentiment index (CSI)		
	Coef	S.E	*p*-value	Coef	S.E	*p*-value
Lagged INV	0.669***	(0.0992)	0.000	0.669***	(0.0992)	0.000
Q	0.00938	(0.00751)	0.211	0.00939	(0.00751)	0.211
BSI, log	0.0174***	(0.00592)	0.003			
CF	–0.00241	(0.00646)	0.709	–0.00242	(0.00646)	0.708
GROW	–4.95e–10	(5.03e–10)	0.325	–4.93e–10	(5.03e–10)	0.327
TANG	–0.0877**	(0.0429)	0.041	–0.0877**	(0.0429)	0.041
CSI, log				0.0172***	(0.00588)	0.003
Year Dummies		Yes				
Number of observations		741			741	
Number of groups		60			60	
Observations per group avg		12.35			12.35	
Number of instruments		51			51	
Number of firms		60			60	
AR(2): *p*-value		0.259			0.259	
Hansen test: *p*-value		0.149			0.148	

Notes Robust standard (S.E) errors in parentheses. Asterisks ***, **, and * indicates significant at 1%, 5%, and 10%, respectively

the previous findings for the whole and large sample firms. They show that the business sentiment index (BSI) and consumer sentiment index (CSI) are statistically significant at a 5% significance level. Both coefficients are positive, signifying that the higher the market sentiment is associated with a positive capital expenditure movement. Concurrently, the asset tangibility has also significantly influenced firms' investment spending for both models in the opposite direction. The higher asset tangibility led to lower firms' capital investment. The q ratio is also statistically significant at the 5% significance level, positive for both sentiment indicators.

The results of the specification tests suggest that the model is sufficiently specified. The *p*-value of the second-order serial correlation tests is greater than 0.1, indicating no serial correlation (autocorrelation) within the transformed residuals. Additionally, the *p*-value of the Hansen test for testing over-identification is also above 0.1, indicating that the instruments (moment conditions) used are valid in the baseline model. Besides, the system GMM results show that the signs and magnitude of the independent variable's coefficient remained similar (i.e., positive and significant at least the 5% level) for the whole sample and sample splitting (large and small-medium firms).

In summary, the results for the large and small-medium sample firms provide clear evidence that both market sentiment indicators (business sentiment index and consumer sentiment index) and asset tangibility significantly influence firm-level investment spending. The results are in line with Zhu et al. (2017), Jiang et al. (2018),

Table 3 System GMM estimation for the small and medium firm sample

Independent variables	Business sentiment index (BSI)			Consumer sentiment index (CSI)		
	Coef	S.E	*p*-value	Coef	S.E	*p*-value
Lagged INV	0.164	(0.106)	0.123	0.164	(0.106)	0.123
Q	0.0579***	(0.0169)	0.001	0.0579***	(0.0169)	0.001
BSI, log	0.0123**	(0.00593)	0.038			
CF	−0.00303	(0.00402)	0.450	−0.00303	(0.00402)	0.450
GROW	0.0228	(0.0271)	0.400	0.0228	(0.0271)	0.400
TANG	−0.0957*	(0.0509)	0.060	−0.0957*	(0.0509)	0.060
CSI, log				0.0122**	(0.00588)	0.038
Year Dummies		Yes				
Number of observations		6692			6692	
Number of groups		613			613	
Observations per group		10.92			10.92	
Number of instruments		76			76	
Number of firms		613			613	
AR(2): *p*-value		0.121			0.121	
Hansen test: *p*-value		0.102			0.096	

Notes Robust standard (S.E) errors in parentheses. Asterisks ***, **, and * indicates significant at 1%, 5%, and 10%, respectively

and Danso et al. (2019), who revealed that market sentiment and firm investment have a positive relationship.

4.1 Long-Run Effects of Firm Investment

Table 4 provides the long-run elasticity of firm investment concerning BCI, CSI, Tobin's Q, and asset tangibility for all sample sets (whole sample and sample splitting). The long-run coefficients for BCI, CSI, Tobin's Q, and asset tangibility are relatively higher than the short-run coefficients for all samples. Besides, the impacts of BCI, CSI, and asset tangibility are also somewhat higher for large firms than for small and medium firms. Therefore, these findings indicate that market sentiment's impact is more significant on large firms than on small and medium firms. Chowdhury et al. (2014) also noted that large-cap stocks tend to be more prone to sentiment.

Table 4 Long-run estimation

Key variables	Whole firm		Small and medium firms		Large firms	
	Coef	Std. Err	Coef	Std. Err	Coef	Std. Err
Business Sentiment Index	0.018**	0.008	0.014*	0.008	0.053***	0.017
Tobin Q	0.059***	0.017	0.069***	0.017	0.0283	0.0217
Tangibility	−0.124*	0.069	−0.114*	0.069	−0.265*	0.139
Customer Sentiment Index	0.018**	0.008	0.015*	0.008	0.052***	0.017
Tobin Q	0.059***	0.017	0.069***	0.017	0.0284	0.0217
Tangibility	−0.124*	0.069	−0.114*	0.069	−0.265*	0.139

Note The long-run coefficient is estimated using delta method

5 Summary and Conclusions

This study examines the impact of market sentiment on capital expenditure (firms' investment) in Malaysia using a dynamic panel data approach from 2000 to 2018. A sample of 673 firms with the unbalanced panel and system GMM estimations are used to estimate the augmented Tobin-Q investment model. Instead of analysing a full sample, the firms split into large and small-medium sub-samples to further examine their investment behaviour on market sentiment. The main results show that market sentiment indicators (business sentiment index and consumer sentiment index), asset tangibility, and Tobin-Q significantly influence investment spending. The findings also show that market sentiment's impact is relatively higher for large firms than for small and medium firms. This finding is consistent with Chowdhury et al. (2014), who found that large-cap firms tend to be more prone to market sentiment. Large firms tend to be more sensitive to the market sentiment in making an investment decision.

This study has proposed four crucial implications for the policy purpose. First, since market sentiment is vital in influencing capital expenditure, the policy should encourage a friendly environment for Malaysia's businesses and consumers. This strategy is essential because capital expenditure is generally so volatile than other aggregate expenditure components; therefore, encouraging more capital investment is vital to improving business and consumer sentiment. Besides, stability in capital expenditure due to the excellent market sentiment is also a prerequisite to sustaining long-term economic growth. Second, since Tobin-Q is statistically significant on firm investment, and a higher value of Tobin's Q indicates higher economic performance (Copeland & Weston, 1988), this signals that the firm's stock market performance is also an essential driver of their decision on capital expenditure. Thus, stock market stability and improvement in firm market capitalisation (due to increased share prices) have provided a positive signal for firms to invest more. Third, to the firm's managers, observing the current condition of the market sentiment (businesses and consumers) is crucial for their capital expenditure planning. This is vital for the firm's management team to plan their business and capital investment strategy prudently. Finally, since large firms' capital expenditure is responded to more than small-medium firms on the market sentiment, the policymakers should assist the large firms during the pessimistic outlook. This is important to ensure that the large firms are not severely affected by the bad sentiment since they play a significant role in the economy.

However, this present study also has some limitations that future researchers can extend. First, it is interesting for future researchers to consider the various alternative of the firm-investment model, such as neo-classical, Tobin's Q, cash-flow, and Euler equation in modelling the determinants of firm investment. This uptake is crucial for further understanding how the firm behaves according to the various economic, finance, non-economic, and non-finance factors in deciding their investment. Second, the future study may consider using unlisted firms, particularly the small and medium enterprises (SMEs), to understand how they determine their capital expenditure. This proposal is because the business's nature and the firm's characteristics differ from the listed firms. Lastly, future research can also consider using a more recent econometric method, for example, the threshold regression, for further examination of how the level of BCI and CSI have a different impact on the capital investment decision of the firms.

Acknowledgements Thankfully, the authors acknowledge financial support from the University Kebangsaan Malaysia (UKM) research grant (Grant number: EP-2020-005, YTI-UKM).

References

Abdulazeez, S., Rohani, M. R., Nisham, T. M., Hasniza, M. T., & Hanita, K. S. (2020). Determinants of capital structure: Evidence from Malaysian firms. *Asia-Pacific Journal of Business Administration, 12*(3/4), 283–326.

Arellano, M., & Bover, O. (1995). Another looks at the instrumental variable estimation of error-components models. *Journal of Econometrics, 68*(1), 29–51.

Arellano, M., & Bond, S. (1991). Some tests of specification for panel data: Monte Carlo evidence and an application to employment equations. *The Review of Economic Studies, 58*(2), 277–297.

Baker, M., & Stein, J. C. (2004). Market liquidity as a sentiment indicator. *Journal of Financial Markets, 7*(3), 271–299.

Baker, M., & Wurgler, J. (2006). Investor sentiment and the cross-section of stock returns. *The Journal of Finance, 61*(4), 1645–1680.

Baker, M., & Wurgler, J. (2007). Investor sentiment in the stock market. *Journal of Economic Perspectives, 21*(2), 129–152.

Barberis, N., Shleifer, A., & Vishny, R. (1998). A model of investor sentiment. *Journal of Financial Economics, 49*(3), 307–343.

Bharadwaj, A., Bharadwaj, S., & Konsynski, B. (1999). Information technology effects on firm performance as measured by Tobin's q. *Management Science, 45*(7), 1008–1024.

Berk, J. B., Richard, C. G., & Naik, V. (2019). Optimal investment, growth options, and security returns. *The Journal of Finance, 54*(5), 1553–1607.

Ben-David, I., Graham, J. R., & Harvey, C. R. (2013). Managerial miscalibration. *The Quarterly Journal of Economics, 128*(4), 1547–1584.

Bhagat, S., Moyen, N., & Suh, I. (2005). Investment and internal funds of distressed firms. *Journal of Corporate Finance, 11*, 449–472.

Blundell, R., & Bond, S. (1998). Initial conditions and moment restrictions in dynamic panel data models. *Journal of Econometrics, 87*(1), 115–143.

Blundell, R., Bond, S., & Windmeijer, F. (2000). Estimation in dynamic panel data models: Improving on the performance of the standard GMM estimator. *Advances in Econometrics.*

Campbell, T. C., Gallmeyer, M., Johnson, S. A., Rutherford, J., & Stanley, B. W. (2011). CEO optimism and forced turnover. *Journal Financial Economics., 101*, 695–712.

Chari, S., Hegde-Desai, P., & Borde, N. (2017). A review of literature on short term overreaction generated by news sentiment in stock market. *GOA Business School.*

Chen, Y., Zhao, H., Li, Z., & Lu, J. (2020). A dynamic analysis of the relationship between investor sentiment and stock market realised volatility: Evidence from China. *PLoS ONE, 15*(12), e0243080. https://doi.org/10.1371/journal.pone.0243080

Chaiyuth, P., Sirimon, T., & Robert, B. (2019). Investor attention and stock market activities: New evidence from panel data. *International Journal of Financial Studies, 7*(30), 1–20.

Chhaochharia, V., Kim, D., Korniotis, G. M., & Kumar, A. (2018). Mood, firm behaviour, and aggregate economic outcomes. *Journal of Financial Economics, 132*, 427–450.

Chirinko, R. S., Fazzari, S. M., & Meyer, A. P. (1999). How responsive is business capital formation to its user cost? An exploration with microdata. *Journal of Public Economics, 74*(1), 53–80.

Chowdhury, S. S., Rashida, S., & Rahman, A. (2014). Effect of sentiment on the Bangladesh stock market returns.

Chowdhury, A., Uddin, H., & Anderson, K. (2021). Trading behaviour and market sentiment: Firm-level evidence from an emerging Islamic market. *Global Finance Journal*, 100621 (article in press). https://doi.org/10.1016/j.gfj.2021.100621

Concetto, L. C., & Ravazzolo, F. (2019). Optimism in financial markets: Stock market returns and investor sentiments. *Journal Risk Financial Management, 12*, 85.

Cook, R. D. (2000). Detection of influential observation in linear regression. *Technometrics, 42*, 65–68.

Copeland, T., & Weston, J. F. (1988). *Financial theory and corporate finance.* Addison-Wesley Publishing.

Cuomo, M. T., Tortora, D., Mazzucchelli, A., Festa, G., Di Gregorio, A., & Metallo, G. (2018). Impacts of code of ethics on financial performance in the Italian listed companies of bank sector. *Journal of Business Accounting and Finance Perspectives, 1*(1), 157–179.

Daniel, K., David, H., & Avanidhar, S. (1998). Investors, psychology and security market under- and overreactions. *Journal of Finance., 53*, 18391885.

Danso, A., Lartey, T., Amankwah-Amoah, J., Adomako, S., Lu, Q., & Uddin, M. (2019). Market sentiment and firm investment decision-making. *International Review of Financial Analysis., 66*, 101369.

Dang, T. V., & Xu, Z. (2018). Market sentiment and innovation activities. *Journal of Financial and Quantitative Analysis, 53*(3), 1135–1161.

Du, D., & Hu, Q. (2020). Why does stock-market investor sentiment influence corporate investment? *Review of Quantitative Finance and Accounting, 54*, 1221–1246.

Edelen, R. M., Marcus, A. J., & Tehranian, H. (2010). Relative sentiment and stock returns. *Financial Analysts Journal, 66*(4), 20–32.

Gao, L., & Suess, S. (2012). Market sentiment in commodity futures returns. *Journal of Empirical Finance, 33*, 84–103.

Giannini, R., Irvine, P., & Shu, T. (2017). Non local disadvantage: An examination of social media sentiment. *The Review of Asset Pricing Studies, 8*(2), 293–336.

Goel, A. M., & Thakor, A. V. (2008). Overconfidence, CEO selection, and corporate governance. *Journal of Finance, 63*(6), 2737–2784.

Graham, J. R., Harvey, C. R., & Puri, M. (2013). Managerial attitudes and corporate actions. *Journal of Financial Economics, 109*(1), 103–121.

Gupta, K., Banerjee, R., & Onur, I. (2017). The effects of R&D and competition on firm value: International evidence. *International Review of Economics and Finance, 51*, 391–404.
Gujarati, D. N. (2003). *Basic econometrics*. McGraw Hill Book Co.
Haritha, P. H., & Rishad, A. (2020). An empirical examination of investor sentiment and stock market volatility: Evidence from India. *Financ Innov, 6*, 34. https://doi.org/10.1186/s40854-020-00198-x
Harrison, A., Love, I., & Mcmillan, M. (2004). Global capital flows and financing constraints Ann E. Harrison. *Journal of Development Economics, 75*(1), 269–301.
Hassan, M. K., Rashid, M., & Castro, E. (2016). Foreign direct investment and investor sentiment: A causal relationship. *Global Economy Journal, 16*(4), 697–719.
Hirshleifer, D. (2015). Behavioral finance. *Annual Review of Financial Economics, 7*, 133–159.
Hilliard, J., Narayanasamy, A., & Zhang, S. (2019). The role of market sentiment in asset allocations and stock returns. *Journal of Behavioral Finance, 21*, 423–441.
Ho, C., & Hung, C.-H. (2009). Investor sentiment as conditioning information in asset pricing. *Journal of Banking & Finance, 33*(5), 892–903.
Hong, H., & Stein, J. (1999). A unified theory of underreaction, momentum trading and overreaction in asset markets. *Journal of Finance, 54*, 2143–2184.
Hribar, P., Melessa, S. J., Small, R. C., & Wilde, J. H. (2017). Does managerial sentiment affect accrual estimates? Evidence from the banking industry. *Journal of Accounting and Economics, 63*(1), 26–50.
Hsiao, C. (2006). Wise working paper series WISEWP0602 panel data analysis-advantages and challenges. In *Proceedings, presented papers, and dissertations*.
Ishijima, H., Kazumi, T., & Maeda, A. (2015). Sentiment analysis for the Japanese stock market. *Global Business and Economics Review., 17*, 237–255.
Ismail, M. A., Ibrahim, M. H., Yusoff, M., & Zainal, M.-P. (2016). Financial constraints and firm investment in Malaysia: An investigation of investment cash flow relationship. *International Journal of Economics and Management, 4*(1), 29–44.
Ismail, M. A., & Yunus, M. M. (2015). Cash flow-investment relationship in Malaysia: A panel threshold regression analysis. *Jurnal Pengurusan, 45*, 49–59.
Jiang, F., Lee, J., Martin, X., & Zhou, G. (2018). Manager sentiment and stock returns. *Journal of Financial Economics*.
Jiun Chia, R. C., Sen Liew, V. K., & Rowland, R. (2020). Daily new COVID-19 cases, The movement control order, and Malaysian stock market returns. *International Journal of Business and Society (IJBS), 21*(2), 553–568.
Karim, Z. A., & Azman-Saini, W. N. W. (2013). Firm-level investment and monetary policy in Malaysia: Do the interest rate and broad credit channels matter? *Journal of the Asia Pacific Economy, 18*(3), 396–412.
Karim, Z. A., Mokhtar, A., & Zaini, M. A. S. (2004). Hubungan antara kadar pulangan nominal dengan permintaan deposit sistem perbankan islam di Malaysia. *Jurnal Ekonomi Malaysia, 38*, 3–27.
Kenneth, L. F., & Statman, M. (2000). Investor sentiment and stock returns. *Financial Analysts Journal, 56*(2), 16–23.
Kim, D.-H., Lin, S.-C., & Suen, Y.-B. (2016). Trade, growth and growth volatility: New panel evidence. *International Review of Economics & Finance, 45*(3), 384–399.
Kuan, C. L., Ismail, A., Zayet, M., Tasnim, M. A., & Shuhidan, M. (2017). Prediction of Malaysian stock market movement using sentiment analysis. *Journal of Physics: Conference Series, 1*.
Koo, J., & Maeng, K. (2005). The effect of financial liberalization on firms' investment in Korea. *Journal of Asian Economics, 16*, 281–297.
Laeven, L. (2002). Financial constraints on investments and credit policy in Korea. *Journal of Asian Economics 13*, 251–269.
Law, S. H. (2018). Applied panel data analysis short panels. *PENERBIT UPM*.

Matemilola, B. T., Bany-Ariffin, A. N., Azman-Saini W. N., & Nassir, M. A. (2018). Does top managers' experience affect firms' capital structure? *Research in International Business and Finance, 45*, 488–498.

Malmendier, U., & Tate, G. (2008). Who makes acquisitions? CEO overconfidence and the market's reaction. *Journal Financial Economics, 89*(1), 20–43.

Moseki, K. K., & Rao, M. (2018). Empirical measures of symmetry of market sentiments. *Cogent Economics & Finance, 6*. https://doi.org/10.1080/23322039.2018.1430113

Mushinada, V. N. C., & Veluri, V. (2018). Investors overconfidence behaviour at Bombay Stock Exchange. *International Journal of Managerial Finance, 14*, 613–632.

Nickell, S. (1982). The determinants of occupational success in Britain. *The Review of Economic Studies, 49*, 43–53.

Norman, G. R., Monteiro, S. D., Sherbino, J., Ilgen, J. S., Schmidt, H. G., & Mamede, S. (2017). The causes of errors in clinical reasoning: Cognitive biases, knowledge deficits, and dual process thinking. *Academic Medicine, 92*(1), 23–30.

Pikulina, E., Renneboog, L., & Tobler, P. N. (2017). Overconfidence and investment: An experimental approach. *Journal of Corporate Finance, 43*, 175–192.

Ramli, N. A., & Latan, H., & Solovida, G. (2019). Determinants of capital structure and firm financial performance—A PLS-SEM approach: Evidence from Malaysia and Indonesia. *The Quarterly Review of Economics and Finance, 71*, 148–160.

Raza, S. A. (2015). Foreign direct investment, workers' remittances and private saving in Pakistan: An ARDL bound testing approach. *Journal of Business Economics and Management, 16*(6), 1216–1234.

Raza, S. A., & Jawaid, S. T. (2014). Foreign capital inflows, economic growth and stock market capitalisation in Asian countries: An ARDL bound testing approach. *Quality & Quantity, 48*(1), 375–385.

Raza, S. A., Jawaid, S. T., Afshan, S., & Karim, M. Z. A. (2015). Is stock market sensitive to foreign capital inflows and economic growth? Evidence from Pakistan. *Journal of Chinese Economic and Foreign Trade Studies, 8*(3), 142–164.

Raza, S., Mansoor, M., & Iraqi, K. (2019). Influence of investor sentiments on stock market capitalization of different economic sectors in a developing economy: Evidence from Pakistan. *Journal of Finance & Economics Research, 4*, 31–43.

Ru, G., & Xin, Y. (2018). How to measure capital investment efficiency: A literature synthesis. *Accounting and Finance, 60*, 299–334.

Rungsomboon, S. (2005). Deterioration of firm balance sheet and investment behavior: Evidence from panel data on Thai firms. *Asian Economic Journal, 19*, 335–356.

Roodman, D. (2009). How to do Xtabond2: An introduction to difference and system GMM in Stata. *The Stata Journal: Promoting Communications on Statistics and Stata, 9*, 86–136.

Schmeling, M. (2009). Investor sentiment and stock returns: Some international evidence. *Journal of Empirical Finance, 16*(3), 394–408.

Singhal, R., Fu, L., & Parkash, M. (2016). Tobin's q ratio and firm performance. *International Research Journal of Applied Finance, 7*, 1–10.

Stauffer, D., & Sornette, D. (1999). Self-organised percolation model for stock market fluctuations. *Physica a: Statistical Mechanics and Its Applications, 271*(3), 496–506.

Tuyon, J., Ahamd, Z., & Matahir, H. (2016). The role of investor sentiment in Malaysian stock market. *Asian Academy of Management Journal of Accounting and Finance*, 43–75.

Toit, D. C., & Moolman, E. (2003). A neoclassical investment function of the South African economy. *Economic Modelling., 21*, 647–660.

Vuong, N. B., & Suzuki, Y. (2020). Impact of financial development on sentiment-return relationship. *Asia-Pacific Markets-Borsa Istanbul Review, 20*(2), 95–107.

Wang, W. (2018). Investor sentiment and the mean-variance relationship: European evidence. *Research in International Business and Finance, 46*, 227–239.

Yu, J., & Yuan, Y. (2011). Investor sentiment and the mean–variance relation. *Journal of Financial Economics, 100*(2), 367–381.

Zainudin, Z., Zaki, Z. M., Abdul Hadi, A. R., Hussain, H. I., & Kantakji, M. H. (2019). Investor sentiment and firm financial performance of Malaysian IPO firms: Pre and post financial crisis. *International Journal of Financial Research, 10*(5), 450–458.

Zhaohui, Z., & Wensheng, H. (2013). Investor sentiment and firms' investment: An empirical study based on catering channel. *Journal of Applied Sciences, 13*, 1199–1205.

Zhu, Z., Song, X., & Huang, W. S. (2017). Top management team demography, investor sentiment, and the investment levels of listed companies. *Asia-Pacific Journal of Accounting & Economics, 25*, 1–15.

Zhou, G. (2018). Measuring investor sentiment. *Annual Review of Financial Economics, 10*, 239–259.

Crypto or Stock? A Comparative Analysis for Beginners

Wai-Yan Wong, Shu-Fen Chuah, Ai-Xin Lee, and Phui-Chee Chong

Abstract Crypto or stock? Investors should understand what they are investing in when weighing cryptocurrencies or stocks. Although cryptocurrencies such as Bitcoin, Ethereum and Cardano have surged in value in recent years, savvy investors have to scrutinise what they are getting into and keep an eye out before jumping in. Therefore, this chapter begins by introducing cryptocurrencies and stocks to help the readers understand these fundamentals. In this chapter, we will look into the definition of cryptocurrency and stocks, the fundamentals of cryptocurrencies and stocks and the interconnectedness between these two investments in recent years.

Keywords Cryptocurrency · Stock market · Bitcoin · Shares

1 Introduction

1.1 What is Cryptocurrency?

Cryptocurrency is a digital and encrypted type of currency. The term "crypto" originates from the cryptographic techniques used to secure transactions. Unlike the traditional currencies such as the US Dollar, Euro or Malaysian Ringgit, cryptocurrencies use cryptographic techniques that do not require any central authority (i.e., banks or government) to manage and oversee such transactions. In other words, it

W.-Y. Wong (✉) · P.-C. Chong
Faculty of Economics and Management, Universiti Kebangsaan Malaysia, Bangi, Selangor, Malaysia
e-mail: wongwy@ukm.edu.my

S.-F. Chuah
Faculty of Business, Economics and Social Development, Universiti Malaysia Terengganu, Kuala Terengganu, Terengganu, Malaysia

A.-X. Lee
School of Management, Universiti Sains Malaysia, Penang, Malaysia

Z. Abdul Karim et al. (eds.), *Contemporary Issues in Finance, Investment and Banking in Malaysia*,
https://doi.org/10.1007/978-981-99-5447-6_3

uses a decentralised financial system, which is cheaper and faster and provides greater transparency.

Cryptocurrency can be used to buy goods and services. Nowadays, the use of cryptocurrency is prevailing and has been widely accepted by many retailers. For example, major retailers such as Microsoft, Home Depot and Automobili Lamborghini accept cryptocurrency payments, making purchases much more effortless. With cryptocurrency, one can also make purchases from non-fungible tokens (NFT), where one can buy or sell any unique digital assets online using cryptocurrency.

1.2 Types of Cryptocurrencies

Cryptocurrency is still very new to many of us although it has existed since 2009 after Satoshi Nakamoto published a paper entitled "Bitcoin: A Peer-to-Peer Electronic Cash System". Since then, cryptocurrencies have aroused significant attention from the public, and they continue to grow extensively. To date, there are more than 10,000 cryptocurrencies in the market (refer to Fig. 1).

The most notable cryptocurrencies are Bitcoin, Ethereum and Tether. The top 10 cryptocurrencies by market capitalisation include Bitcoin (BTC), Ethereum (ETH), Tether (USDT), USD Coin (USDC), Binance Coin (BNB), Binance USD (BUSD), Cardano (ADA), Ripple (XRP), Solana (SOL) and Polkadot (DOT) (refer to Table 1).

Laycock (2022) found a significant increase in cryptocurrency sentiment worldwide along with the popularity of cryptocurrency. Global cryptocurrency ownership has also increased from an average of 11.2% in November 2021 to 14.6% in April 2022. Malaysia owns 15.2%, higher than the global average and is ahead of Brazil

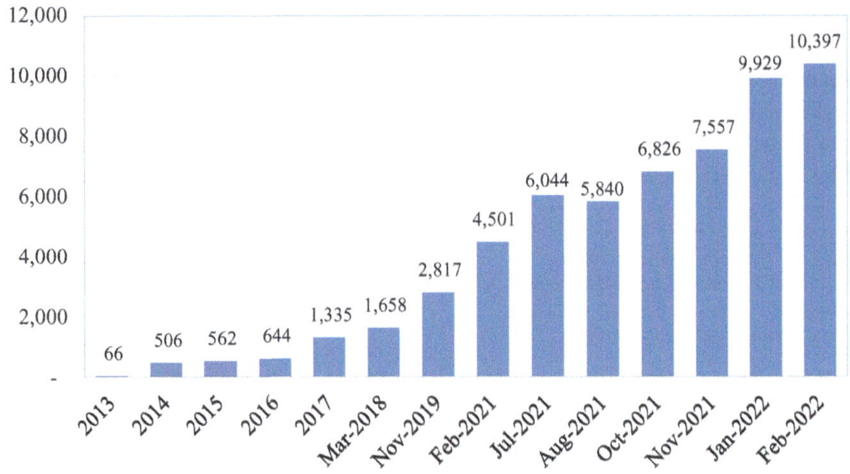

Fig. 1 Number of cryptocurrencies worldwide (2013 to Feb 2022) (*Source* Statista [2022])

Table 1 List of cryptocurrencies by market capitalisation

Rank	Name	Symbol	Market capitalisation ($)
1	Bitcoin	BTC	414,985,382,594
2	Ethereum	ETH	141,911,421,347
3	Tether	USDT	69,969,909,097
4	USD Coin	USDC	54,373,174,290
5	Binance Coin	BNB	36,407,966,900
6	Binance USD	BUSD	17,650,166,271
7	Cardano	ADA	17,088,593,615
8	Ripple	XRP	15,769,405,151
9	Solana	SOL	11,165,492,085
10	Polkadot	DOT	7,786,771,849

Source CoinMarketCap (2022)

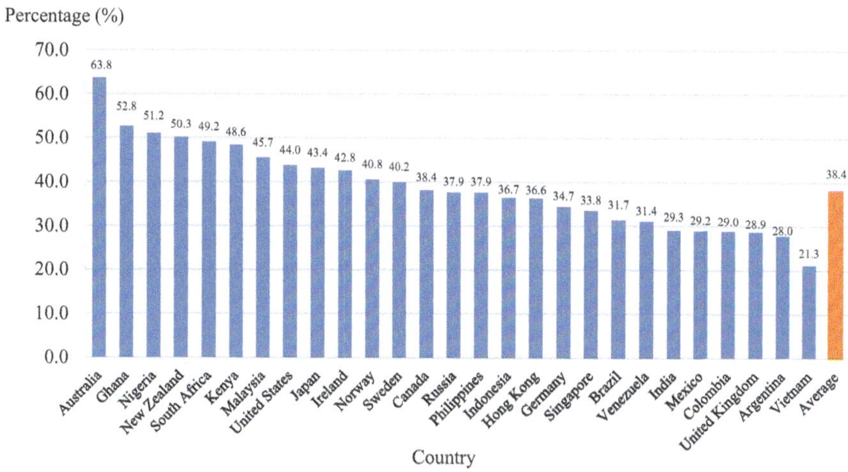

Fig. 2 Percentage of Bitcoin ownership by country (as at April 2022) (*Source* Laycock [2022])

(15.1%) and Argentina (14.7%). Amongst all, Bitcoin (BTC) is the most widely held cryptocurrency by Malaysia (45.7%), followed by Ripple (XRP) at 24.8% and Dogecoin (DOGE) at 22.9%. Malaysia ranked 7th in terms of Bitcoin ownership, ahead of many developed countries such as the United States (44%), Japan (43.4%) and Ireland (42.8%) (refer to Fig. 2).

1.3 Fundamentals of Cryptocurrencies

The cryptocurrency market is not as stable compared to other financial markets. Unlike stocks, cryptocurrency does not have intrinsic value. The value of cryptocurrency can increase and fall significantly in just nano seconds. Since cryptocurrency is not backed by underlying assets or cash flows, the value of cryptocurrency is typically determined by the market sentiment over the fundamental of the economic model, i.e., supply and demand. The value of cryptocurrency is driven only when someone desires to buy more in the future. Generally, cryptocurrencies such as Bitcoin are scarce. When people wish to own, but there is a limited supply, the value of cryptocurrency will rise to meet the expected demand (Royal, 2022).

Despite the rise of cryptocurrency and its popularity, financial concerns have come to light due to its volatility and decentralised system nature. Some countries such as Bangladesh, China, Iraq and Morocco have banned using cryptocurrencies. Therefore, everyone must be vigilant about the merit and uncertainty associated with using cryptocurrencies.

2 What is Stock?

Stocks or common stocks (also known as shares) are the security representing a partial ownership interest in a corporation. It represents a legal ownership stake in a corporation. Generally, investors can purchase stocks through the primary or secondary market. When a corporation issues stocks to the public for the first time, they are sold in the primary market. This type of new stock issuance is commonly known as Initial Public Offering (IPO).

Subsequently, investors can trade stocks in the secondary market. The secondary market is also known as the stock market or stock exchange for most investors. New York Stock Exchange (NYSE), Nasdaq and Bursa Malaysia are examples of secondary markets where an investor can buy or sell stocks from another investor. In short, the primary market is where a corporation interacts with an investor while the secondary market is where an investor interacts with another investor. The owner of the stock (known as the stockholder) is now the owner of the issuing company and is eligible for a corresponding share of the company's profits (usually in the form of dividends, depending on the company's dividend policy).

2.1 Types of Stocks

Generally, there are two main types of stock: common and preferred. The stockholders (also known as shareholders) have certain rights based on the types of stocks

Table 2 Common stock vs. preferred stock

	Common stock	Preferred stock
Ownership	Yes	Yes
Voting Rights	Yes	No
Dividend Income	Variable	Fixed
Order of Claims	After debtholders and preferred stockholders	After debtholders

they own. Although both common stockholders and preferred stockholders are entitled to ownership or stake in a company, there are some differences between common and preferred stocks. A comparison of individual characteristics between the two is illustrated in Table 2.

Although both common and preferred stockholders have a legal ownership stake in a company, only the common stockholders have voting rights. The stockholders voting rights allow them to cast their vote on certain corporate decisions such as the appointment of the board of directors, auditors, new stock issuance, etc. Having said that, preferred stockholders do not have voting rights and cannot vote on any company decisions.

Similarly, common stockholders and preferred stockholders receive dividend payments from a company. However, the dividend paid to common stockholders varies, depending on the company's profits. For example, a company may pay out RM2 dividends when the company is doing well and decide not to pay out anything when the company profits have been unfruitful. The preferred stockholders, on the other hand, received fixed dividends.

The order of claims on a company's earnings also varies according to the type of stockholders. Generally, debtholders are the first to claim. Followed by preferred stockholders, common stockholders are the last to be paid out. In the event of company liquidation, the distribution of company assets also differs depending on the type of stockholders. The first in line for payments is the company's debtholders or creditors. Preferred stockholders are the second who will be given priority in receiving payout before the common stockholders.

2.2 *Fundamentals of Stocks*

Unlike cryptocurrencies, stocks have intrinsic value. The intrinsic value tells us how well the company is performing and enlightens the "true" value of a company. It is a common fundamental analysis conducted by investors to access the "true" value of a stock and determine whether a stock is undervalued or overvalued. Be mindful that a stock price does not necessarily be equivalent to its intrinsic value.

The stock price is the stock's current value determined by the market. There are many factors affecting the price of a stock (for example, supply and demand, investor sentiments, economic conditions, government policy, etc.). However, the most significant factor that has to do with stock price is the supply and demand in the market. The stock price will eventually reflect the current demand for stock with the available supply. Let's say many people wish to buy Apple Inc. stock rather than sell the stock (demand more than supply). This wish will drive the stock price of Apple Inc. higher. The stock price would otherwise fall when the stock supply is more than demand. Nevertheless, the stock price of a company in the long run very much depends on its capability to increase its earnings over time. In other words, a company's stock price will increase in the long run as a result of the underlying company's success.

3 Differences Between Crypto and Stocks

In this section, we will discuss the difference between crypto and stocks. In this section, we will discuss the difference between crypto and stocks. There are mainly four differences that we will focus on in this section; ownership, exchange, volatility and regulation.

3.1 Ownership

According to Market Business News (MBN), ownership is known as the state, act or right of owning something. There are many forms of ownership, private or collective owners of the property.[1] For stock ownership, investors can become part of the owners of the company if they buy a percentage of the shares in the company via the stock exchange. Equity is a way to describe ownership, and equities are an alternative name for stocks. Different types of stocks will determine voting rights, dividend payments and **capital appreciation**. Voting right refers to the right of a shareholder of a corporation to vote at the company's annual shareholder meeting as they are a partial owner of the company (Hayes, 2021). Shareholders have the power to vote on corporate actions, policies, board members and other issues. On the other hand, dividend payments refer to the distribution of some company earnings to their shareholders. **Capital appreciation, known as capital gains, refers to an increase or rise value of an asset in the market.** The process of owning stock starts from opening an account at a brokerage to make trades and holding on stocks in the buyer's name. In order to do so, buyers need to provide their personal information, security number and street address to the brokerage firms.

[1] Refer to https://marketbusinessnews.com/financial-glossary/ownership/.

For crypto, the ownerships are commonly acquired in stable coins, DeFi tokens, NFTs and asset-backed tokens.[2] In other terms, crypto is known as digital currencies based on blockchain technology. For crypto ownership, it does not represent partial ownership of the company that issued it and is backed by no hard assets or cash flows. As crypto buyers, it is more difficult to track ownerships and they will hold the assets in a virtual wallet or on a storage device.[3] The ownership of crypto will be verified by a private key that is given to the owner. With that private key, you can sign a specific message to prove you are a owner of cryptocurrencies (Wengroff, 2021). In less than 5 min, owners can transfer their ownership of crypto-asset exchanges to private wallets without any complicated process (Pedro, 2019). Therefore, it can be said that it will be easier for an individual to own crypto rather than stocks.[4] However, it must be noted that crypto prices are speculation driven by sentiment. The detail about crypto prices will be further discussed in the following part (volatility).

3.2 Exchange

There are differences between the stock exchange and the crypto exchange. Generally, stock exchange refers to a market where an individual can buy or sell their stocks. It can be exchanged in a physical location or on an electronic trading platform.[5] Crypto exchange, on the other hand, acts as an intermediary between a buyer and a seller, in which they will earn money through commissions and transaction fees.[6]

Every country usually has its specific platform on the stock exchange. For example, the listed stock exchanges are the New York Stock Exchange (NYSE) and the Nasdaq in the United States. Table 3 below shows the list of exchange name and their respective country (Kennon, 2022).

For crypto, the exchanges for buying and selling cryptocurrency are newer.[7] In other words, exchange in crypto is relatively unstable compared to stock. Crypto is not controlled by the government hence, several problems might occur. For example, hacking risk is inherently higher for crypto than stock market, which comes from the use of keys and the transactions. This means that if someone accidentally have access to your private keys, they can access your crypto account and the currency may be stolen (Hartwiq, 2021). These kinds of issues may affect the value of cryptocurrencies

[2] Refer to https://www.softwaretestinghelp.com/types-of-cryptocurrency/#:~:text=Answer%3A%20There%20are%20about%20nine%20types%20of%20cryptocurrencies.,or%20use%20case%2C%20and%20functioning%20of%20the%20cryptocurrency.

[3] Refer to https://online.maryville.edu/blog/cryptocurrency-vs-stocks/.

[4] Refer to https://www.cointree.com/learn/cryptocurrency-exchange-vs-stock-exchange/.

[5] Refer to https://corporatefinanceinstitute.com/resources/knowledge/finance/stock-exchange/.

[6] Refer to https://corporatefinanceinstitute.com/resources/cryptocurrency/cryptocurrency-exchanges/.

[7] Refer to https://online.maryville.edu/blog/cryptocurrency-vs-stocks/.

Table 3 Types of stock exchange

Stock exchange	Location (Country)
Tokyo Stock Exchange or Japan Exchange Group	Tokyo, Japan
Shanghai Stock Exchange	Shanghai, China
Hong Kong Exchange	Hong Kong
Euronext	France, Portugal, Netherlands, Belgium
Shenzen Stock Exchange	Shenzen, China
London Stock Exchange Group	UK, Italy
TMX Group	Toronto, Canada
BSE India Ltd	Mumbai, India

and cause its overall higher transaction fees. Transaction fees are needed when an individual wants to sell or buy crypto. There are no fixed transaction fees, and it's all depending on the market. There are three types of transaction fees in crypto: exchange fees, network fees and wallet fees.[8] Exchange fees in crypto refer to fees that are charged to an individual if they decide to exchange crypto for money. Network fees refer to fees that need to be bore by an individual before he or she wishes to send or receive digital assets. Wallet fees occur only if an individual wants to withdraw or send their crypto from one wallet to another.

3.3 Volatility

All stocks or crypto have their level of volatility. In finance, term volatility refers to how frequently and drastically an asset's price changes over time. If an asset is highly volatile, its prices fluctuate a lot within a time period and vice versa. In this section, we will discuss the difference between crypto and stocks in terms of volatility.

Investing in stocks will be much less volatile than investing in crypto as stocks have been introduced and emerged in the market for a long time since 1611. Therefore, it is safer to invest as we have enough data to analyse the stocks (Waugh, 2021). Those data can predict future market performance and mitigate risk before we invest. We need to note that a stock's value will be affected by its performance, outlook, valuation and cash flow. Compared to crypto, the stock market seems like a more diverse trade market where investors can track and predict the investment return. Individual stocks refer to the ownership or purchasing of stocks in one specific company. This could be riskier to invest in as you need to study in depth of a particular company. How can we measure volatility in stocks? There are several that can be used to measure volatility in stocks, standard deviation, maximum drawdown and beta. A standard deviation is a popular tool used to measure stock volatility. It measures the amount of variability or dispersion around an average to expected risk and the significance

[8] Refer to https://phemex.com/academy/what-is-bitcoin-transaction-fees.

of certain price movements. Beta is one of the measurement tools to measure the relationship between volatility in stocks and the overall market.

Crypto is relatively new compared to stock in the global market. Therefore, crypto investments are more volatile than investing in stock as they are not backed by physical assets or anything. The main reason crypto prices are speculation is because it is highly driven by sentiment. As sentiment changes, crypto prices will shift. Investors may choose to invest in crypto as short-, medium- and long-term investments (Thaker & Mand, 2021). In terms of tools or indicators that can be used to measure volatility in crypto, there are **Bollinger Bands**, Average True Range and CBOE Volatility Index.[9] There are differences between these three measurements. **Bollinger Bands are used to identify the trends and detect if there were over brought or oversold crypto in the market.** The Average True Range is used to analyse crypto market volatility and measure how much crypto prices change on average in a particular period of time .[10] According to IMF, crypto prices are moving in sync with stocks, raising the risk of contagion across financial markets.[11] At the same time, it will also be harder for crypto to be used as a hedging instrument (Adrian et al., 2022).

3.4 Regulation

Financial regulation is a form of regulation supervised by the governments and financial institutions.[12] With the proper regulation, governments can provide a safer environment for investors and protect them during investment. Without any regulation, it could lead to a collapse or a severe recession in the open market. Every country has administrative and regulatory bodies to investigate and be involved in regulatory duties. In this section, we will discuss the difference between crypto and stocks in terms of their regulations.

Generally, stocks have a stronger and more established regulation than crypto. There will be many government agencies regulated in all the stock exchanges, brokers and companies. Every country has its government agencies as well. For example, Securities and Exchange Commission (SEC) in the United States (US), the Central Bank of Hungary in Hungary, the China Securities Regulatory Commission in China, and the Financial Supervisory Service in Korea. Most of them play the same role and regulation in the stock market. In the United States, the SEC protects investors and

[9] Refer to https://zignaly.com/crypto-knowledge-base/volatility-indicators/.

[10] Refer to https://cryptoadventure.com/why-average-true-range-is-important-in-crypto-trading/#:~:text=A%20popular%20and%20efficient%20technical%20indicator%20in%20analyzing,price%20on%20average%20during%20a%20particular%20time%20frame.

[11] Refer to https://www.business-standard.com/article/markets/crypto-prices-moving-in-sync-with-stocks-posing-systemic-risks-122011200477_1.html.

[12] Refer to Capital Com (https://capital.com/financial-regulation-definition).

provides fair investment activities in the market (Chen, 2022). SEC is the top regulatory agency responsible in the United States for overseeing all stock exchanges and the securities industry (Little, 2021). Companies must provide relevant information via agencies to investors before they can make any offer or sale of a security. It must be registered and follow the rules and regulations of the Securities and Exchange Commission. However, most governments did not directly control the stock market. But they will impose some policies which directly or indirectly impact the stock market.[13] Studies like Somani (2020) examine the effects of various government actions on stock market performance during a financial crisis. The findings show that the US government had performed many actions to stabilise and strengthen the economy during the crisis.

In crypto, it has lower regulation than stocks as the former is relatively new in the market and it is still not widely accepted or regulated by governments, where some countries have even banned crypto. For example, China banned all crypto transactions in their country in late September 2021. They argue that crypto transactions will lead to financial crime and an unstable economy (Shin, 2022). In 2021, China pressured mining farm operators and large mining operations to shut down and to leave China's market (Sharma, 2022). Other countries which banned crypto include Egypt, Iraq, Qatar, Oman, Morocco, Algeria, Tunisia and Bangladesh (Quiroz, 2022). In Malaysia, Bitcoin is not recognised as legal tender by Central Bank Malaysia (Bank Negara Malaysia, 2014), which means that any risk invested in Bitcoins is at its own risk and not covered by Bank Negara Malaysia.

4 The Interconnectedness Between Crypto and Stocks

Theoretically, crypto is nothing but a currency or an exchange medium that has no formal backing for its value and is subject to market forces, such as investors' sentiment and beliefs (Garratt & Wallace, 2018). Unless there is mass adoption and people believe that crypto could act as a medium of exchange, else one possible value to crypto is always zero, which means crypto has no inherent value at all. Bitcoin, which has been around since 2009, is the first and also the biggest crypto today. On the other hand, the Amsterdam stock exchange, created in 1611, was the first stock exchange in the world (Petram, 2011). Apparently, stocks have a much longer history than crypto, but crypto, particularly Bitcoin, has started to gain faith and gone into the mainstream in recent years. In fact, though invented as a currency at first, crypto is now being treated as an investment product (Sun et al., 2021). Some even name crypto as the new gold, digital gold, or gold 2.0 (Baur & Hoang, 2021). In answering the question "Why is gold valuable"? Butt and Hough (2009, p. 279) once explained, "Gold's value lies in its financial role—but in the end, it is valuable because we, the human race, continue to believe it is so, for whatever reason!" Butt and Hough (2009, pp. 279) Similarly, more and more people believe in digital assets

[13] https://stern-capital.com/does-the-president-control-the-stock-market.

such as the new gold—crypto and perceive them as the future of the capital market (Sandner, 2021), the next revolutionary financial invention after credit cards and e-wallets. Statistically, the global cryptocurrency market peaked at $2.9 trillion in November 2021 (Howcroff, 2022). In contrast, the Bitcoin market alone was worth $1.03 trillion, and the gold market $11.8 trillion (Reiff, 2021). The global stock market was estimated at $120.4 trillion (Securities Industry and Financial Markets Association, 2021) during the same period.

Following the increase in market capitalisation of crypto, the interconnectedness between crypto and stocks has come under the spotlight in recent years. Generally, there is a mixed relationship between crypto and stocks over the time following the major events in the crypto world. In other words, we found their relationships change following the timeline when people perceive crypto differently, depending on market conditions, as supported by López-Cabarcos et al. (2021). Hence, the following discussions will be presented according to the different time periods when the events took place. In addition, it should be noted that most of our discussion surrounds Bitcoin since it is not only the oldest crypto but also makes up the greatest market capitalisation of crypto. Four events will be discussed:

- Event 1: Stability period between 2009 and 2016
- Event 2: 2017 boom and 2018 crash
- Event 3: Constantly record new highs—2019 to early 2022
- Event 4: Crypto's biggest bear market

4.1 *Event 1: Stability Period Between 2009 and 2016*

From the invention of Bitcoin in 2009 till the end of 2016, Bitcoin prices remained stable at under $1500 (Chan et al., 2019), despite Bitcoin price crashes have been observed on several occasions in 2011, 2013 and 2015. For example, Bitcoin was priced at $29.58 on 9 June 2011 but dropped to $2.14 on 18 November 2011 and again reached a peak of $1,127.45 on 29 November 2013 but plunged to the bottom record of $172.15 on 13 Jan 2015 (Morris, 2021). In spite of the volatility, Bitcoin prices are relatively stable, under $1,500 USD and researchers such as Chan et al. (2019), Bouri et al. (2017) and Shahzad et al. (2019) report that Bitcoin could be used to hedge against to the stock market in some extent. When individuals use Bitcoin to hedge against the stock market, individuals strategically trade so that a gain or loss in the stock market is offset by the changes to the value of the Bitcoin. Simply put, an asset exhibits a strong hedging feature when it is negatively correlated to another asset. Baur and Lucey (2010) and Chan et al. (2019) explain that the relationship between Bitcoin and the stock market could be illustrated in Table 4, while the interconnectedness between Bitcoin and stock markets during the stability period is reported in Table 5.

Bitcoin has a mixed relationship with the stock market, depending on the market conditions, with the majority of them suggesting a negative relationship between Bitcoin and stock market movement. In addition, researchers such as Filtz et al. (2017)

Table 4 Relationship between Bitcoin and the stock market

Relationship between Bitcoin and the stock market	Role of Bitcoin
Significant negative correlation	Strong hedge
Significant positive correlation	Diversifier
Insignificant correlation	Weak hedge

Table 5 The interconnectedness between crypto and stocks during the stable period

Study period	Frequency of data	Stock markets	Results	Conclusion	Authors
19 July 2010–22 May 2015	Daily	Financial Times Stock Exchange (FTSE) Index	Insignificant relationship	Weak hedge	Dyhrberg (2016)
July 2011–Dec 2015	Daily and weekly	i. Nikkei 225 & MSCI Pacific	i. Daily returns are significantly negatively correlated. Relationship fades for weekly data	Strong hedge	Bouri et al. (2017)
		ii. Shanghai A-Share	ii. Weekly returns are significantly negatively correlated	Strong hedge	
		iii. S&P 500, FTSE 100, DAX 30, MSCI World, MSCI Europe	iii. Significant positive for both daily and weekly data	Diversifier	
Oct 2010–Oct 2017	Daily, weekly and monthly	S&P 500, Nikkei, Shanghai A-Share, TSX Index and Euro STOXX	i. Significant negative for monthly data only	Strong hedge	Chan et al. (2019)
			ii. Uncorrelated in the daily and weekly returns	Weak hedge	
19 July 2010–22 Feb 2018	Daily	5 MSCI stock indices: World, Developed, Emerging Markets, China, and the US	MSCI World and MSCI China Index: no evidence of predictability from a stock index to that asset in the low quantiles of both the stock and the asset returns	Weak hedge	Shahzad et al. (2019)

explain that Bitcoin and stock markets have a weak relationship, likely because these two markets have different pools of investors. Anyhow, investors, particularly in the Japanese and Chinese markets, reap benefits from Bitcoin volatility and consider Bitcoin a safe haven asset (Bouri et al., 2017; Chan et al., 2019; Shahzad et al., 2019). It should also be noted that the frequency of data matters in examining the interconnectedness between Bitcoin and stock markets (Bouri et al., 2017; Chan et al., 2019), and Bitcoin may hedge against stock markets only when investors hold Bitcoins for longer periods (Chan et al., 2019). At this point of time, Bitcoin is frequently being treated like a gold, given their many similarities. For instance, both of them have a scarcity of supply (i.e. only 21 million Bitcoin available in the market), their supply is not controlled by a government, and both of them have high price volatility (Dyhrberg, 2016).

4.2 Event 2: 2017 Boom and 2018 Crash

The year 2017 marks an important year for crypto as Bitcoin achieved its significant breakthrough. The price has skyrocketed from around $1000 in January 2017 to $20,000 in December 2017 (Higgins, 2017). At the same time, a statement such as "Bitcoin becomes just like everything else on Wall Street as correlation with stocks jumps to 2-year high" started to top the news headline (Cheng, 2018), suggesting that the role of Bitcoin has changed from gold-alike to stock-alike. A study from DataTrek Research (Cheng, 2018) shows that on a 90-day basis, the correlation between the daily percent returns of the cryptocurrency and the S&P 500 is 33% (Fig. 3). One of the possible reasons for this high correlation could be because Bitcoin started gaining public attention in January 2016, especially the institutional investors, following the launching of Bitcoin futures by CME, the world's largest futures exchange, in December 2017 (Arnold, 2018; Cheng, 2018).

Despite achieving a high record in Bitcoin price, the market crashed and Bitcoin was worth only around $3,300 in December 2018. The positive correlation between Bitcoin and the stock market is supported by Bovaird (2018) who reported that both stocks and digital currencies followed each other closely. Both markets experienced remarkable gains in 2017 and dropped earlier in 2018. However, this positive relationship holds only for the short term and the correlation between the two is relatively weak for the long term. Using data from 4 January 2016 to 30 September 2019, López-Cabarcos et al. (2021) suggest that Bitcoin volatility is more unstable in speculative periods, while stock indices such as S&P 500 and VIX influence Bitcoin volatility in stable periods. Yaya et al. (2019) also stated that other crypto prices are cointegrated with Bitcoin, both pre-and-post the crash, and the crypto markets are more efficient after the crash. After all, investors continue adding crypto to their investments to hedge or diversify their portfolios.

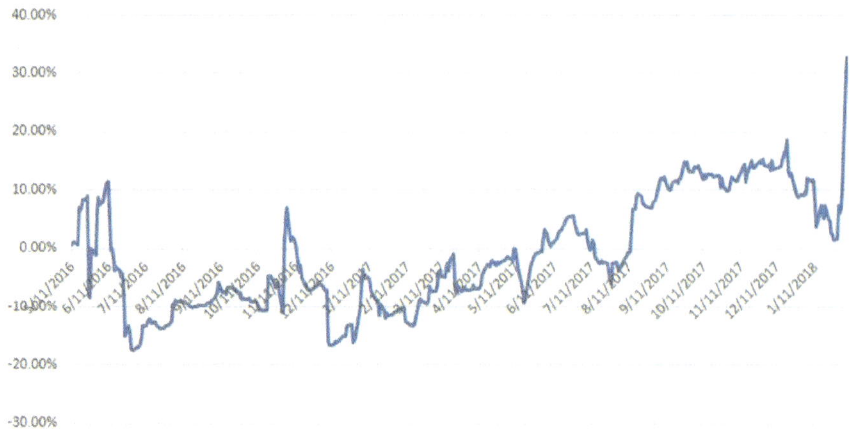

Fig. 3 90-day correlation of S&P and Bitcoin daily returns (*Source* DataTrek Research, as reported in Cheng [2018])

4.3 *Event 3: Constantly Record New Highs—2019 to Early 2022*

Bitcoin continues to soar upward and record new highs from 2019 to early 2022, with a peak of $67,802 in November 2021 (Vakil, 2022), while Ethereum and stock markets such as Nasdaq 100 and S&P 500 present a similar upward trend, as shown in Fig. 4. Using data from 2019 and 2020, Corbet et al. (2020) found that both crypto returns and volumes traded have increased following the COVID-19 outbreak, suggesting crypto has acted as value storage and provides a safe haven rather than a diversification effect during the period of exceptional financial market stress. However, this hedging effect does not last long as people live longer with COVID-19. The report released by Bank of America shows that since July 2021, crypto has moved with the stock market, and Bitcoin acts as a risk asset rather than an inflation hedge (Locke, 2022). This finding is also supported by Fulton (2022). Fulton (2022) reported that data from CoinDesk and Blockchain Center show that Bitcoin is showing a correlation to S&P 500 in the last quarter of 2021, in which the 90-day correlation between them grew from no significant correlation (0.2) to fairly strong correlation (0.6). Moreover, the correlation between Bitcoin and Nasdaq 100 was also near all-time highs, and Bitcoin continues to fall alongside with stocks after the Federal Reserve announced the increases in interest rates (Locke, 2022).

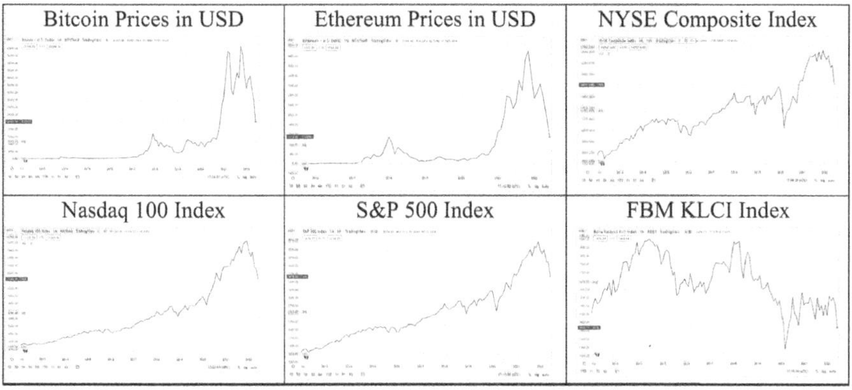

Fig. 4 Performance of Bitcoin, Ethereum, NYSE, Nasdaq 100, S&P 500, and FBM KLCI (*Notes* Line chart generated via TradingView for the period 1 January 2012 to 1 June 2022, except Ethereum which started on 1 August 2015)

4.4 Event 4: Crypto's Biggest Bear Market

In a recent report released by 21 Shares on 1 June 2022, bitcoin is said to have moved in sync with S&P 500, with their correlation reaching an all-time high of 0.69. However, when viewed for the longer term, their correlation is relatively low and estimated to be around 0.15 over the last eight years. Hence, crypto is uncorrelated to the stock market and continues to be one of the best-performing assets in the past decade. The report also revealed that including the top five crypto assets into the investment portfolio can drastically improve risk-adjusted returns while adding a 5% large market capitalisation crypto provides a better risk-return trade-off than investing solely in Bitcoin.

Today, we have more than 19,000 cryptos, and thousands of them are predicted to collapse soon (Kharpal, 2022). Bitcoin, which was priced at $67,802 in November 2021, has now dipped to $22,000 only, while the total market capitalisation of the crypto market has lost more than $2 trillion, with the latest value estimated to be at $926 billion (as dated 13 June 2022) (Howcroff, 2022). Crypto, is said in its biggest bear market in history since its first inception in 2009. As shown in Fig. 4, stock markets including FBM KLCI have posed a similar downward trend in the recent performance but further analysis is needed to confirm the relationship. It is vital for us to understand the interconnectedness between crypto and stocks over time as this allows us to quantify risks possessed by crypto, which ultimately shed the light on whether we should include or exclude crypto from the investment portfolio.

5 Conclusion and Summary

In this chapter, we provide a comparison analysis on the differences between conventional stock and cryptocurrencies. Our chapter starts off with the introduction of stocks and crypto, emphasising on the types of stocks and crypto currently in the market. According to Statista (2022), there are more than ten thousand crypto existing in the current market, with the main capitalisation being Bitcoin, Ethereum, Tether and USD Coin. For stocks, they are mainly separated into common stock and preferred stock, with the former being more common.

We also discussed about the fundamentals of both instruments, discussing about where their value is derived from. Cryptocurrency does not have intrinsic value and its value can fluctuate dramatically. Its value is not backed by underlying assets or cash flows, and therefore, the value of cryptocurrency is typically determined by the market sentiment. Unlike cryptocurrencies, stocks have intrinsic value, where it could reflect how well the company is performing.

We also compare the main differences between crypto and stocks from four perspectives which are ownership, exchange platform, volatility and regulation. Finally, we provide a comparison analysis on the movement of crypto and stock price in recent years. We show their interconnectedness during four events. During the period of 2009–2016, Bitcoin prices were generally stable under $1,500 (Chan et al., 2019) and many researches have concluded it is a good hedge for stocks as they have a negative relationship with stock market. However, this has changed since 2017 due to its boom and subsequent crash in 2018. In recent years, we have seen higher correlation in the movements of crypto and stocks. Therefore, crypto is not a good hedge for stocks as it used to be.

Acknowledgements Acknowledgement to "Geran Inovasi Pengajaran dan Pembelajaran (GIPP) with Project Code: EP-2022-007" and "Ministry of Higher Education Malaysia for Fundamental Research Grant Scheme with Project Code: FRGS/1/2021/SS01/UKM/02/4".

References

Adrian, T., Iyer, T., & Qureshi, M. S. (2022). Crypto prices move more in sync with stocks, posing new risks. https://blogs.imf.org/2022/01/11/crypto-prices-move-more-in-sync-with-stocks-posing-new-risks/

Arnold, A. (2018, October 19). How institutional investors are changing the cryptocurrency market. *Forbes*. https://www.forbes.com/sites/andrewarnold/2018/10/19/how-institutional-investors-are-changing-the-cryptocurrency-market/?sh=79eacae91ffe

Bank Negara Malaysia. (2014). Statement on Bitcoin. *BNM*. https://www.bnm.gov.my/-/statement-on-bitcoin

Baur, D. G., & Hoang, L. T. (2021). A crypto safe haven against Bitcoin. *Finance Research Letters*, *38*, 101431.

Baur, D. G., & Lucey, B. M. (2010). Is gold a hedge or a safe haven? An analysis of stocks, bonds and gold. *Financial Review*, *45*(2), 217–229.

Bouri, E., Molnár, P., Azzi, G., Roubaud, D., & Hagfors, L. I. (2017). On the hedge and safe haven properties of Bitcoin: Is it really more than a diversifier? *Finance Research Letters, 20*, 192–198.
Bovaird, C. (2018, October 16). Is the correlation between stocks and bitcoin real? *Forbes.* https://www.forbes.com/sites/cbovaird/2018/10/16/is-the-correlation-between-stocks-and-bitcoin-real/?sh=692528f76146
Butt, C. R., & Hough, R. M. (2009). Why gold is valuable. *Elements, 5*(5), 277–280.
Chan, W. H., Le, M., & Wu, Y. W. (2019). Holding Bitcoin longer: The dynamic hedging abilities of Bitcoin. *The Quarterly Review of Economics and Finance, 71*, 107–113.
Chen, J. (2022). Securities and Exchange Commission (SEC). https://www.investopedia.com/terms/s/sec.asp
Cheng, E. (2018, February 8). Bitcoin becomes just like everything else on Wall Street as correlation with stocks jumps to 2-year high. *CNBC.* https://www.cnbc.com/2018/02/08/bitcoins-correlation-with-stocks-jumps-to-2-year-high.html#:~:text=Investing%20Club-,Bitcoin%20becomes%20just%20like%20everything%20else%20on%20Wall%20Street%20as,jumps%20to%202%2Dyear%20high&text=On%20a%2090%2Dday%20basis,co%2Dfounder%20of%20DataTrek%20Research.
CoinMarketCap. (2022, May 1). Historical snapshot. *CoinMarketCap.* https://coinmarketcap.com/historical/20220501/
Corbet, S., Hou, Y. G., Hu, Y., Larkin, C., & Oxley, L. (2020). Any port in a storm: Cryptocurrency safe-havens during the COVID-19 pandemic. *Economics Letters, 194*, 109377.
Dyhrberg, A. H. (2016). Bitcoin, gold and the dollar—A GARCH volatility analysis. *Finance Research Letters, 16*, 85–92.
Filtz, E., Polleres, A., Karl, R., & Haslhofer, B. (2017). *Evolution of the bitcoin address graph.* In *Data science–Analytics and applications* (pp. 77–82). Springer Vieweg.
Fulton, R. J. (2022, June 14). Is bitcoin correlated to the S&P 500? Nasdaq. https://www.nasdaq.com/articles/is-bitcoin-correlated-to-the-sp-500
Garratt, R., & Wallace, N. (2018). Bitcoin 1, bitcoin 2,...: An experiment in privately issued outside monies. *Economic Inquiry, 56*(3), 1887–1897.
Hartwiq, B. (2021). Cybersecurity in cryptocurrency: Risks to be considered. https://www.dataversity.net/cybersecurity-in-cryptocurrency-risks-to-be-considered/
Hayes, J. (2021). Hayes statement on the passage of the John R. Lewis voting rights advancement act. https://hayes.house.gov/2021/8/hayes-statement-passage-thejohn-lewis-voting-rights-advancement-act
Higgins, S. (2017, December 29). From $900 to $20,000: Bitcoin's historic 2017 price run revisited. *Coindesk.* https://www.coindesk.com/markets/2017/12/29/from-900-to-20000-bitcoins-historic-2017-price-run-revisited/
Howcroff, E. (2022, June 13). Cryptocurrency market value slumps under $1 trillion. *Reuters.* https://www.reuters.com/business/finance/cryptocurrency-market-value-slumps-under-1-trillion-2022-06-13/
Kennon, J. (2022). What is a stock exchange? *The Balance.* https://www.thebalance.com/what-is-a-stock-exchange-358113
Kharpal, A. (2022, June 3). Crypto firms say thousands of digital currencies will collapse, compare market to early dotcom days. *CNBC.* https://www.cnbc.com/2022/06/03/crypto-firms-say-thousands-of-digital-currencies-will-collapse.html
Laycock, R. (2022, January 11). Finder cryptocurrency adoption index. *Finder.Com.* https://www.finder.com/finder-cryptocurrency-adoption-index
Little, K. (2021). How is the stock market regulated? *The Balance.* https://www.thebalance.com/who-s-watching-your-back-in-stock-market-3141308
Locke, T. (2022, May 7). Bitcoin isn't an inflation hedge, and it hasn't been for a long time, Bank of America says. *Yahoo News.* https://www.yahoo.com/news/bitcoin-isn-t-inflation-hedge-182941333.html
López-Cabarcos, M. Á., Pérez-Pico, A. M., Piñeiro-Chousa, J., & Šević, A. (2021). Bitcoin volatility, stock market and investor sentiment. Are they connected?. *Finance Research Letters, 38*, 101399.

Morris, C. (2021, June 25). South African brothers disappear along with $3.6 billion in Bitcoin. *Fortune*. https://fortune.com/2021/06/24/bitcoin-ameer-raees-cajee-theft-south-africa/
Pedro, F. (2019). What's the difference between trading cryptocurrency and stocks? *Yahoo*. https://finance.yahoo.com/news/difference-between-trading-cryptocurrency-stocks-140043344.html
Petram, L. O. (2011). *The world's first stock exchange: How the Amsterdam market for Dutch East India Company shares became a modern securities market*, 1602–1700. Eigen Beheer.
Quiroz, M. (2022, January 5). Crypto is fully banned in China and 8 other countries. *Fortune*. https://fortune.com/2022/01/04/crypto-banned-china-other-countries/
Reiff, N. (2021, November 26). How much of all money is in bitcoin? *Investopedia*. https://www.investopedia.com/tech/how-much-worlds-money-bitcoin/
Royal, J. (2022). Cryptocurrency vs. stocks: What's the better choice for you? *Bankrate*. https://www.bankrate.com/investing/crypto-vs-stocks/
Sandner, P. (2021, August 24). Digital assets: The future of capital markets. *Forbes*. https://www.forbes.com/sites/philippsandner/2021/08/24/digital-assets-the-future-of-capital-markets/?sh=271003406a57
Securities Industry and Financial Markets Association. (2021). Capital markets fact book. *SIFMA*. https://www.sifma.org/wp-content/uploads/2021/07/CM-Fact-Book-2021-SIFMA.pdf
Shahzad, S. J. H., Bouri, E., Roubaud, D., Kristoufek, L., & Lucey, B. (2019). Is Bitcoin a better safe-haven investment than gold and commodities? *International Review of Financial Analysis, 63*, 322–330.
Sharma, R. (2022). Is there a cryptocurrency price correlation to the stock market? *Investopedia*. https://www.investopedia.com/news/are-bitcoin-price-and-equity-markets-returns-correlated/
Shin, F. (2022). What's behind China's cryptocurrency ban? *World Economic Forum*. https://www.weforum.org/agenda/2022/01/what-s-behind-china-s-cryptocurrency-ban/#:~:text=In%20late%20September%202021%2C%20the%20People%E2%80%99s%20Bank%20of,financial%20system%20owing%20to%20their%20highly%20speculative%20nature.
Somani, S. (2020). The effects of government policies on the stock market. *University of South Carolina*. https://www.sc.edu/about/offices_and_divisions/research/news_and_pubs/caravel/archive/2015/2015-caravel-stock-market.php
Statista. (2022, March 22). Number of cryptocurrencies worldwide from 2013 to February 2022. *Statista*. https://www.statista.com/statistics/863917/number-crypto-coins-tokens/
Sun, W., Dedahanov, A. T., Shin, H. Y., & Li, W. P. (2021). Factors affecting institutional investors to add crypto-currency to asset portfolios. *The North American Journal of Economics and Finance, 58*, 101499.
Thaker, H. M. T., & Mand, A. A. (2021). Bitcoin and stock markets: A revisit of relationship. *Journal of Derivatives and Quantitative Studies, 29*(3), 234–256.
Vakil, C. (2022, May 11). Bitcoin value cut in half from its high. *Yahoo News*. https://finance.yahoo.com/news/bitcoin-value-cut-half-high-161751152.html
Waugh, E. (2021). Crypto vs. stocks: Which investment has less risk? *Experian*. https://www.experian.com/blogs/ask-experian/crypto-vs-stocks-which-investment-has-less-risk/
Wengroff, J. (2021). Can you prove that you own your crypto assets? *Transitnet*. https://transitnet.io/blog/can-you-prove-that-you-own-your-crypto-assets/#:~:text=The%20most%20reliable%20way%20to%20prove%20ownership%20of,transaction%2C%20even%20a%20small%20one%20%28as%20explained%20above%29.
Yaya, O. S., Ogbonna, A. E., & Olubusoye, O. E. (2019). How persistent and dynamic inter-dependent are pricing of Bitcoin to other cryptocurrencies before and after 2017/18 crash? *Physica a: Statistical Mechanics and Its Applications, 531*, 121732.

The Size Effect in Malaysia's Stock Returns

Syajarul Imna Mohd Amin, Aisyah Abdul-Rahman, and Bakri Abdul Karim

Abstract The size effect has been the most significant anomaly in stock price. Unlike developed stock markets, Malaysia's market is smaller, less liquid, more volatile, prone to higher risk premiums and has higher cost of funds. These features could be attributed to informational inefficiency, high trading costs, and less competition. Nonetheless, investors have become interested in the Malaysian stock market for international diversification and potentially high returns. Thus, this research aims to examine the size effect in Malaysia's cross-section of stock returns, involving 828 stocks listed in the FTSE Bursa Malaysia KLCI Index from January 2011 to December 2020. Fama–MacBeth-profitability regressions suggest that small firms and dividend payers perform better than large firms and non-dividend payers. Moreover, the small significant positive coefficient of lagged profitability suggests that Malaysian stock's returns are not highly persistent. The findings would benefit investors, fund managers, and top management for portfolio diversification and risk management in Malaysia's stock.

Keywords Firm size · Profitability shocks · Expected stock returns · Fama–MacBeth · Malaysia

1 Introduction

The size effect has been the most significant anomaly discovered in asset pricing literature, and it has been the longest-debated issue in academic discourse. Despite the attention it has received, there is still much debate and misunderstanding on the

S. I. M. Amin (✉) · A. Abdul-Rahman
Faculty of Economics and Management, Universiti Kebangsaan Malaysia, Bangi, Selangor, Malaysia
e-mail: imna@ukm.edu.my

B. A. Karim
Faculty of Business and Economics, Universiti Malaysia Sarawak, Kota Samarahan, Sarawak, Malaysia

Z. Abdul Karim et al. (eds.), *Contemporary Issues in Finance, Investment and Banking in Malaysia*,
https://doi.org/10.1007/978-981-99-5447-6_4

issue of size anomalies in the context of market efficiency. The size effect is the phenomenon in which small firms are found to earn higher returns compared to large firms. Researchers view the discovery of the size effect as a violation of the CAPM propositions in that firm-specific factor, i.e., size is a second source of price risk other than the market factors. Size effect documents are common in US stock markets such as the NYSE and AMEX markets (Banz, 1981) and the NASDAQ market (Lamoureux & Sanger, 1989). More recent literature has evidenced that the size effect disappeared after the early 1980s (Dichev, 1998; Chan et al., 2000; Horowitz et al., 2000; Amihud, 2002). Hou and Van Dijk (2019) discovered that the size effect disappeared only from ex post realized returns after the early 1980s and that size became a robust effect in ex ante expected returns.

There is disagreement on the appropriate use of realized return to measure expected return in asset pricing formulation (Blume & Friend, 1973; Elton, 1999; Froot & Frankel, 1989; Sharpe, 1978). Campbell (1991) decomposed realized stock returns into the sum of expected returns, news about future cash-flows (cash-flow shocks) and future discount rate. In a later study, Chen et al. (2013) suggested that news about future cash-flow is the dominant determinant of stock return. Based on these arguments, Hou and Van Dijk (2019) hypothesized that the disappearance of the size effect could be explained by three possibilities: (1) there were differences in future cash-flow between small and large firms; (2) size is not related to expected returns, neither before nor after the early 1980s; (3) there was no systematic difference between future cash-flows of small firms and large firms.

While some studies evidenced that the size effect had disappeared after the early 1980s, recent literature found it resurrected. Nonetheless, the size effect is highly reported in the US markets, and has also been tested in several studies in other developed markets (Chiah et al., 2016; Ejaz & Polak, 2018; Hashem & Su, 2019). Consistent with the US evidence, Hou and Djik (2019) confirmed that there was a significantly negative (positive) profitability shock to small (large) firms and, statistically significant size premium in developed Europe after the 1980s. Previous empirical work, however, may not be applicable to a developing market due to differences in regulatory framework and the size and maturity of stock returns. Scholars concern on whether size effect is relevant in stock markets outside the US. Unlike the US stock market, emerging stock markets like Malaysia are still infantile. The Malaysian market is rather smaller, less liquid, more volatile, and prone to higher risk premiums, and higher costs of funds. These features could be attributed to informational inefficiency, high trading costs, and less competition. Nonetheless, investors have become interested in the Malaysian stock market for international diversification and for potential high returns.

Given the prominence of the size effect on stock prices, it needs a critical scrutiny, especially in the case of emerging markets for the advancement of knowledge to benefit investors, scholars, and policymakers. Therefore, this research contributes to the construct validity of the size effect, which is still scarce in emerging markets. Indeed, more research in a diverse sample is required to develop the validity of the theory of asset pricing anomaly. Thus, this study intends to reaffirm the findings of US stock markets based on the Malaysian stock market, which is operating in an emerging market. Due to the dearth of local studies on this issue, our study would add to the much needed literature on the size effect. Furthermore, this study may provide policymakers with additional empirical evidence on the importance of size effect as a tool for stabilizing markets.

2 Literature Review

Previous studies suggest that size plays a significant role in determining stock prices in the US market (see Banz, 1981; Basu, 1983; Fama & French, 1992). Similarly, the size effect is found to be significant in many stock return studies in Asian markets (see Shum & Tang, 2005; Rouwenhorst, 1999; Wong, 1989). With a few exceptions, the general finding is that size effect does exist: small firms show a greater reaction than large firms. This finding is consistent with the information asymmetry theory, which says that small firms are subject to greater information asymmetry than large firms, because the former are typically not invested in by large institutional traders. Hence, there is a general lack of media and analyst coverage.

Early evidence of the size effect is provided by Ikenberry et al. (1995). They find that the cumulative abnormal returns, CAR (–2, +2) for the smallest quintile firms is 8.19% compared to 2.09% for the largest quintile, while the pre-event price drop as measured by CAR (–20, –3) for small firms is –3.91% compared to –1.21% for large firms. Other studies that provide evidence on the signalling size effect include Otchere and Ross (2002) in Australia; Zhang (2002) in Japan; Firth and Yeung (2005), and Zhang (2005) in Hong Kong; Jung et al. (2005) in Korea; and Koerniadi et al. (2007) in New Zealand.

In a recent study, Hou and Van Djik (2019) found a strong positive relationship between profitability shocks and contemporaneous stock returns. For the full 1963–2014 sample period, the value-weighted average returns difference between the quintile of firms with the highest profitability shocks and the quintile of firms with the lowest profitability shocks was close to 2% per month. This result suggests that the cross-sectional profitability model captures the market's cash-flow expectations: firms that are more (less) profitable than expected earn significantly higher (lower) stock returns. It also suggests that profitability shocks can drive a large wedge between realized and expected returns. The study evidenced that the average profitability shock is close to zero for both small firms and big firms before 1983. But after 1983, small firms experienced large negative profitability shocks, whereas big firms experienced large positive shocks. The latter result suggests that the realized returns of small (big) firms for the post-1983 period are lower (higher) than expected. As a result, the observed size premium in ex post realized returns during this period underestimates the "true" size premium in ex ante expected returns.

In terms of expected return indicators, there are several alternative proxies that have been used in asset pricing tests in the past literature. Brav et al. (2005) extract measures of expected returns for individual stocks from analysts' target prices.

Campello et al. (2008) construct measures of expected stock returns using corporate bond yields. Claus and Thomas (2001), Gebhardt et al. (2001), and Pástor et al. (2008) estimate the implied cost of capital (ICC) based on market prices and analysts' earnings forecasts and use it to test the risk-expected return relationship. Hou et al. (2012) estimate expected returns using a modified version of the ICC in which earnings forecasts are obtained from a cross-sectional profitability model rather than from analysts' forecasts. In their seminal work, Hou and Van Dijk (2019) used adjusted realized return for the price impact of cash-flow shocks to measure expected returns. Compared to deriving expected returns from market prices (like in the ICC literature), the advantage of adjusting realized returns is that it provides insights into the patterns (and sources of) in-sample cash-flow shocks that drive the differences between realized and expected returns. Furthermore, while the ICC measures a firm's long-term average expected stock return (the internal rate of return), the adjusted expected return approach allows for the estimation of the one-period-ahead expected return by adjusting realized returns for the price impact of cash-flow shocks over that period.

Given the current state of the literature, the question of whether the size effect exists outside of the US markets has to be answered empirically. This research attempts to fill the gap in the literature by testing the theory of size anomaly in the context of the Malaysian stock market and compare the findings with those in the US markets.

3 Data and Methodology

3.1 Data Description

This study used 828 stocks in the FTSE Bursa Malaysia KLCI Index. The FTSE Bursa Malaysia KLCI, also known as the FBM KLCI, is a major stock market index which tracks the performance of the 30 largest companies by full market capitalization listed on the Main Board of Bursa Malaysia. We collected the monthly stock returns from January 2011 to December 2020. In addition, following Hou and Van Dijk (2019), we also use the following variables. Size is the market equity at the end of December of the year t. Earning is operating income and depreciation. Book equity is stockholder equity value. BE/ME is book equity divided by market equity value at the end of year t–1. Market value of a firm is calculated by adding its total assets and the difference between market equity and book equity. Lastly, total assets and dividends are also collected. All data is extracted from Thomson Datastream.

In order to form portfolios, we sort firms into Top 25%, Middle (both 50% and 75%) and Bottom (below 25%) based on their size, and we calculate the value-weighted and equal-weighted monthly returns on the portfolios.

4 Results and Discussion

Table 1 provides the summary statistics (panel A) and the average value-weighted (panel B) and equal-weighted (panel C) returns, which are in excess of the 1-month Treasury-bill rate of the portfolios. In addition, the differences between the bottom and top portfolios are also reported. Both value-weighted realized returns and equal-weighted realized returns for the bottom portfolio are higher than top portfolio. Over the sample period, the results show that small firms perform better than large firms. The value-weighted spread between small firms and big firms is 0.9% per month with a *t*-stat of 3.38. The equal-weighted spread between small firms and big firms is 0.7% per month with a *t*-stat of 1.92.

Table 2 shows the average coefficients and their time series *t*-statistics from annual Fama and MacBeth (1973) cross-sectional regressions of profitability (earnings scaled by lagged total assets, E_{t+1}/A_t) on variables that are hypothesized to capture differences in expected profitability across firms. V_t/A_t is the market-to-book ratio of a firm's assets. DD_t is a dummy variable that equals 1 for dividend payers and 0 for nonpayers. D_t/B_t is the ratio of dividends to book equity. We estimate the regressions for each year between 2011 and 2020.

The results are quite similar to those reported in Fama and French (2006), Hou and Robinson (2006), and Hou and Van Dijk (2019). Profitability is positively related to *D*/*B* suggesting that firms that pay out more dividends are more profitable (Tables 3 and 4). In addition, the coefficient on *DD* is positive, thus it shows that dividend payers are more profitable than nonpayers. However, in terms of *V*/*A*, the results

Table 1 Summary statistics and average returns of top-mid-bottom size

	Big 25%	2	3	Small 25%	
A. Summary statistics					
Number of firms	207	207	207	207	
Average Size (RM billion)	6.979	0.338	0.112	0.038	
Maximum Size (RM billion)	95.101	0.708	0.225	0.096	
Minimum Size (RM billion)	0.716	0.227	0.096	0.014	
B. Value-weighted average return					
Value-Weighted realized return (%)	0.35	0.10	0.10	1.25	0.9
t-statistic	2.15	2.56	2.57	2.77	3.38
C. Equal-weighted average returns					
Equal-Weighted realized returns (%)	0.58	1.05	1.04	1.28	0.7
t-statistic	2.20	2.55	2.51	2.68	1.92

Note Realized returns in excess of the 1-month Treasury-bill rate and expressed as a percentage per month

Table 2 Cross-sectional profitability regression

	Coefficient	*t*-Statistics
Intercept	0.04***	5.02
V_t/A_t	–0.02***	–38.6
DD_t	0.03***	2.47
D_t/B_t	0.34***	6.40
E/At–1	0.002	0.25
Adj R^2	0.43	

show a negative coefficient, which is not in line with Fama and French (2006), Hou and Robinson (2006), and Hou and Van Dijk (2019). In addition, the results also indicate that the coefficient on lagged profitability is small and positive but not significant. The average adjusted R^2 is 43%, indicating that the model is acceptable (Table 5).

Table 6. shows the performance of each portfolio based on its size. Using the Treynor-Mazuy Model (1966), the results show that all portfolios have a positive Alpha, indicating that the portfolio has selectivity ability. In addition, the small-sized portfolio seems to generate greater returns than big-sized portfolio. According to Jiang et al. (2021), refers to the market timing ability, which a positive value shows market timing ability. The results indicate that the big-sized portfolio has good timing ability as compared to small-sized portfolio.

Table 3 Average returns of portfolio based on profitability shocks

	High	2	3	Low	High-Low
A. Value-weighted average profitability shocks and returns					
VW profitability shock	0.724	–0.027	–0.342	–1.866	2.59
t-statistics	0.82	–0.091	–1.38	–2.71	4.37
VW realized return	–0.28	–0.37	0.53	0.66	
t-statistics	–0.06	–0.19	2.09	4.45	
B. Equal-weighted average profitability shocks and returns					
EW profitability shock	0.495	–0.048	–0.337	–1.866	2.03
t-statistics	0.76	–0.16	–1.31	–2.59	3.12
EW realized return	0.72	0.92	0.95	1.34	
t-statistics	2.11	2.54	2.09	4.5	

Note Realized returns in excess of the 1-month treasury-bill rate and expressed as a percentage per month

Table 4 Average expected profitability and profitability shocks of size

	Big	2	3	Small	Small-Big
A. Value-weighted average expected profitability and profitability shocks					
VW expected profitability	−0.448	−0.305	0.368	0.467	0.915
t-statistics	−0.84	−0.78	−0.98	−1.34	
VW profitability shocks	−0.289	−0.323	−0.335	−0.48	−0.191
t-statistics	−0.82	−0.81	−0.96	−1.12	
B. Equal-weighted average expected profitability and profitability shocks					
EW expected profitability	0.518	0.363	0.361	0.641	0.123
t-statistics	0.97	0.93	1.08	1.27	
EW profitability shock	0.341	0.390	0.368	0.467	0.126
t-statistics	0.97	0.98	1.09	1.13	

Table 5 Cross-sectional regression of realized returns on size

	Coefficient	*t*-Statistics
Intercept	0.047	7.70
Ln(size)	−0.00187	−6.12
Ln (BE/ME)	−0.00061	−0.95
Adj R^2	0.004	

Table 6 Market timing

	Big	2	3	Small
Alpha	0.0010	0.006	0.0069	0.011
t-statistics	0.25	1.15	1.19	1.33
β_t	−1.18	−1.67	−1.58	−1.27
t-statistics	−2.74	−2.90	−2.46	−1.41
βpt	50.85	15.01	−3.88	−30.50
t-statistics	0.73	0.16	0.97	0.84

5 Summary and Conclusion

This chapter provides the empirical evidence of the size effect in Malaysia's cross-section of stock returns, involving 828 stocks listed in the FTSE Bursa Malaysia KLCI Index from January 2011 to December 2020. The study used Fama-MacBeth-profitability regressions and found that small firms provide higher stock returns than large firms. Besides, dividend-paying firms are more profitable than non-dividend-paying firms. Moreover, it is evidenced that Malaysian stock returns are not highly persistent. The findings imply that Malaysia's stocks provide a good testament for portfolio diversification and risk management.

Acknowledgements The authors appreciate the financial support from the Yayasan Tun Ismail Ali (YTI-UKM) Grant (code: EP-2020-006).

References

Amihud, Y. (2002). Illiquidity and stock returns: Cross-section and time-series effects. *Journal of Financial Markets, 5*, 31–56.

Banz, R. W. (1981). The relationship between return and market value of common stocks. *Journal of Financial Economics, 9*, 3–18.

Basu, S. (1983). The relationship between earnings' yield, market value and return for NYSE common stocks: Further evidence. *Journal of Financial Economics, 12*(1), 129–156.

Blume, M. E., & Friend, I. (1973). A new look at the capital asset pricing model. *Journal of Finance, 28*, 19–33.

Brav, A., Lehavy, R., & Michaely, R. (2005). Using expectations to test asset pricing models. *Financial Management, 34*, 5–37.

Campbell, J. Y. (1991). A variance decomposition for stock returns. *Economic Journal, 101*, 157–179.

Campbell, J. Y., & Ammer, J. (1993). What moves the stock and bond markets? A variance decomposition for long-term asset returns. *Journal of Finance, 48*, 3–37.

Campello, M., Chen, L., & Zhang, L. (2008). Expected returns, yield spreads, and asset pricing tests. *Review of Financial Studies, 21*(3), 1297–1338.

Chan, L. K. C., Karceski, J., & Lakonishok, J. (2000). New paradigm or same old hype in equity investing? *Financial Analysts Journal, 56*, 23–36.

Chen, L., Da, Z., & Zhao, X. (2013). What drives stock price movement? *Review of Financial Studies, 26*(4), 841–876.

Chiah, M., Chai, D., Zhong, A., & Li, S. (2016). A better model? An empirical investigation of the Fama-French five-factor model in Australia. *International Review of Finance, 16*(4), 595–638.

Claus, J., & Thomas, J. (2001). Equity premia as low as three percent? Evidence from analysts' earnings forecasts for domestic and international stock markets. *Journal of Finance, 56*(5), 1629–1666.

Dichev, I. D. (1998). Is the risk of bankruptcy a systematic risk? *Journal of Finance, 53*(3), 1131–1147.

Ejaz, A., & Polak, P. (2018). Australian Stock Exchange and sub-variants of price momentum strategies. *Innovations, 15*(1), 224–235.

Elton, E. J. (1999). Expected return, realized return, and asset pricing tests. *Journal of Finance, 54*, 1199–1220.

Fama, E. F., & MacBeth, J. D. (1973). Risk, return, and equilibrium: Empirical tests. *Journal of Political Economy, 81*, 607–636.

Fama, E. F., & French, K. R. (1992). The cross-section of expected stock returns. *Journal of Finance, 47*, 427–465.

Firth, M., & Yeung, C. S. (2005). An empirical investigation of share buybacks in Hong Kong. *Journal of Emerging Market Finance, 4*(3), 207–225.

Froot, K., & Frankel, J. A. (1989). Forward discount bias: Is it an exchange risk premium? *Quarterly Journal of Economics, 104*, 139–161.

Gebhardt, W. R., Lee, C. M. C., & Swaminathan, B. (2001). Towards an implied cost of capital. *Journal of Accounting Research, 39*, 135–176.

Hashem, N., & Su, L. (2019). Internationalization and the cross-section of stock returns: evidence from multinational corporations publicly listed in the UK. *International Journal of Business and Economics, 18*(3), 245–263.

Horowitz, J. L., Loughran, T., & Savin, N. E. (2000). Three analyses of the firm size premium. *Journal of Empirical Finance, 7*, 143–153.

Hou, K., & Van Dijk, M. A. (2019). Resurrecting the size effect: Firm size, profitability shocks, and expected stock returns. *The Review of Financial Studies, 32*(7), 2850–2889.

Hou, K., & Robinson, D. T. (2006). Industry concentration and average stock returns. *Journal of Finance, 61*, 1927–1956.

Hou, K., van Dijk, M. A., & Zhang, Y. (2012). The implied cost of capital: A new approach. *Journal of Accounting and Economics, 53*, 504–526.

Ikenberry, D., Lakonishok, J., & Vermaelen, T. (1995). Market underreaction to open market share repurchases. *Journal of Financial Economics, 39*(2–3), 181–208.

Jiang, G. J., Zaynutdinova, G. R., & Zhang, H. (2021). Stock-selection timing. *Journal of Banking & Finance, 125*, 106089.

Jung, S. C., Lee, Y. G., & Thornton Jr, J. H. (2005). An empirical comparison between operations of stabilization funds and stock repurchases in Korea. *Pacific-Basin Finance Journal, 13*(3), 319–341.

Koerniadi, H., Liu, M. H., & Tourani-Rad, A. (2007). Share repurchases in New Zealand. *In issues in corporate governance and finance* (pp. 481–498). Emerald Group Publishing Limited.

Lamoureux, C. G., & Sanger, G. C. (1989). Firm size and turn-of-the-year effects in the OTC/NASDAQ market. *The Journal of Finance, 44*(5), 1219–1245.

Otchere, I., & Ross, M. (2002). Do share buy back announcements convey firm-specific or industry-wide information? A test of the undervaluation hypothesis. *International Review of Financial Analysis, 11*(4), 511–531.

Pástor, L., Sinha, M., & Swaminathan, B. (2008). Estimating the intertemporal risk-return tradeoff using the implied cost of capital. *Journal of Finance, 63*, 2859–2897.

Rouwenhorst, K. G. (1999). Local return factors and turnover in emerging stock markets. *The Journal of Finance, 54*(4), 1439–1464.

Sharpe, W. F. (1978). New evidence on the capital asset pricing model: Discussion. *Journal of Finance, 33*, 917–920.

Shum, W. C., & Tang, G. Y. (2005). Common risk factors in returns in Asian emerging stock markets. *International Business Review, 14*(6), 695–717.

Wong, K. A. (1989). The firm size effect on stock returns in a developing stock market. *Economics Letters, 30*(1), 61–65.

Zhang, H. (2002). Share repurchases under the commercial law 212-2 in Japan: Market reaction and actual implementation. *Pacific-Basin Finance Journal, 10*(3), 287–305.

Zhang, H. (2005). Share price performance following actual share repurchases. *Journal of Banking & Finance, 29*(7), 1887–1901.

The Impact of the COVID-19 Pandemic on the Malaysian Stock Market

Zulkefly Abdul Karim, Lay Qin Yi, Bakri Abdul Karim, and Siti Farah Dilla Zakaria

Abstract The COVID-19 pandemic has been shattering the world since the beginning of 2020 and has caused an enormous impact on the stock markets. Malaysia, a small and open economy, was equally affected by the pandemic. This is reflected in the Movement Control Order (MCO) implementation, which ceased most of the economic activities and consequently affected the Malaysian stock market. Therefore, this study aims to examine the impact of COVID-19 on the FTBM Kuala Lumpur Composite Index (KLCI) and 13 other sectoral indices using the Autoregressive Distributed Lag (ARDL) model. Using the sample period from 5 February 2020 to 31 December 2020, the main results showed that the increase in COVID-19 cases in Malaysia and globally still positively impacted the KLCI and all sectoral indices during this period. The findings of this study bring implications for investors, investment institutions, and policymakers in the following aspects. First, this study helps investors in determining strategies to manage their portfolios. This study also assists investment institutions in identifying risks in each sector during the pandemic. Finally, this study helps policymakers set policies to maintain stock market stability while facing market shocks like this pandemic. This study is relevant in increasing perspectives to help all stakeholders execute the best decisions, especially with the COVID-19 pandemic still active worldwide.

Keywords Stock market · Pandemic COVID-19 · Asset pricing · ARDL

Z. A. Karim (✉)
Faculty of Economics and Management, Universiti Kebangsaan Malaysia, Bangi, Selangor, Malaysia
e-mail: zak1972@ukm.edu.my

L. Q. Yi
Hong Leong Bank Berhad, Kuala Lumpur, Malaysia

B. A. Karim
Faculty of Business and Economics, Universiti Malaysia Sarawak, Kota Samarahan, Sarawak, Malaysia

S. F. D. Zakaria
Tun Ismail Ali Distinguished Chair (YTI-UKM), Universiti Kebangsaan Malaysia, Bangi, Selangor, Malaysia

Z. Abdul Karim et al. (eds.), *Contemporary Issues in Finance, Investment and Banking in Malaysia*,
https://doi.org/10.1007/978-981-99-5447-6_5

1 Introduction

Since COVID-19 was declared a pandemic by the World Health Organization (WHO) on 11 March 2020, this pandemic has profoundly impacted stock markets worldwide. As of March 2020, the U.S. stock market has experienced tremendous turmoil due to panic selling. The U.S. Securities Commission's circuit breaker system froze stock market trading when the price of the S&P 500 index fell more than 7% from the previous day's price. In addition, the Dow Jones Index experienced the most prominent daily decline in U.S. history on 12 March 2020 and 16 March 2020 (Funakoshi & Hartman, 2020). In Malaysia, as of 29 July 2022, the total number of COVID-19 cases was 4.67 million, with a total death toll of 35,956 (Ministry of Health Malaysia, 2020). Due to the worsening pandemic, the first Movement Control Order (MCO) was declared on 18 March 2020 to prevent the pandemic from spreading further in Malaysia. Then, MCO was extended and relaxed to a different phase in 2020 and 2021, including the Conditional Movement Control Order (CMCO) and Recovery Movement Control Order (RMCO). During MCO, all economic activities have been stopped except for essential services such as water, electricity, energy, telecommunications, postal, transportation, irrigation, oil, gas, fuel, lubricants, broadcasting, finance, banking, health, pharmacy, fire, prison, port, airport, security, defence, cleaning, retail and food supply. Besides that, the KLCI has experienced a downward trend and reached its lowest point of 1,219.71 on 19 March 2020.

In response to the economic downturn due to COVID-19, the Bank Negara Malaysia (BNM) has also lowered the Overnight Policy Rate (OPR) to stimulate the economy. The reduction in the OPR rate has caused market uncertainty and a reduction in the investment portfolio discount rate under the Capital Asset Pricing Model (CAPM) framework. To maintain the discount rate, the market will adjust the equity risk premium (ERP) to reflect increased market volatility, adjust debt costs to reflect increasing credit spreads and adjust company-specific risks to reflect credit risk, liquidity risk, and forecasting risk. The discount rate will increase again when risk and volatility have been adjusted according to market conditions (KPMG, 2020). Investors will most likely ask for higher returns to compensate for the higher uncertainties and risks they face to protect their portfolios.

As a small and open economy, the Malaysian stock market is also affected by the COVID-19 pandemic and stock market conditions of other countries, especially the large stock markets which dominate the global stock market. As of April 2020, the U.S. stock market accounted for 46% of the world, with the New York Stock Exchange (NYSE) and National Association of Securities Dealers Automated Quotations (NASDAQ) contributing 31.5% and 14.5% of the share, respectively. They are followed by the Chinese stock market, which accounts for 14.4% of the world stock market (World Federation of Exchanges, 2020). The US and China also contribute significantly to Foreign Direct Investment (FDI) in Malaysia. The US is the largest foreign investor in Malaysia after Singapore, with a total investment from the US of RM6.0 billion in 2020, which is 13.45% of total FDI inflows. China is the fourth FDI contributing country after Singapore and Thailand in 2020, with a total of RM2.6 billion, 17.69% of total FDI flows (Department of Statistics Malaysia, 2020). While the US and China play an essential role in the global economy as well as the Malaysian economy, it is imperative to determine to what extent can large-capacity stock market conditions such as these countries be able to affect the stock market conditions in Malaysia.

This study examines the effect of COVID-19 on sectoral index returns in Malaysia, which has not been studied by Chia et al. (2020) and Gamal et al. (2021). Although studies on developing stock markets have been conducted by researchers such as Rabhi (2020), Mert and Omer (2020) and El-Khatib and Samet (2020), developing stock markets still receive less attention compared to advanced countries. Given this background, this study contributes to the literature on stock market studies in Malaysia from the following aspects. First, it fills the gap of the study in terms of population by covering a more comprehensive sample. This study also fills the research gap in terms of data analysis in which this study has a more extended study period compared to the study of Lee et al. (2020) and Saad et al. (2020). Finally, this study also fills in the study's gaps in methodology. It examines the effect of COVID-19 on the stock market using Autoregressive Distributed Lag (ARDL) analysis which has not been used by previous studies in Malaysia such as Chia et al. (2020), Lee et al. (2020) and Saad et al. (2020).

2 Stock Market and Pandemic COVID-19

Past studies have shown that stock markets worldwide performed poorly and experienced negative returns when COVID-19 started to spread (Hassan & Gavilanes, 2021). Liu et al. (2020) also showed that the impact of COVID-19 on traditional Chinese industries is negative and more serious. Studies in developing countries have also found that the growth of daily COVID-19 cases has negatively affected stock market performance (El-Khatib & Samet, 2020; Mert & Omer, 2020; Rabhi, 2020). Mert and Omer (2020) found that the negative impact of the COVID-19 outbreaks on developing stock markets started to diminish after the peak of this pandemic in March 2020. The effect of COVID-19 on developing stock markets in Asia is more significant than on developed stock markets in Europe. Although most studies in developed and developing countries have shown that COVID-19 negatively affects the stock markets, Onali (2020) showed that changes in the number of cases and deaths in the US and six other countries that suffered the worst COVID-19 crisis do not have an impact on the US stock market returns.

The Malaysian stock market was also affected by the COVID-19 pandemic. The number of COVID-19 cases harms the Malaysian stock market (Chia et al., 2020; Gamal et al., 2021; Lee et al., 2020; Saad et al., 2020). For example, Chia et al. (2020) showed that for each additional case of newly confirmed COVID-19, the index return decreased by 0.003–0.005%. Lee et al. (2020) showed that the plantation sector was less affected by the COVID-19 condition, while Saad et al. (2020)

showed that the health services and financial services sectors were less affected by the COVID-19 pandemic. According to Lee et al. (2020), the worsening COVID-19 epidemic in China tends to improve the performance of the health services, industrial services products, telecommunications and media and utilities sectors in Malaysia. On the contrary, the worsening COVID-19 outbreak in the US tends to improve the performance of the industrial products and services and utility sector but lower the performance of the telecommunications and media and transportation and logistics sectors in Malaysia.

Liu et al. (2020) showed that the COVID-19 pandemic also positively impacted the health services and information technology sectors in the case of China stock market. In contrast, the transport, accommodation and catering sectors have been severely affected during this pandemic. In addition, this pandemic also hurts the mining, electricity and heating sectors and the environment (Liu et al., 2020). Moreover, using Hang Seng Index and the Shanghai Stock Exchange Composite Index, Al-Awadhi et al. (2020) found that the pandemic negatively impacted the beverage sector more than the transportation sector. Meanwhile, Shen and Zhang (2021) divided the Chinese stock market into two groups which are "Stay at Home" and "Out of Home" stocks. The results show that, for "Out of Home" stocks, there was a significant negative impact of COVID-19 and the cumulative abnormalities continue to decline. For the "Stay at Home" stocks, there is no significant negative impact and the accumulated abnormal returns continue to increase. Studies by Liu et al. (2020) in China and Harjoto et al. (2021) in the US also showed that shares of large-capitalized companies experience more negative effects on their returns than shares of small-capitalized companies. Both studies also found that the impact of COVID-19 is more harmful to small-capitalized indices than to large-capitalized indexes in the stock market.

3 Research Methodology

3.1 Data and Variables Description

This study uses daily data from 5 February 2020 to 31 December 2020. The study uses data from the FTBM Kuala Lumpur Composite Index (KLCI) and 13 sectoral indices covering the consumer, construction, energy, financial, healthcare, industrial products, plantation, real estate, REIT, technology, telecommunications and media, transportation and logistics, and utility. Data are collected from various online sources. Data related to COVID-19 are extracted from a database on the official WHO website.

Daily stock returns as the dependent variable are calculated using the following formula:

$$R_t = \frac{\mathrm{I}_t - \mathrm{I}_{t-1}}{\mathrm{I}_{t-1}} \times 100\% \tag{1}$$

In Eq. (1), R_t is the return for the KLCI index (or sectoral index) on day t, while I_t and I_{t-1} refer to the average index price for day t and t−1, respectively.

The independent variables of this study are the Malaysian new cases of COVID-19 (MC), world covid cases (WC), Shanghai Composite Index (SH) and NASDAQ Composite Index (NASDAQ). The Shanghai Composite Index and the NASDAQ Composite Index are considered international market benchmarks and are expected to influence the movement of the stock price in the Malaysian market.

3.2 Baseline Model

The baseline regression models of this study are:

$$R_{KLCI} = \alpha + \beta_1 LogMC_t + \beta_2 SH_t + \beta_3 NASDAQ_t + \in \quad (2)$$

$$R_I = \alpha + \beta_1 LogMC_t + \beta_2 SH_t + \beta_3 NASDAQ_t + \in \quad (3)$$

$$R_{KLCI} = \alpha + \beta_1 LogWC_t + \beta_2 SH_t + \beta_3 NASDAQ_t + \in \quad (4)$$

$$R_I = \alpha + \beta_1 LogWC_t + \beta_2 SH_t + \beta_3 NASDAQ_t + \in \quad (5)$$

The baseline model in Eq. (2)–(5) is used to estimate the determinants of stock return, return of KLCI (R_{KLCI}), and return of the sectoral index (R_I). Models (2) and (3) examine the impact of the Malaysian covid case (MC), while models (4) dan (5) investigate the effect of world covid cases (WC) on the Malaysian stock market. MC and WC will be regressed separately in the baseline model to avoid the correlation among these variables. The baseline model in Eqs. (2)–(5) will be estimated using Autoregressive Distributed Lag (ARDL) model by considering the lagged optimum for each model using Akaike information criteria.

4 Result and Discussions

4.1 Descriptive Statistics

Table 1 shows the descriptive statistics for the daily returns of the Malaysian stock sectoral indexes. The health services sector records the highest average daily returns at 0.49%, while the REIT sector records the lowest average daily returns at −0.049%. These findings indicate that during COVID-19, the demand for medical care products has increased. Therefore, the share price for medical care companies has increased

Table 1 Descriptive statistics of stock returns (%)

Sectoral Index	Mean	Minimum	Maximum	Median	SD
KLCI	0.0339	−5.2613	6.8508	0.0439	1.2714
Construction	−0.0073	−11.8395	8.5112	0.1116	2.0756
Consumer Products and Services	−0.0002	−5.7519	3.8626	0.0265	1.1935
Energy	−0.0270	−25.3943	14.2269	−0.1015	3.6258
Financial Services	0.0332	−7.2300	8.5992	0.0078	1.7034
Health Services	0.4889	−7.9797	9.8475	0.2855	2.7632
Industrial Products and Services	0.1150	−10.7373	7.8145	0.2393	1.9295
Plantation	0.0173	−6.5189	7.3318	−0.0150	1.3310
Property	0.0090	−7.4290	5.2403	0.0144	1.5505
REIT	−0.0492	−6.4731	2.9507	−0.0338	0.9656
Technology	0.2845	−12.0424	10.5838	0.2553	2.4820
Telecommunication and Media	0.0255	−6.2901	5.9313	0.0444	1.5317
Transportation and Logistics	0.0557	−7.0109	7.0521	0.0780	1.7070
Utilities	0.0187	−6.2563	3.9945	0.0306	1.2066

due to the bullish sentiment for the medical care shares. In contrast, during COVID-19, demand for real estate, investment, and trust has dropped, thus has affected the share prices of the REIT companies. The energy sector has the highest standard deviation of 3.63, while the REIT with the lowest standard deviation at 0.97, indicates that during COVID-19, the share prices of energy are highly volatile. In contrast, the share price of REITs is less volatile. Table 2 shows the correlations among index returns. All pairs recorded positive coefficients. However, the pairs of KLCI-Financial Services and KLCI -Industrial Product record the highest correlation at 0.82. The lowest correlation is among the pair REIT-Health Services at 0.21.

4.2 *Empirical Results*

Tables 3 and 4 show the estimation results of the baseline model in Eqs. (2)–(5) to examine the impact of COVID-19 on the Malaysian stock market using an ARDL model analysis. Specifically, Table 3 summarizes the impact of Malaysian COVID-19 cases, whereas Table 4 summarizes the impact of World COVID-19 cases on the Malaysian stock market return (aggregate return and sectoral return). The coefficients of the ARDL model for all sector indexes are significant at least at the 10% level. In addition, the F-statistics of all models are also significant at the 1% level. These

Table 2 Correlations between sectoral stock index returns

Indexes/Sectors	(i)	(ii)	(iii)	(iv)	(v)	(vi)	(vii)	(viii)	(ix)	(x)	(xi)	(xii)	(xiii)	(xiv)
(i)	1.0000													
(ii)	0.7100	1.0000												
(iii)	0.8100	0.7700	1.0000											
(iv)	0.6200	0.6900	0.6800	1.0000										
(v)	**0.8200**	0.6100	0.7300	0.5900	1.0000									
(vi)	0.4000	0.3400	0.2900	0.2500	0.1000	1.0000								
(vii)	**0.8200**	0.7400	0.8100	0.6800	0.7000	0.3300	1.0000							
(viii)	0.7200	0.6600	0.6900	0.5800	0.5800	0.2800	0.7600	1.0000						
(ix)	0.6700	0.7700	0.7300	0.6800	0.6300	0.3500	0.7300	0.5800	1.0000					
(x)	0.5800	0.5900	0.6800	0.5200	0.6000	**0.2100**	0.5700	0.4500	0.7000	1.0000				
(xi)	0.6400	0.6400	0.6500	0.6300	0.5100	0.4000	0.7000	0.5700	0.6400	0.4900	1.0000			
(xii)	0.6100	0.6400	0.6500	0.6300	0.5600	**0.2300**	0.6300	0.5300	0.6200	0.4900	0.5700	1.0000		
(xiii)	0.6800	0.6800	0.7100	0.6300	0.5900	0.3400	0.7100	0.6300	0.6800	0.5700	0.6300	0.6000	1.0000	
(xiv)	0.7200	0.7200	0.7500	0.6200	0.6100	0.3800	0.7300	0.6300	0.7600	0.6600	0.6900	0.5700	0.6600	1.0000

Notes (i) KLCI; (ii) Construction (iii) Consumer Products and Services; (iv) Energy; (v) Financial Services; (vi) Health Services; (vii) Industrial Products and Services; (viii) Plantation; (ix) Real Estate; (x) REIT; (xi) Technology; (xii) Telecommunications and Media; (xiii) Transportation and Logistics; and (xiv) Utilities findings indicate that all explanatory used in the baseline model such as COVID-19 cases and movement of international stock market return are important in influencing the movement of Malaysian equity return (market return and sectoral return).

Based on the results in Table 3, COVID-19 new cases in Malaysia have a significant negative relationship with KLCI returns. Its coefficient indicates that a 1% change in the COVID-19 new cases in Malaysia leads to a 0.33% decline in the return of the KLCI index. The results of this study are in line with previous studies in Malaysia which show that the number of COVID-19 cases hurts the Malaysian stock market (Chia et al., 2020; Gamal et al., 2021; Lee et al., 2020; Saad et al., 2020). In addition, the returns of the Shanghai Composite Index and NASDAQ have a significantly positive relationship with the returns of the KLCI. This result is in line with those by Ramdhan et al. (2020) and Narayan et al. (2014). For example, Ramdhan et al. (2020) showed that China and Malaysian stock markets are strongly integrated.

On the other hand, the COVID-19 new cases in Malaysia have a significant positive relationship with the index returns of all sectors except the Energy, Health Services, Industrial Products and Services, and Plantation and Technology sectors (Models 4, 6, 7, 8, and 11). The biggest positive change has been seen in the Telecommunications and Media sector where a 1% change in the COVID-19 new cases in Malaysia leads to a 10.77% increase in the Telecommunications and Media index return. The results of this study are consistent with the previous studies by Liu et al. (2020) and Al-Awadhi et al. (2020). Liu et al. (2020) noted that when travel bans are carried out, information technology plays an important role in the sharing of current information as well as the dissemination of COVID-19 pandemic prevention and control information. At the same time, face-to-face in-person classes have also been postponed and learning and teaching sessions have been moved to online. This move has gradually restored investor confidence in the Telecommunications and Media sector. In addition, the smallest positive change is seen in the REIT and Real Estate sector index returns where a 1% change in the COVID-19 new cases in Malaysia leads to a 0.44% increase in the REIT index return and 0.75% in the Real Estate index return respectively. As shown by Akinsomi (2020), COVID-19 only hurts REITs during travel bans. Thus, when the Movement Control Order expired in May 2020, the returns of the RIET sector index had risen steadily again.

The Shanghai Composite Index has a significant positive relationship with returns of all sectors in Malaysia except the Construction, Health Services, and Telecommunications and Media sectors (Models 2, 6, and 12). This finding indicates that the improvement in economic performance in China has a significant positive impact on all sector returns except the Construction, Health Services, and Telecommunications and Media. As for the NASDAQ index, the U.S. stock market has a significant positive impact on all sectoral returns in Malaysia except for Energy, and Telecommunications and Media sectors. These findings show that the Malaysian stock market is very sensitive to the development of the international stock market, in particular the movement of China and the U.S. stock market.

As shown in Table 5, the coefficients of the ARDL model for all sector indices are significant at least at the 10% significance level. Moreover, the F-statistics of all models are also significant at the 1% significance level. These findings indicate that,

Table 3 ARDL estimation results (Malaysian COVID-19 cases)

Model	1	2	3	4	5	6	7
Model Selected	ARDL (9, 8, 7, 5)	ARDL (9, 8, 5, 9)	ARDL (10, 5, 0, 9)	ARDL (8,10,10,10)	ARDL (8, 5, 2, 7)	ARDL (7, 9, 8, 5)	ARDL (9, 8, 8, 8)
C	0.1317 (0.6546)	−0.7189 (0.1366)	−0.3579 (0.1970)	1.1967 (0.4597)	−0.5904 (0.2008)	0.8749 (0.3878)	0.0867 (0.8477)
Ln(MC)	−0.0033 (0.0021)*	0.0572 (0.0005)*	0.0320 (0.0082)*	−0.0626 (0.0382)**	0.0882 (0.0064)*	−0.2011 (0.0829)***	−0.0683 (0.0494)**
SH	0.3723 (0.0079)*	−0.2442 (0.0008)*	0.4925 (0.0001)*	5.0170 (0.0063)*	0.1549 (0.0529)***	−3.5826 (0.0750)***	0.4599 (0.0381)**
NASDAQ	0.3463 (0.0004)*	2.3446 (0.0015)*	1.2144 (0.0156)**	−2.1455 (0.0713)***	0.6443 (0.0160)**	0.9350 (0.0894)***	1.7860 (0.0004)*
R-squared	0.8570	0.9021	0.8337	0.9207	0.6796	0.6435	0.8994
Durbin Watson	2.1440	1.5824	2.1859	1.5449	1.8782	2.0114	1.9642
F-Statistics	6.9302 (0.0000)*	7.5899 (0.0000)*	7.2439 (0.0000)*	3.6820 (0.0070)*	4.5820 (0.0000)*	2.3698 (0.0045)*	6.2138 (0.0000)*

8	9	10	11	12	13	14
ARDL (9, 7, 1, 8)	ARDL (8, 7, 7, 7)	ARDL (10, 10, 10, 8)	ARDL (10, 5, 5, 5)	ARDL (8, 7, 7, 4)	ARDL (4, 2, 1, 5)	ARDL (2, 9, 0, 1)
0.8591 (0.0850)***	−0.2140 (0.6246)	0.0829 (0.7479)	1.6136 (0.0130)**	−0.2916 (0.3997)	−0.2511 (0.4523)	0.0687 (0.7577)
−0.0176 (0.0865)***	0.0074 (0.0060)*	0.0044 (0.0344)**	−0.2262 (0.0070)*	0.1077 (0.0000)*	0.0479 (0.0552)***	0.0121 (0.0323)**
0.2035 (0.0902)***	0.1666 (0.0892)***	2.7773 (0.0591)***	0.9089 (0.0247)**	-0.6244 (0.0094)*	0.4314 (0.0531)***	0.2170 (0.0245)**

(continued)

Table 3 (continued)

8	9	10	11	12	13	14
1.1047 (0.0024)*	1.2094 (0.0026)*	1.4292 (0.0069)*	1.1562 (0.0000)*	-0.1813 (0.0131)**	0.7614 (0.0000)*	0.2573 (0.0013)*
0.8063	0.7606	0.9668	0.8338	0.7555	0.4510	0.3708
2.1452	1.8216	2.0435	2.5322	1.8701	2.1009	1.8881
6.2446 (0.0000)*	3.7728 (0.0000)*	6.3994 (0.0028)*	7.8862 (0.0000)*	5.2219 (0.0000)*	5.7510 (0.0000)*	4.4012 (0.0000)*

Notes The number affixed to the model refers to the number of lags used in the model for each variable; MC refers to the New Case of COVID-19 Malaysia; SH refers to the returns of the Shanghai Composite Index and NASDAQ refers to the returns of the NASDAQ Composite Index. Model 1 refers to the KLCI; Model 2 refers to Construction; Model 3 refers to Consumer Products and Services; Model 4 refers to Energy; Model 5 refers to Financial Services; Model 6 refers to Health Services; Model 7 refers to Industrial Products and Services; Model 8 refers to Plantation; Model 9 refers to Real Estate; Model 10 refers to REITs; Model 11 refers to Technology; Model 12 refers to Telecommunications and Media; Model 13 refers to Transportation and Logistics, and Model 14 refers to Utilities

Table 4 ARDL estimation results (World COVID-19 Cases)

Model	1	2	3	4	5	6	7
Selected Models	ARDL (3, 1, 7, 8)	ARDL (12, 8, 7, 8)	ARDL (1, 0, 0, 9)	ARDL (9, 8, 0, 2)	ARDL (1, 0, 0, 5)	ARDL (10, 7, 7, 7)	ARDL (12, 4, 8, 6)
C	−0.4461 (0.7107)	−1.3567 (0.5531)	−2.1162 (0.0622)***	−1.3973 (0.6025)	−0.7032 (0.5421)	5.6315 (0.0739)***	−0.5746 (0.7705)
Ln(WC)	0.0305 (0.0866)***	0.08117 (0.1030)	0.1648 (0.0698)***	0.1083 (0.0644)***	0.0593 (0.5452)	−0.4677 (0.0809)***	0.0707 (0.0281)**
SH	−0.1258 (0.0030) *	0.6181 (0.0001)*	0.3326 (0.0003)*	0.6552 (0.0371)**	0.3399 (0.0069)*	−1.1986 (0.0163)**	1.2541 (0.0082)*
NASDAQ	0.6642 (0.0000)*	3.3494 (0.0000)*	0.4445 (0.0000)*	1.2960 (0.0021)*	0.5141 (0.0009)*	2.5926 (0.0252)**	1.2021 (0.0000)*
R SQUARE	0.5233	0.9101	0.5743	0.5016	0.2643	0.6493	0.7994
Durbin Watson	1.9125	1.8049	1.9997	2.1720	1.9185	2.4184	2.0548
F-statistik	4.3919 (0.0000)*	7.4606 (0.0000)*	11.5189 (0.0000)*	4.0723 (0.0000)*	5.9486 (0.0000)*	2.2866 (0.0056)*	4.9512 (0.0000)*

8	9	10	11	12	13	14
ARDL (4, 1, 0, 1)	ARDL (1, 1, 0, 5)	ARDL (6, 1, 0, 7)	ARDL (1, 1, 7, 8)	ARDL (2, 1, 0, 1)	ARDL (10, 12, 12, 12)	ARDL (1, 1, 7, 8)
−0.2506 (0.7643)	−0.6316 (0.4677)	0.7605 (0.3623)	1.2696 (0.5246)	0.4227 (0.6776)	28.2081 (0.0093)**	1.0978 (0.3074)
0.0900 (0.0454)**	0.0395 (0.0737)***	−0.1087 (0.0212)**	−0.1128 (0.0276)**	0.0890 (0.0887)***	−1.9377 (0.0545)**	−0.0996 (0.0335)**
0.2679 (0.0028)*	0.3430 (0.0004)*	0.1540 (0.0438)**	-0.5757 (0.0000)*	0.3814 (0.0002)*	−0.2625 (0.0490)**	−0.1116 (0.0001)*

(continued)

Table 4 (continued)

8	9	10	11	12	13	14
0.3664 (0.0000)*	0.7752 (0.0000)*	0.7954 (0.0000)*	1.9939 (0.0000)*	0.3177 (0.0012)*	−7.8435 (0.0272)**	1.0473 (0.0002)*
0.3735	0.4701	0.5703	0.6229	0.2769	0.9957	0.5553
1.9869	2.2071	2.2142	1.9665	2.1678	2.0046	2.1079
9.8709 (0.0000)*	13.1319 (0.0000)*	7.2606 (0.0000)*	8.2622 (0.0000)*	9.3580 (0.0000)*	14.3031 (0.0242)**	6.2458 (0.0000)*

the world's COVID-19 new cases are significantly and positively related to KLCI returns. The return of the KLCI index will grow by 3.04% for every 1% change in the global COVID-19 new cases. This is somewhat consistent with the findings of the Onali (2020) study, which found that COVID-19 conditions in other countries had less of an impact on the local stock market and tended to have a positive impact. The NASDAQ Composite Index also has a substantial positive link with KLCI returns, despite the Shanghai Composite Index's significant negative relationship with the KLCI.

In addition, the global COVID-19 new cases have a significant positive relationship with the index returns of all sectors except the Financial Services, Health Services, REITs, Technology, Transport and Logistics, and Utilities sectors (Models 5, 6, 10, 11, 13, and 14). The most significant positive impact is seen in the returns of the Consumer Products and Services sector, where a 1% change in the world's COVID-19 new cases leads to a 16.48% increase in the returns of the Consumer Products and Services sector index. In addition, a 1% change in the world of COVID-19 new cases leads to a 10.835% increase in the returns of the Energy sector. Based on the report of Tenaga Nasional Berhad (2020), electricity consumption for the Residential sector has jumped between 20 and 50% during this pandemic period. This is because, during the MCO, the citizen just stays at home during this period, and therefore electricity consumption has increased significantly for their daily activities.

The relationship between the world's COVID-19 new cases and the returns of the Financial Services sector index is insignificant. This is in line with the study of Saad et al. (2020) which also shows that changes in the global COVID-19 cases do not significantly impact the returns of the Financial Services sector. Besides, except for the Health Services, Technology, Transport and Logistics, and Utilities sectors (Models 6, 11, 13, and 14), the Shanghai Composite Index has a significant positive relationship with all sector's returns. As for the NASDAQ, the returns of all sectors have a significant positive relationship except for the Transport and Logistics sector (Model 13). These findings indicate that the majority of sub-sector stock returns in the emerging market (i.e., Malaysia) are very responsive to the performance of the most influential international stock market. This signals to the stock market players to observe the international risk factors for their decision of investment in Malaysia equity market.

5 Summary and Conclusion

This study examines the impact of COVID-19 and the development of US and China stock market on the Malaysian stock market and its sectors. Daily data covering the period from 5 February 2020 to 31 December 2020 and ARDL model are used in this study. The results show that to a great extent COVID-19 cases in Malaysia and the world have a positive effect on Malaysian sectors, specifically Consumer Products, Financial Services, Real Estate, and Telecommunication and Media. However, the KLCI index is only affected by the local COVID-19 cases, not the world COVID cases. Meanwhile, the stock market returns of the US and China also have a positive impact on the KLCI and most sectoral indices.

The results of this study shall have significant implications to investors, fund managers and policymakers. Investors can identify the impact of COVID-19 on each sector and make their investment decision to maximize returns. The study also assists fund managers to re-structure their investment portfolios during pandemic period. In addition, this study also assists policymakers in formulating policies to ensure stock market stability from the catastrophic of COVID-19.

This study has limitations as it only explores the impact of COVID-19 on Malaysian stock market. Besides that, it only uses COVID-19 daily case data until the end of 2020 and relies on four variables in the model. Thus, further studies are recommended to extend the analysis using a longer sample period, more countries and regions and explore more proxies of the COVID-19 outbreak.

Acknowledgements Thankfully, the authors acknowledge financial support from the Universiti Kebangsaan Malaysia (UKM) research grant (Grant number: EP-2020-061).

References

Akinsomi, O. (2020). How resilient are REITs to a pandemic? The COVID-19 effect. *Journal of Property Investment & Finance.*

Al-Awadhi, A. M., Alsaifi, K., Al-Awadhi, A., & Alhammadi, S. (2020). Death and contagious infectious diseases: Impact of the COVID-19 virus on stock market returns. *Journal of Behavioral and Experimental Finance, 27*, 100326.

Chia, R. C. J., Liew, V. K. S., & Rowland, R. (2020). Daily new COVID-19 cases, the movement control order, and Malaysian stock market returns. *International Journal of Business and Society, 21*(2), 553–568.

Department of Statistics Malaysia. (2020). *Consumer Price Index Malaysia December 2020.*

El-Khatib, R., & Samet, A. (2020). *Impact of COVID-19 on emerging markets.* Available at SSRN 3685013.

Funakoshi, M., & Hartman, T. (2020, April). Mad March: How the stock market is being hit by COVID-19. In *World Economic Forum.*

Gamal, A. A. M., Al-Qadasi, A. A., Noor, M. A. M., Rambeli, N., & Viswanathan, K. K. (2021). The impact of COVID-19 on the Malaysian stock market: Evidence from an Autoregressive Distributed Lag Bound testing approach. *Journal of Asian Finance Economics and Business, 8*(7), 1–9.

Harjoto, M. A., Rossi, F., & Paglia, J. K. (2021). COVID-19: Stock market reactions to the shock and the stimulus. *Applied Economics Letters, 28*(10), 795–801.

Hassan, S., & Gavilanes, J. M. R. (2021). First to react is the last to forgive: Evidence from the stock market impact of COVID 19. *Journal of Risk and Financial Management, 14*(1), 26.

Liu, H., Wang, Y., He, D., & Wang, C. (2020). Short term response of Chinese stock markets to the outbreak of COVID-19. *Applied Economics, 52*(53), 5859–5872.

Ministry of Health Malaysia. (2020). Press Release 31 December 2020—Current Situation of Coronavirus Infection 2019 (COVID-19) in Malaysia.

KPMG. (2020). *Private equity valuation issues in the midst of COVID-19.*

Lee, K. Y. M., Jais, M., & Chan, C. W. (2020). Impact of COVID-19: Evidence from Malaysian stock market. *International Journal of Business and Society, 21*(2), 607–628.

Mert, T., & Omer, S. G. (2020). The impact of COVID-19 on emerging stock markets. *Finance Research Letter, 36*, 1–6.

Narayan, S., Sriananthakumar, S., & Islam, S. Z. (2014). Stock market integration of emerging Asian economies: Patterns and causes. *Economic Modelling, 39*, 19–31.

Onali, E. (2020). *COVID-19 and stock market volatility*. SSRN 3571453.

Rabhi, A. (2020). Stock market vulnerability to the COVID-19 pandemic: Evidence from emerging Asian Stock Market. *Journal of Advanced Studies in Finance (JASF), 11*(22), 126–131.

Ramdhan, N., Yousop, N. M., Ahmad, Z., & Abdullah, N. M. H. (2020). Malaysia Stock Market Integration: The effect of leader and emerging market. *Journal of Advanced Research in Business and Management Studies, 2*(1), 1–10.

Saad, N. M., Mohamad, N. E. A., & Haniff, M. N. (2020). Relationship between share price and COVID cases among all sectors in main market of Bursa Malaysia. *Global Business & Management Research, 12*(4).

Shen, D., & Zhang, W. (2021). Stay-at-home stocks versus go-outside stocks: The impacts of COVID-19 on the Chinese stock market. *Asia-Pacific Financial Markets, 28*(2), 305–318.

Tenaga Nasional Berhad. (2020). https://www.tnb.com.my/assets/press_releases/20200646BM.pdf

World Federal of Exchanges. (2020). *Total equity market—market capitalisation.*

Reaction and Efficiency of the Cryptocurrency Market During the COVID-19 Pandemic: The Effect of Size and Supply

Ruzita Abdul Rahim, Nur Arissa Maisarah Nadhri, Noor Azryani Auzairy, and Syahida Zainal Abidin

Abstract The COVID-19 pandemic might be bad news for all economic units, but it has become an unprecedented push factor for cryptocurrencies. These digital currencies have received overflowing investment through capital withdrawn from traditional investment instruments such as stocks and bonds. This chapter investigates the reaction and efficiency of Bitcoin and 40 altcoins from the World Health Organization's announcement of the COVID-19 pandemic on 11 March 2020 and the first vaccination approval on 31 December 2020. Using the event study approach for the observation period from 1 January 2019 until 31 October 2021, we find that their reactions are significant and increasingly positive on the longer event windows. We also find that the size effect is highly significant in the cryptocurrency market compared to the stock markets. Cryptocurrencies with saturated supply react more drastically than those with unlimited supply, but the impact of supply is less pronounced than size. Meanwhile, Bitcoin appears to be more efficient than all altcoins except for the five largest cap. The results of this study would be beneficial for investors, particularly those searching for a safe haven or hedger in the cryptocurrency market.

Keywords Cryptocurrencies · COVID-19 · Event study · Investor reaction · Market efficiency · Pandemic · Vaccine

1 Introduction

Since Bitcoin's debut in 2009, cryptocurrencies have piqued the interest of many academics and policymakers. Satoshi Nakamoto, the pseudo name of its creator, aims for this first cryptocurrency to operate on a decentralised peer-to-peer (P2P) network to move away from the jurisdiction and monitoring of central banks and authorities.

R. A. Rahim (✉) · N. A. M. Nadhri · N. A. Auzairy · S. Z. Abidin
Faculty of Economics and Management, Universiti Kebangsaan Malaysia, Bangi, Selangor, Malaysia
e-mail: ruzitaar@ukm.edu.my

Z. Abdul Karim et al. (eds.), *Contemporary Issues in Finance, Investment and Banking in Malaysia*,
https://doi.org/10.1007/978-981-99-5447-6_6

Powered by Blockchain and other Fintech, cryptocurrencies offer benefits such as real-time transactions at significantly lower fees than conventional online payment mechanisms. By 30 December 2021, CoinmarketCap has registered 17,205 cryptocurrencies with a total market capitalisation of USD1.736 trillion. Since Bitcoin is worth USD902.10 billion, it accounts for 48% of the cryptocurrency market. Its dominance in the cryptocurrency market explains why most studies focus on it, although more altcoins have been accepted as mainstream investments.

COVID-19, caused by the Severe Acute Respiratory Syndrome Coronavirus (SARS-CoV-2), has allowed scholars to examine the behaviour of cryptocurrencies more exclusively. Like the first SARS (SARS-CoV-1) that originated in Guangdong, China, COVID-19 was first detected in China, this time in the Wuhan Province, on 17 November 2019. Within a few months of its first case, the virus that spreads airborne and can spread through small droplets of the saliva of infected humans (and animals) has infected 118,000 people in 114 countries before the World Health Organization (WHO) declared the COVID-19 outbreak a pandemic, public health emergency of international concern on 11 March 2020. Following that announcement, governments worldwide imposed strict physical containment measures or total lockdowns to control the spread of COVID-19 infection. The rising number of cases worldwide when the healthcare systems were unprepared to serve the overflowing patients have sparked serious concerns over the severity of the illness, the risk of getting infected and infecting people around us and even death once infected. Meanwhile, lockdowns and other containment measures to curb COVID-19 have caused unprecedented disruption to the global economy. Financial markets were the first to report the effects as a reaction to the deteriorating fundamental values and capital flight driven by investors' fear and panic.

The impact of COVID-19 on financial markets is significant for traditional financial assets and cryptocurrencies. There was a massive sale of cryptocurrencies on 8 March 2020, which resulted in a total capitalisation loss of USD21 billion (~5%) in 24 h. The market crash created Black Monday in the stock markets on the 9th of March 2020 (Umar et al., 2021a). At this point, most European countries have been quarantined or contained with fewer measures. WHO's pandemic declaration has exacerbated the existing state of the cryptocurrency market. Within two days of the announcement, the cryptocurrency market lost nearly half of its market value due to a sharp decline in the prices of major cryptocurrencies. This unprecedented situation has attracted scholars to examine the COVID-19 pandemic from various perspectives. Most studies focus on its effects on human health (e.g., Cummings et al., 2022; Dai et al., 2022; Jiang et al., 2021), while others analyse the economic impact (e.g., Atalan, 2020; Hossain, 2021; Jia et al., 2021).

Concerning the latter, Nusratullin et al. (2021) stated that the pandemic had demonstrated its ability to harm the global economy on an unprecedented scale, resulting in enormous economic costs by affecting banking, governments, and financial markets. Several studies have examined the behaviour of financial assets during the current pandemic. The findings indicate that financial assets display a strong dynamic return connection (Li et al., 2021). Herwany et al. (2021) found that stocks on the Indonesia Stock Exchange plummeted on the 22nd day after the COVID-19 outbreak. Interestingly, Khan et al. (2020) discovered that the Shanghai Composite Index recovers in the longer event window after being severely impacted in the short event window. They relate the recovery to the Chinese government's effective measures to contain the spread of the virus, which helped to re-establish investor faith in the stock market. Other studies relate the stock markets' revival to the recently developed COVID-19 vaccine. Cao et al. (2020) and Rouatbi et al. (2021) asserted that mass vaccination contributes to stabilising the global equity markets from the massive drop and volatilities due to the pandemic. To examine this proposition, Khalfaoui et al. (2021) examined the impact of the COVID-19 vaccination on S&P 500 returns.

Relative to the stock markets, a relatively small number of studies analyse the impact of COVID-19 on cryptocurrencies. Among the few is a study by Mnif et al. (2020), which found that Bitcoin had the most efficient market prior to the COVID-19 outbreak. However, its market became less efficient than Ethereum and other cryptocurrencies after the COVID-19 episode. Salisu and Ogbonna (2021) concluded that the return volatility of cryptocurrencies exhibits riskier properties during the pandemic. Still, the trend is similar to behaviour during previous financial crises, such as the Global Financial Crisis. Lahmiri and Bekiros (2020) and Kim and Lee (2021) found that the COVID-19 pandemic has had a negative impact on cryptocurrencies, making their prices extremely volatile and unpredictable. On the contrary, Ftiti et al. (2021) and Zhu et al. (2021) argued that the pandemic is the primary factor supporting the growing trend in cryptocurrencies. Caferra and Vidal-Tomás (2021) discovered that COVID-19 only caused a short-term impact on the cryptocurrency market. Pertaining to the effects of vaccination on cryptocurrency, Kim and Lee (2021) found the immunity drug created only a short-term decrease in the cryptocurrency market complexity during COVID-19.

Because the crypto market is still emerging, it has yet to see a full-fledged macroeconomic crisis like the COVID-19 outbreak. Meanwhile, empirical studies offer contradictory evidence regarding the cryptocurrency market's reaction to the announcement of the COVID-19 pandemic. In addition, there is limited evidence about cryptocurrency's reaction to vaccination. Thus, this chapter examines the market reaction to the COVID-19 pandemic and vaccine announcements. This chapter contributes to the cryptocurrency literature by expanding the coverage from Bitcoin to 40 altcoins. Based on the reviewed literature, no study has exclusively examined cryptocurrencies except for Lahmiri and Bekiros (2020). Their study examined the stability and irregularity of 45 cryptocurrencies before and during the COVID-19 crisis. Meanwhile, this study examines the reaction and efficiency of 41 cryptocurrency markets towards the COVID-19 pandemic and vaccine news. This study will add more evidence to the currently mixed findings established about market efficiency while also introducing the size and supply effect on the reaction. The results have important implications for investors and practitioners since COVID-19 is still a real threat to global economic recovery.

The remaining chapter is structured as follows. Section 2 reviews previous studies. Section 3 explains the event study and the sample cryptocurrencies. It is followed by a section that reports and discusses the results and a final section that concludes and discusses the implications of the study.

2 Review of Past Studies

Most studies on the impact of COVID-19 have proven that the modern-age pandemic has significantly driven down the market value of traditional assets such as stocks, bonds, precious metals, crude oil, and other commodities (Umar & Gubareva, 2021). However, an exclusive study on cryptocurrencies is necessary because this digital asset is unique in many aspects. We have reviewed some past studies (Table 1) and found that only Lahmiri and Bekiros (2020) have exclusively examined cryptocurrencies. Firstly, cryptocurrency is not regulated by any central authority, unlike other assets. Its decentralised property allows it to break free from the spillover effect of the economic downturn and corporate disruptions during the pandemic (Vidal-Tomas & Ibanez, 2018). Powered by blockchain and Fintech, this digital asset gets its "fifteen-minute fame" as the pandemic-induced movement restrictions led economic units to switch to digital solutions. However, once cryptocurrencies are offered as an investment tool, their prices cannot be detached from other investment instruments. Active investors and traders are constantly looking for opportunities to make more profits, and cryptocurrencies are no exception. This notion is particularly true among cryptocurrencies that have made it to the mainstream. Just two years ago, the mainstream list included only major cryptocurrencies such as Bitcoin, Ethereum, Tether, USD Coin and Stellar (XRP). By July 2022, major investment platforms such as Invest ing.com have included 1,093 cryptocurrencies. Their list represents about 6% of the total cryptocurrencies on the CoinMarketCap platform.

The switch between investment instruments causes constant flows between assets, including cryptocurrencies, thereby increasing interdependencies. Some studies, such as Corbet et al. (2020), have discovered that the correlation between stock markets and Bitcoin rises dramatically during this period of tremendous financial stress. The COVID-19 pandemic is likely to heighten the interconnectedness between cryptocurrencies and other assets, considering it has caused immense pressure on the global economy. Empirically, Umar et al. (2021b) have examined the effects of COVID-19-related media coverage on the returns and connectivity of cryptocurrencies and fiat currencies. Umar et al. (2021b) evaluated the three most relevant cryptocurrencies (Bitcoin, Ethereum and Ripple) against the major fiat currencies (Euro, Great Britain Pound [GBP] and Chinese Yuan). Their results show that (i) before the first wave, the media coverage index has predicted the effect on crypto-fiat currencies connectivity, (ii) cryptocurrencies are the clean shock sender whereas the fiat currencies are the net receiver, and (iii) volatility records similar results except for Euro, which shows unambiguous net receiver property in certain months. Umar and Gubareva (2021) argued that more studies are paying attention to the influence of media information on infectious diseases on investors' decisions. The reaction of the cryptocurrencies towards news has been examined earlier by Xin and Chong (2017),

Table 1 Summary of past studies

Author(s)	Article title	Methodology	Results
Corbet et al. (2020)	The contagion effects of the COVID-19 pandemic: evidence from gold and cryptocurrencies	GARCH model	Volatility relationship between main Chinese stock markets and Bitcoin evolves significantly with the emergence of COVID-19
Umar et al. (2021a, 2021b)	The impact of COVID-19-related media coverage on the return and volatility connectedness of cryptocurrencies and fiat currencies	Time-varying parameter vector autoregression (TVP-VAR) model	Media coverage index (only before the first wave) and the cryptocurrency is a clean shock sender
Xin and Chong (2017)	The technology and economic determinants of cryptocurrency exchange rates: The case of Bitcoin	Autoregressive distributed lag (ARDL) model	Changes in economic fundamentals have an impact on Bitcoin returns
Umar and Gubareva (2021)	The relationship between the COVID-19 media coverage and the environmental, social and governance leaders equity volatility: a time frequency wavelet analysis	Squared wavelet coherence (SWC) and Wavelet coherence phase difference (WCPD) techniques	Predominantly high coherence implies high correlation during a systemic event (COVID-19). Financial market volatility underscores the importance of alternative assets for hedging
Lahmiri and Bekiros (2020)	The impact of COVID-19 pandemic upon stability and sequential irregularity of equity and cryptocurrency markets	Largest Lyapunov Exponent (LLE) based on Rosenstein's method and Approximate Entropy (ApEn)	Cryptocurrency market is increasingly unstable, and level of irregularity becomes increasingly uncertain
Demir et al. (2020)	The relationship between cryptocurrencies and COVID-19 pandemic	ARDL analysis	There is a link between COVID-19 and the price of the cryptocurrency
Vukovic et al. (2021)	COVID-19 Pandemic: Is the Crypto Market a Safe Haven? The Impact of the First Wave	OLS, quantile, and robust regressions analysis	Cryptocurrencies do not react to COVID-19 first wave but are exposed to overflowing risky assets
Mnif and Jarboui (2021)	COVID-19, bitcoin market efficiency, herd behaviour	Inefficiency index (MLM) and Multifractal Detrended Fluctuation Analysis (MFDFA)	Bitcoin is multifractal before the pandemic and becomes less fractal after the outbreak. Efficiency of Bitcoin is sensitive to scales, COVID-19 outbreak, and related events highlighting investor sentiment effects

(continued)

Table 1 (continued)

Author(s)	Article title	Methodology	Results
Jarboui and Mnif (2021)	Cryptocurrency bubble risk and the FOMC announcements during COVID-19 black swan event	Event study; abnormal returns (AR) and cumulative abnormal returns (CARs)	First FOMC event has a significant negative effect after 4 days of the announcement for all cryptocurrencies except Tether. CARs are significant in some event windows
Fama (1970)	Efficient Capital Markets: A Review of Theory and Empirical Work	Submartingale model	Autocorrelations are consistently positive but ~0, a tendency for runs over random processes
Urquhart (2016)	The Inefficiency of Bitcoin	A battery of robust tests	Bitcoin market is inefficient but showing good progress
Cheah et al. (2018)	Long memory interdependency and inefficiency in Bitcoin markets	Fractionally cointegrated VAR framework	Bitcoin market exhibits moderate to high inefficiency, implying room for speculation
Mnif et al. (2020)	How the cryptocurrency market has performed during COVID-19? A multifractal analysis	A multifractal detrended fluctuation approach	COVID-19 crisis has had a positive impact on the efficiency of the cryptocurrency market
Wang and Wang (2021)	COVID-19 and financial market efficiency: Evidence from an entropy-based analysis	Multiscale entropy-based for scales of hourly and 1–30 business days	At all scales, four markets' efficiency decreases sharply and persistently from Feb-March 2020
Vidal-Tomas and Ibanez (2018)	Semi-strong efficiency of Bitcoin	Robust test	Bitcoin becomes more efficient over time in relation to its own events but is unaffected by monetary policy news

who argued that changes in economic fundamentals impact Bitcoin returns. They discovered that the long-term Bitcoin exchange rate is more sensitive to economic fundamentals than technological changes.

Despite the increasing attention on cryptocurrencies, studies that exclusively examine the impact of the COVID-19 pandemic on the cryptocurrency market are scant. Among the few studies is Lahmiri and Bekiros (2020), who examined 45 cryptocurrencies. The results show that the cryptocurrency market is increasingly unstable while its irregularity becomes increasingly uncertain. The instability and irregularity in cryptocurrency are also more severe than in 16 stock markets. They concluded that the cryptocurrency market was highly affected during the COVID-19 pandemic, and investing in it was extremely risky. Their finding contradicts Corbet et al. (2020), who suggested that, like precious metals (gold), cryptocurrencies can serve as hedgers for stocks when the COVID-19 pandemic is progressing into an epidemic.

Demir et al. (2020) found a positive relationship between COVID-19 cases and the price of cryptocurrencies. They explained that this relationship is due to the government imposing movement restrictions when the number of cases and deaths increases. Conversely, Vukovic et al. (2021) found quite different results from other studies (e.g., Corbet et al., 2020; Demir et al., 2020; Lahmiri & Bekiros, 2020) in their sample cryptocurrencies (Bitcoin, Ethereum, Ripple [XRP], Tether and Bitcoin Cash). During the first wave of the COVID-19 pandemic, cryptocurrencies did not respond. Instead, Vukovic et al. (2021) observed that cryptocurrencies are exposed to overflowing capital from other risky assets during the COVID-19 pandemic. An exception is Tether, the only stablecoin among the five largest market capitalisation cryptocurrencies. It is said that because Tether is backed by the US Reserve (US dollar), it does not significantly react to (affected by) the COVID-19 pandemic. From an investment viewpoint, that will make Tether a safe place (Corbet et al., 2020) for investors to invest without worrying about a sudden price fall. However, its safe haven property is not likely to be against the US stock market and oil since all five cryptocurrencies are significant and positively related to the S&P 500 index, except for Tether and oil.

Mnif and Jarboui (2021) examined three critical events, including the Federal Reserve's announcement of quantitative easing with no maximum limit. In their study, the cumulative average residual approach (CAR) is utilised to test the market efficiency hypothesis while also determining the total impact of an event on the Bitcoin market. The result shows that the Fed's expansive policy causes a positive significant abnormal return in longer event windows. For the Fed's Payment Protection Program, the event does not generate significant abnormal returns except for a significant positive effect on Bitcoin. Jarboui and Mnif (2021) investigated the impact of the eight Federal Open Market Committee (FOMC) statement announcements during the COVID-19 pandemic on selected cryptocurrencies (Bitcoin, Ethereum, Tether, Litecoin, and Ripple). Except for Tether, the empirical evidence reveals that the first FOMC event has a significantly negative effect (CAR) on the sample cryptocurrencies after four days of the announcement.

The present study aims to establish the cryptocurrency market efficiency through the reaction of a sample to the COVID-19 pandemic and vaccine news. The COVID-19 pandemic presents a tremendous opportunity for this study because it presents an unprecedented shock that affects each aspect of the economy on a global scale. Unlike economic shocks from a specific country or region, COVID-19 is a worldwide phenomenon, just like cryptocurrencies. Theoretically, an efficient market (investors collectively) will mean that asset prices will quickly and fully reflect all relevant information. Fama (1970) classified market efficiency into three forms; weak, semi-strong, and strong, depending on the information reflected in the asset prices. Regardless of the levels, the main implication of an efficient market is that investors will not be able to make abnormal returns consistently using the information in question. In other words, the investors will not be able to outsmart the other investors in anticipating future returns using the information. Motivated by evidence of inefficiencies in the cryptocurrency market such as documented by Vukovic et al. (2021) and Urquhart (2016) re-examined the issue and found that the cryptocurrency market is relatively isolated from shocks transmitted from the other asset classes. It also shows a weaker response to macroeconomic news than traditional assets and fiat currencies. However, results from the sub-periods show that Bitcoin is efficient in the latter. Thus, Urquhart (2016) concluded that Bitcoin is an inefficient market on the verge of becoming efficient. This evidence is consistent with that of Cheah et al. (2018), who argued that the Bitcoin market exhibits moderate to high inefficiency, implying the possibility of speculative profits for investors.

Regarding their reaction to the COVID-19 pandemic, Mnif et al. (2020) found that the COVID-19 crisis has positively influenced the efficiency of the cryptocurrency market. Their study, which employed a multifractal detrended fluctuation approach, the magnitude of the long memory index, and the generalised Hurst exponent, found that Bitcoin was more efficient before the COVID-19 crisis. At the same time, other cryptocurrencies (Ethereum, Ripple, Litecoin, and Binance) are more efficient during and after the pandemic. The mixed results are consistent with Wang and Wang (2021), who examined the effects of the COVID-19 epidemic on the efficiency of Bitcoin and traditional financial markets. Using the refined composite multiscale fuzzy entropy (MFE) at all scales, they discovered that the efficiency of Bitcoin, S&P 500, gold, and the US Dollar markets declined rapidly and consistently between February and March 2020. In the literature we reviewed, we recognise that the scant evidence on the cryptocurrency market has not exclusively considered digital currencies except for Lahmiri and Bekiros (2020). They focused on the stability and irregularity of cryptocurrencies during the COVID-19 crisis. The present study differs by focusing on the reaction of 41 cryptocurrencies towards the COVID-19 pandemic and vaccine news to add more evidence to the currently mixed findings established so far about market efficiency.

3 Methodology

3.1 Data and Sample Cryptocurrencies

To establish empirical evidence on the reaction and efficiency of the cryptocurrency market, we used an event study to determine how Bitcoin and 40 selected altcoins reacted to news related to COVID-19 and its vaccination. Data for the 41 randomly selected cryptocurrencies, including Bitcoin, is gathered from the CoinMarketCap database (coinmarketcap.com). In Table 2, we present the profiles of the sample cryptocurrencies. The mean, minimum, and maximum prices are based on the average open-close-high-low price data from 31 December 2018 (to calculate the return on 1 January 2019) to 30 October 2021.

We examined two major events related to COVID-19; the first event is the day the World Health Organization (WHO) declared the new coronavirus outbreak a global

Table 2 Profiles of sample cryptocurrencies, with market price stated in USD

Cryptocurrency	Unit	Price (USD)				Market capitalisation	Cap
		Mean	Std. Dev.	Min	Max		
Bitcoin	BTC	19,964	17,800	3,401	66,002	371,432,502,830	89.78%
Ethereum	ETH	896.41	1,118	105	4,358	103,699,996,987	No limit
Tether	USDT	1.00	0.00	0.98	1.03	20,198,444,490	No limit
Ripple	XRP	0.45	0.33	0.14	1.79	19,895,039,596	48.35%
USD Coin	USDC	1.00	0.01	0.98	1.04	6,188,280,889	No limit
Stellar	XLM	0.17	0.15	0.04	0.71	3,731,215,057	48.26%
TRON	TRX	0.04	0.03	0.01	0.16	2,667,753,597	No limit
VeChain	VET	0.03	0.05	0.00	0.24	2,207,664,967	74.18%
Filecoin	FIL	28.45	37.69	2.57	199.82	1,796,946,571	34.12%
INO COIN	INO	2.84	1.96	0.17	12.05	481,635,131	No limit
Fantom	FTM	0.45	0.00	3.17	5.17	479,787,394	80.31%
XDC Network	XDC	0.02	0.04	0.00	0.18	279,131,227	No limit
SwissBorg	CHSB	0.26	0.38	0.01	1.51	253,537,445	No limit
WhiteCoin	XWC	0.39	0.53	0.00	2.49	239,830,719	74.42%
Voyager Token	VGX	0.98	1.57	0.02	6.96	219,279,299	99.68%
loTeX	IOTX	0.02	0.02	0.00	0.12	130,808,940	95.40%
WAX	WAXP	0.09	0.08	0.02	0.45	123,146,918	No limit
Gnosis	GNO	75.65	89.51	9.12	455.06	108,609,822	15.05%
Centrality	CENNZ	0.06	0.03	0.01	0.18	64,868,357	No limit
Populous	PPT	1.10	1.10	0.19	6.63	58,098,188	100.0%
Walton Chain	WTC	0.89	0.60	0.17	2.76	49,495,500	78.07%
PIVX	PIVX	0.59	0.37	0.18	2.38	35,752,976	No limit
The Midas Touch Gold	TMTG	0.01	0.01	0.00	0.07	35,100,124	No limit
Powerledger	POWR	0.08	0.03	0.04	0.13	33,511,421	No limit
Groestlcoin	GRS	0.42	0.34	0.11	2.09	32,179,715	74.98%
Bluzelle	BLZ	0.11	0.11	0.01	0.56	28,327,310	No limit
Oxen	OXEN	0.52	0.39	0.11	2.04	26,194,630	No limit
PLATINCOIN	PLC	9.38	9.88	1.65	47.03	25,504,743	No limit
Ignis	IGNIS	0.03	0.02	0.01	0.08	22,789,036	76.16%
TenX	PAY	0.19	0.08	0.05	0.45	21,593,708	No limit
Bread	BRD	0.21	0.11	0.05	0.52	18,473,484	No limit
Particl	PART	2.23	0.96	0.78	5.33	17,955,473	No limit
Measurable Data Token	MDT	0.02	0.02	0.00	0.12	12,611,214	67.62%
Blocknet	BLOCK	1.71	0.85	0.58	6.02	11,518,905	No limit

(continued)

Table 2 (continued)

Cryptocurrency	Unit	Price (USD)				Market capitalisation	Cap
		Mean	Std. Dev.	Min	Max		
SALT	SALT	0.13	0.05	0.04	0.25	10,167,614	No limit
Propy	PRO	0.15	0.05	0.07	0.25	7,991,005	No limit
Validity	VAL	0.02	0.02	0.00	0.11	6,667,885	49.24%
AppsCoins	APPC	0.06	0.02	0.03	0.11	5,577,717	No limit
Morpheus.Network	MRPH	0.16	0.05	0.06	0.35	5,176,823	98.50%
Adshares	ADS	0.22	0.39	0.01	1.72	4,271,332	51.95%
Autonio	NIOX	0.05	0.08	0.00	0.44	3,782,494	31.48%

Notes Authors' calculations

pandemic on 11 March 2020. The second event is the day the WHO proclaimed the commencement of the COVID-19 immunisation program on 31 December 2020, after which the vaccines would be administered worldwide. To test the significance of the events, we set four event windows: (1) 3 days event window (−1, +1), (2) 61 days event window (−30, +30), (3) 401 days event window (−200, +200), and (4) 1,035 days windows (−435, +599 days) for pandemic and vaccine announcement, respectively.

3.2 *Measuring Market Reaction*

In an event study, the market reaction is measured using the cumulative abnormal return (CAR). The first step is calculating the returns (*R*) of the studied asset *i*, i.e., cryptocurrencies at time *t* as follows;

$$R_{i,t} = \frac{P_{i,t} - P_{i,t-1}}{P_{i,t-1}}, \text{ where } P_t = \frac{(O + C + L + H)}{4} \tag{1}$$

Unlike most studies that use price data of either closing or opening, we set the price (*P*) of day *t* equal to the average of its opening (*O*), closing (*C*), highest (*H*), and lowest (*L*) prices to capture the high frequency of changes in cryptocurrency prices.

Then, the abnormal return (*AR*) is computed as the difference between the returns of a cryptocurrency and its benchmark. The reasons behind choosing the global equity market index, MSCI World Index (MSCI), as the benchmark is: (1) equity is the former riskiest asset among the traditional financial assets, and (2) cryptocurrency is a global asset, so a global index is most appropriate than the local stock market index. We employ the simple market model, which assumes each cryptocurrency has a beta equal to 1.0 to compute the *AR* for the *i*th cryptocurrency at time *t*, that is:

$$AR_{i,t} = R_{i,t} - R_{B,t} \tag{2}$$

where R_i is the return of cryptocurrency and R_B is the return of the benchmark portfolio (MSCI), calculated similarly as in Eq. (1). Next, the cumulative abnormal return (*CAR*) for the *i*th cryptocurrency for the event window (j, J) is calculated;

$$CAR_i = \frac{\sum_{t=j}^{J} AR_t}{(N)} \tag{3}$$

where N is the total number of days within an event window from $t = j$ to J. We employ a *t*-test to determine whether the reaction (*CAR*) of the *i*th cryptocurrency is significant using the following formula:

$$t = \frac{CAR_{i,N}}{\sigma_{AR,i,N}} \text{ where } \sigma_{AR,i,N} = \sqrt{\sum_{T-j}^{J} \left(AR_{i,t} - \overline{AR_{i,t}}\right)^2 / (N-1)} \tag{4}$$

where *CAR* is significant at 5% level if the estimated *t*-statistics from Eq. (4) for the 3-day, 61-day, 401-day and 1,035-day event windows are greater than the *t* critical values of 3.1828, 1.9996, 1.9659, and 1.9623, respectively. Note that in this study, the *t*-statistics is estimated for the *CAR* of each particular cryptocurrency (i) such that its standard deviation (σ_{AR}) is based on the deviation of its serial *AR*s from the average *AR*. This approach is slightly different from studies that test their samples collectively, unlike this study, which aims to test the reaction at the micro level.

4 Results and Discussion

4.1 Return Properties of Sample Cryptocurrencies

Tables 2 and 5 (Appendix) report the summary and descriptive statistics of returns on the 41 cryptocurrencies, including MSCI as the benchmark, based on the return data from 1 January 2019 to 31 October 2021. As shown in Tables 2 and 5, the mean daily returns for 39 (95.12%) of the 41 cryptocurrencies are positive during this period, ranging from 0.0000 (TenX) to 0.0365 (Autonio). Meanwhile, MSCI records a mean return of 0.0008, the second lowest after TenX, excluding the two altcoins (USD Coin and Tether) with negative mean returns. Bitcoin records a mean return of 0.0031, which is nearly four times higher than that of MSCI. The results, which show that 37 altcoins also report mean returns higher than MSCI, explain the appeal of cryptocurrencies to investors and speculators. However, an investment decision that only considers return tends to trap investors in high risks of losing. The risk-return trade-off theory suggests that, at minimum, the decision must be based on risk and return aspects. Interestingly, 39 cryptocurrencies hit their lowest return on 12 March 2020, the day after WHO's pandemic declaration. On that day, most financial markets experienced a negative shock (Inman, 2020).

All return series have kurtosis coefficients greater than 3.0, with the highest kurtosis values 760.9504 and 597.1117, which are reported by Autonio and Adshares, respectively. A high kurtosis is associated with a high level of risk from an investment perspective because it suggests that the asset has a high probability of substantial and extremely tiny returns. Except for MSCI and five cryptocurrencies (i.e., Bitcoin, USD Coin, Tether, Ethereum, and XRP), all return series exhibit high positive skewness. This finding is consistent with Vaz de Melo Mendes and Carneiro (2020), who found that Bitcoin's asymmetry coefficient (skewness) is significantly negative. It is interesting to see that all five cryptocurrencies that have negative skewness are the ones that have the largest market capitalisation in the market. The reason could be that these digital currencies are well-established and behave like other traditional financial assets such as stock. Negative skewness indicates that an investor can expect frequent small wins and a few huge losses. Although trading techniques based on negative skewness may yield consistent returns, an investor should be mindful that huge losses are still possible.

Similar to Corbet et al. (2020), we measure the volatility property of MSCI and the sample cryptocurrencies based on the standard deviation. Tables 2 and 5 place MSCI on top of the other 41 cryptocurrencies based on their standard deviation. The last row in Table 3 (altcoins > Bitcoin) shows that besides MSCI, which is the least volatile, Bitcoin is the least volatile among cryptocurrencies. Table 5 shows that Bitcoin is followed by USD Coin, Tether, TRON, Gnosis and Stellar. Meanwhile, cryptocurrencies that report higher volatility are Autonio, Adshares, WhiteCoin, The Midas Touch Gold, and PLATINCOIN, as they show the highest standard deviation. This finding supports the assertion that cryptocurrencies are much riskier than MSCI, the riskiest traditional financial assets (stock). Even the most established cryptocurrency, Bitcoin, is twice as riskier than MSCI. Note also that all cryptocurrencies and MSCI record negative minimum values, indicating that the pandemic leaves its trace on all assets.

Investors should not be fooled by the high returns reported by cryptocurrencies because they may not sufficiently compensate for the additional risks born by the investors. The Sharpe ratio provides the most straightforward standardised measure to incorporate risk and return in an investment decision.

$$Sharpe = \frac{(R_i - R_F)}{\delta} \text{ where } \delta^2 = \frac{\sum_{t=n}^{N} (R_t - (E(R)))}{(N-1)},\ \delta = {}^{2}\sqrt{\delta^2} \quad (5)$$

and R_F is the rate of return on risk-free security. We use the gross Sharpe ratio ($R_F = 0$) to draw Fig. 1, which shows that only 12 out of 41 cryptocurrencies outperform MSCI based on the return per unit of risk. The figure also shows several meaningful observations: (1) despite its low return, equity portfolio (MSCI) offers a higher return per unit of risk than most cryptocurrencies, (2) Bitcoin generates one of the highest Sharpe ratios, and that justifies its growing popularity among fund managers, and

Table 3 Descriptive statistics of cryptocurrencies return

Variable	Mean	Std. Dev.	Minimum	Maximum	Skewness	Kurtosis
MSCI	0.0008	0.0120	−0.0991	0.0877	−1.3670	19.5100
Bitcoin	0.0031	0.0281	−0.2005	0.1322	−0.3408	5.8857
Statistics for Altcoins						
Mean	0.0036	0.0655	−0.4087	0.7364	0.6304	36.4036
Std Deviation	0.0030	0.0351	0.2512	1.0122	8.8462	101.8507
Minimum	−0.0010	0.0120	−1.0000	0.0184	−31.7960	1.1118
Maximum	0.0365	0.6969	−0.0991	20.7473	26.1230	760.9504
Cryptos > MSCI	38/41	41/41	0/41	39/41	37/41	20/41
Altcoins > Bitcoin	22/40	40/40	2/40	38/40	36/40	35/40

Note Authors' calculation

(3) lower risk cryptocurrencies are more likely to generate higher Sharpe ratios than higher risk cryptocurrencies. The observations suggest that investors have taken unnecessarily high risks to obtain the same returns as low-risk investments such as Bitcoin or MSCI. Note that two of the largest cryptocurrencies (USD Coin and Tether) report negative Sharpe ratios. In addition, one altcoin (Fantom) performs better than Bitcoin, while several less-known altcoins such as TRON, VeChan, and XDC Network appear to be as competitive as Bitcoin. This information is vital to investors in jurisdictions where the authority has ruled out that investment in cryptocurrencies is at their own risk. For instance, the Malaysian government has ruled out that its central bank or other authorities do not govern cryptocurrencies. They advised that investors must never put their capital at unnecessary risk by trading cryptocurrencies in unregistered exchanges. Its central bank (Bank Negara Malaysia, BNM) has specified that under Malaysia's laws, cryptocurrencies (i) are not legal tender in this country and (ii) their businesses are not protected by the country's prudential and market conduct standards or arrangements otherwise applicable to financial institutions (Jayaseelen & Kok, 2017).

5 Investor's Reaction During the Pandemic

In Fig. 2, we plot the cumulative average abnormal return (CAAR) for 40 altcoins against Bitcoin, calculated from 1 January 2019 until 30 October 2021, to give a broad picture of the situation throughout the observation period. The trend shows that Bitcoin and the sample altcoins had an adverse reaction when the first COVID-19 was detected in Wuhan, China. However, the CAR drop is not much different from many other falls throughout the observation period. The reaction to WHO's announcement was much more significant and indicative of the shock felt by investors. Bitcoin and altcoin samples recorded around an 8% drop in their respective CAR, but one day after

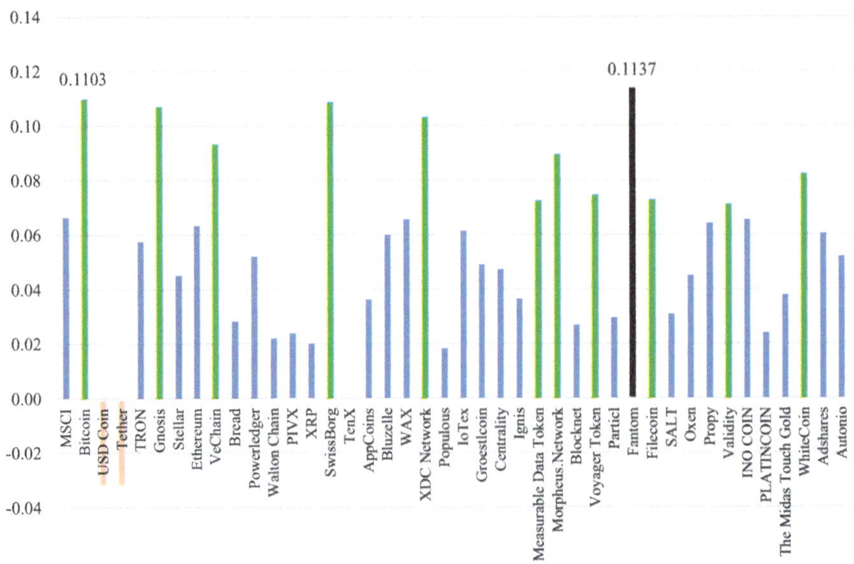

Fig. 1 Performance of MSCI, Bitcoin and 40 altcoins (*Note* Green bars indicate cryptocurrencies with Sharpe ratios higher than MSCI's, the black bar indicates altcoin with a Sharpe ratio higher than Bitcoin's, and red bars are altcoins with negative Sharpe ratios)

the news. Within ten days, both samples recovered the pre-outbreak performance. These indifferent reactions are unconventional because the voluminous evidence indicates that the pandemic significantly affected financial markets, including cryptocurrencies. This finding is primarily due to some badly affected cryptocurrencies offsetting those that performed well during the pandemic. The trend shown in Fig. 2 shows that a more detailed analysis (at the micro level) is necessary to detect the pandemic's impact on cryptocurrencies. The cryptocurrencies' reaction to the vaccine discovery is more pronounced, although with a long delay. Investors reacted very favourably to the positive development in the world's fight on COVID-19. Although some studies (e.g., Ftiti et al., 2021; Zhu et al., 2021) have shown that the prices of Bitcoin and many cryptocurrencies have been rallying after the pandemic, the vaccine discovery has provided another push force in the market. Meanwhile, studies on equity markets (Cao et al., 2020; Khalfaoui et al., 2021; Rouatbi et al., 2021) discovered that vaccination had stabilised the global equity markets.

We quantify the significance of the COVID-19-related news by t-testing the CAR at different event windows. CAR at each event window is computed and tested at the individual cryptocurrency level. Then we count the number of CARs at each event window that is significantly positive and negative and CARS that are insignificant. Table 4 presents the percentage of CARs for Bitcoin and the 40 altcoins related to the announcements of COVID-19 on 11 March 2020 and the first vaccination program on 31 December 2020. In Panel A, Bitcoin's investors react insignificantly to the pandemic announcement in the narrower event windows (−1, +1) and (−30, +30),

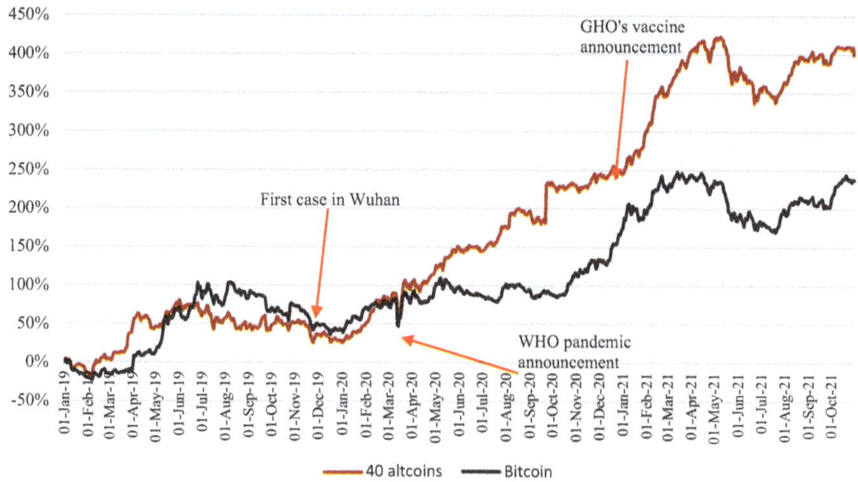

Fig. 2 Bitcoin vs altcoins' CAAR from 1.1.2019 to 31.10.2021 (*Note* The dark blue line represents the CAAR for the 40 altcoins, and the red line represents Bitcoin's CAR)

suggesting that they might have already reflected the global market shock on its price. In other words, this evidence indicates that the markets of Bitcoin and 25% of altcoins are efficient, consistent with the results of earlier studies. Bitcoin CARs on the broader event windows are highly significant and positive. Since only 5% and 0 CARs are insignificant in event windows (−200, +200) and (−435, +599), there seems to be a possibility that cryptocurrencies' investors were perplexed by the news that there was a long delay before they could fully interpret and reflect the news. These results as consistent with the trend of CARs shown earlier in Fig. 2. The CARs of Bitcoin and altcoins do not reach a stable point until around June 2021, which suggests that investors only fully reflect the COVID-19-related news long after all countries started administering their vaccination programs to the public.

Overall, the results from all three event windows indicate that the CARs are more likely to be significantly positive on the broader event windows. In Panel A, the results suggest that investors of most (75%) cryptocurrencies react significantly to the pandemic news. This finding suggests that the pandemic news shocks investors. However, more significant CARS are positive, which indicates that investors tend to react favourably to the pandemic news. This finding contradicts the fact that a pandemic is bad news to investors. However, it does not make the result faulty because cryptocurrencies are known to be a safe haven, an asset with a significantly negative correlation with other assets. This property makes cryptocurrencies a safe getaway for investors who have to reinvest their capital once withdrawn from other assets badly affected by the pandemic. Investors' switching behaviour during this pandemic was one of the reasons the cryptocurrency market recorded multiple high price hikes during this pandemic crisis.

Table 4 Summary of CAR's *t*-test results

Event date	Event window	Bitcoin	40 altcoins		
			+ve/sig (%)	−ve/sig (%)	Xsig (%)
Panel A. WHO declared the pandemic 11 March 2020 ($t = 0$)	(−1, +1)	−ve/Xsig	10.00	37.50	52.50
	(−30, + 30)	−ve/Xsig	40.00	35.00	25.00
	(−200, + 200)	+ve/sig	60.00	35.00	5.00
	(−435, + 599)	+ve/sig	97.50	2.50	0.00
Panel B. GHO announced the vaccine development 31 December 2020 ($t = 0$)	(−1, +1)	+ve/Xsig	17.50	32.50	50.00
	(−30, + 30)	−ve/Xsig	52.50	27.50	20.00
	(−200, + 200)	+ve/sig	47.50	42.50	10.00
	(−730, + 304)	+ve/sig	97.50	2.50	0.00

Note Abbreviations +ve = positive, −ve = negative, sig = significant, and Xsig = insignificant

Panel B shows CAR results on the investors' reaction towards the vaccine development. Again, Bitcoin's investors react insignificantly towards the news in the narrower event windows, supporting our earlier proposition that this cryptocurrency has an efficient market. Similar to the result in Panel A, its CARs on the broader event windows are highly significant and positive. The results for the altcoins suggest that investors in the majority (52.5%) of altcoins behave similarly to Bitcoin. The distribution of significant CARs and negative and positive CARs is very similar to the results of the pandemic announcement in Panel A. The market reacts to the announcement significantly. As expected, it reacts favourably to the positive news. Similar results of more positive CAR during the wide event window have been documented by Mnif et al. (2020). The result is interesting because it shows that the news does not immediately reset the investors' behaviour to leave cryptocurrencies and switch back to traditional financial assets. Once the vaccination program is administered, the immunisation process would allow economies to reopen. However, that is the right decision for investors to make because, during the early phase, the vaccination inventory was only sufficient to be administered to essential workers.

Table 6 provides the list of countries that produce 11 types of COVID-19 vaccines for the world population. Several issues must be considered when considering COVID-19 vaccination. The first and most crucial problem is the mutations of SARS-CoV-2 (the virus that causes COVID-19) that cause new variants of COVID-19. The first variant is Alpha which was detected in the United Kingdom in September 2020, followed by Beta (South Africa in May 2020), Gamma (Brazil in November

2020), Delta (India in October 2020), and the latest is Omicron which is found in multiple countries in November 2021. The newer variants, particularly Omicron, tend to be more infectious and can cause more severe illness. Indeed, the global community is continuously on guard against COVID-19 Omicron to avoid the threat of imposing some kinds of physical containment that will disrupt economic activities. More resources are needed to upgrade the vaccines and administer additional or probably periodical vaccines to the public.

The second issue is the increasing costs of producing and administering vaccines. Considering that Russia, one of the vaccine producers, is currently in a war with Ukraine, the production burdens are placed on the other producers in China, the United Kingdom, Sweden, India, the United States and Germany. With some vaccines getting less demand due to the lower efficacy rate, the remaining producers are getting pressure to produce more inventories ready for global consumption. The end effect of this pressure would be a higher price that governments worldwide have to pay when they are still recovering from the COVID-19 crisis and currently facing global inflation.

5.1 Do Size and Supply Matter in Their Reaction?

Thus far, we have looked at the cryptocurrency market reaction from the broad picture that generally has shown the unique behaviour of Bitcoin from the altcoins. In stock market literature, several firm-specific characteristics such as size, growth, momentum and liquidity (Carhart, 1997; Fama & French, 1993) could explain the asset's behavioural difference. In this chapter, we examine whether size affects investors' reactions. Similar to stocks, cryptocurrencies with larger market capitalisation would be expected to weather any shock better than smaller cryptocurrencies. For larger cryptocurrencies, a small group of investors reacting to a certain shock would not cause a large change in their values. To test the size effect in the sample reactions, we compare the CARs of the 5 largest versus the 5 smallest cryptocurrencies. As shown in Table 6, the five largest altcoins in the sample are Ethereum, Tether, XRP, USD Coin and Stellar, while the smallest are Autonio, Adshares, AppCoins, Validity and Morpheus.Network.

The results displayed in Fig. 3 support the size effect proposition. By plotting the average CARs of BIG versus SMALL cryptocurrencies on the same graph, we can directly compare the different reactions between the two subsamples. As shown in Fig. 3, the reactions (CARs) of the BIG (largest) cryptocurrencies are immaterial relative to the reactions of the SMALL (smallest) cryptocurrencies. Compared to BIG, Bitcoin exhibits larger reactions, which are not likely to be entirely driven by the news about COVID-19. Bitcoin's CAR started its increasing spree in May 2019.

BIG's CARs show a sharp contrast to SMALL's CARs. However, SMALL already begins its price rally in March 2019 before making a quantum leap around October 2020. The dramatic reaction by the SMALL group is contributed mainly by Autonio and Adshares, whose price movements are not likely to be driven by the pandemic.

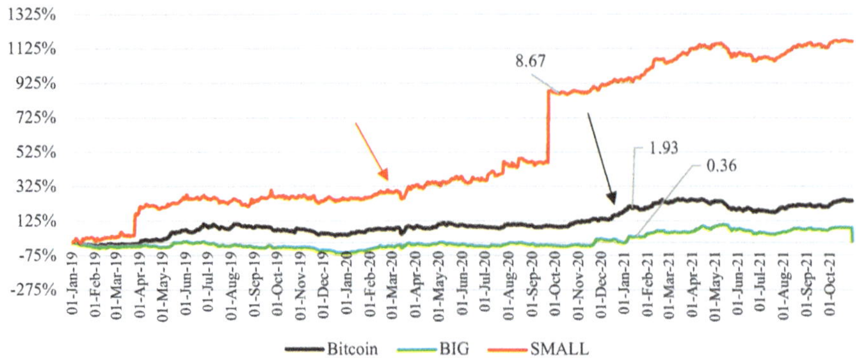

Fig. 3 Comparison between CARs of big and small cryptocurrencies

Overall, there are two major observations that can be made from Fig. 3. First, there is a significant size effect on the reaction of cryptocurrencies towards the news related to COVID-19. Similar to stocks, smaller cryptocurrencies tend to give a much bigger reaction than their larger counterparts. Although the CAR movement is not likely to be driven by the pandemic announcement, the drastic movement happens during a time that coincides with the pandemic period. Second, unlike the results for the whole sample in Table 2, Fig. 3 shows that with the size difference, we could see that cryptocurrencies on both extreme ends of size do not react significantly to the pandemic news. Nonetheless, they react favourably to the vaccine news, more abruptly in the case of smaller cryptocurrencies. Thus, although small-cap cryptocurrencies offer a lot of short-term growth potential, they are usually quite volatile and are considered high-risk investments. These cryptos can crash at any time, and the crash can happen very instantly (Collins, 2019).

We next investigate another unique characteristic of cryptocurrency, which makes it more of an investment than a medium of exchange tool. Although not all cryptocurrency has limited supply, some that do would mean it must have a certain impact on the prices, as the economic supply–demand theory would suggest. In this sample, we have examples of both types. We select the best examples of limited supply based on the highest capacity ratios (i.e. circulating supply/maximum supply). The subsample with the highest capacity ratio (Low Supply) consists of Populus (100%), Voyager Token (99.68%), Morpheus.Network (98.50%), IoTex (95.40%), and Fantom (80.13%). The "High Supply" subsample is represented by cryptocurrencies with the lowest number of units circulating with unlimited supply, i.e., PIVX, Oxen, Particl, Blocknet, and PLATICON. Figure 4 displays the CARs movement of these subsamples, which supports our conjecture.

Several observations are worth mentioning from the CAR trends in Fig. 4. First, there is a reasonably large difference between CARs of low and high-supply cryptocurrencies. Both subsamples behave quite similarly throughout the observation period, except when the WHO announced the vaccine discovery news. Low-supply

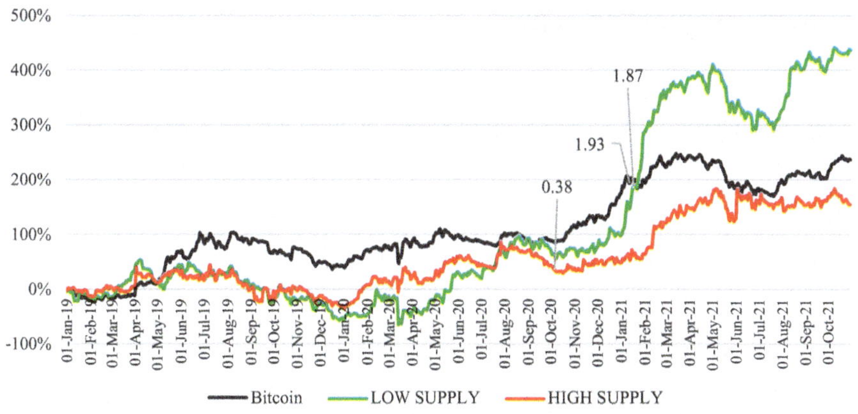

Fig. 4 Comparison between CARs of low and high-supply cryptocurrencies

cryptocurrencies show a greater positive response to the news than high-supply cryptocurrencies. The probable reason is the pressure on price, which becomes more intense when the supply of currency is already saturated, such as in the case of Populus and Voyager Token. Second, the CAR difference due to supply is significantly smaller than the difference due to size, as shown in Fig. 3. This result suggests that small-cap currencies are more prone to shock and, therefore, less suitable for investors but more appealing to speculators.

Third, throughout this study, Bitcoin shows that it acts efficiently, as its CAR quickly stabilises after rebounds from a drop when the news about the pandemic is prompted. However, Bitcoin reacts very favourably towards the vaccine development news, but it takes some time before (inefficiently) reaching the relatively constant phase. The second piece of evidence supports the result by Cheah et al. (2018). They argued that the Bitcoin market exhibits moderate to high inefficiency, implying the possibility of speculative profits for investors. Interestingly, Bitcoin represents the steadiest reaction relative to the 40 altcoins, Small-cap altcoins, and saturated (close to full-cap ratio) altcoins. Altcoins with unlimited supply exhibit reaction that resembles Bitcoin. Meanwhile, Big-cap altcoins indicate the highest efficiency as they are not affected by the COVID-19 news. Based on these findings, it can be concluded that the cryptocurrency market has been relatively inefficient during the COVID-19 pandemic, consistent with the results documented earlier by Mnif et al. (2020), Cheat et al. (2018) and Urquhart (2016). The cryptocurrencies, including Bitcoin, show a delayed reaction to the COVID-19 vaccine announcement, while unlimited altcoins also indicate a delayed reaction towards the announcement pandemic declaration.

6 Summary and Conclusion

This chapter investigates the cryptocurrency market reaction to WHO's announcement of the COVID-19 pandemic on 11 March 2020 and its vaccine on 31 December 2020. The results of this study show that the pandemic announcement does not create a price change that is significantly different from other price changes in these highly volatile digital assets. By including 41 cryptocurrencies, this study contributes to the existing literature that lacks rigorousity by focusing on large and popular cryptocurrencies, thereby unable to capture the effect of size and supply on their behaviour. We find that the reactions are significant in most cryptocurrencies and increasingly positive on the broader event windows. We also find that the size effect is highly significant in the cryptocurrency market and more apparent than the size effect in stock markets. Cryptocurrencies with saturated supply react more drastically than those with an unlimited supply, probably because the demand pressure on price cannot be supported in the absence of new currencies. Still, the impact of supply is significantly less pronounced than size. Meanwhile, Bitcoin appears to be more efficient than all altcoins except for the five largest-cap. The results of this study would be beneficial for investors, particularly those searching for a safe haven or hedger in the cryptocurrency market. Since the pandemic is still an ongoing threat to the world, investors need to be more vigilant about the small altcoins that could burst due to the overheated market.

Acknowledgements The authors wish to acknowledge that this paper is funded by the Ministry of Higher Education Malaysia (FRGS/1/2018/SS01/UKM/02/2).

Appendix

See Tables 5 and 6.

Table 5 Descriptive statistics of sample cryptocurrencies, listed by the standard deviation

Variable	Mean	Std. Dev.	Minimum	Maximum	Skewness	Kurtosis
MSCI	0.0008	0.0120	−0.0991	0.0877	−1.3670	19.5100
Bitcoin	0.0031	0.0281	−0.2005	0.1322	−0.3408	5.8857
USD Coin	−0.0010	0.0312	−1.0000	0.0184	−31.7960	10.1890
Tether	−0.0010	0.0312	−1.0000	0.0235	−31.7655	10.1761
TRON	0.0024	0.0414	−0.2114	0.2251	0.1446	4.1992
Gnosis	0.0045	0.0419	−0.2229	0.2891	0.8841	7.0782
Stellar	0.0021	0.0461	−0.2167	0.5420	2.5793	25.7990
Ethereum	0.0030	0.0471	−1.0000	0.1722	−9.5007	19.9399
VeChain	0.0045	0.0480	−0.2749	0.2785	0.0382	4.0228
Bread	0.0014	0.0490	−0.3174	0.2704	0.0774	5.5628
Powerledger	0.0028	0.0534	−0.2778	0.5478	1.6076	16.8131
Walton Chain	0.0012	0.0540	−0.3197	0.5313	1.0728	13.0559
PIVX	0.0013	0.0541	−0.3256	0.4316	1.1470	12.0512
Ripple	0.0011	0.0549	−1.0000	0.3277	−5.2829	1.1118
SwissBorg	0.0060	0.0550	−0.1958	0.4169	1.2738	5.9095
TenX	0.0000	0.0568	−0.2801	0.6041	1.8237	16.1297
AppCoins	0.0021	0.0573	−0.2897	0.5258	1.2615	12.8051
Bluzelle	0.0036	0.0598	−0.3551	0.3389	0.1465	3.5117
WAX	0.0042	0.0637	−0.2868	0.7195	2.9926	25.3817
XDC Network	0.0067	0.0647	-0.2400	0.4905	1.8349	9.3798
Populous	0.0012	0.0648	-0.2706	0.6635	2.4200	20.8597
IoTex	0.0040	0.0649	−0.3606	0.9468	4.4108	53.6689
Groestlcoin	0.0033	0.0668	−0.2543	0.8431	5.6177	68.9507
Centrality	0.0032	0.0672	−0.2265	0.5944	1.9977	15.4771
Ignis	0.0025	0.0679	−0.3551	0.9612	3.8801	50.2902
Measurable Data Token	0.0050	0.0687	−0.4294	0.9793	3.2076	42.7843
Morpheus.Network	0.0063	0.0700	−0.2127	0.3883	0.9535	3.0041
Blocknet	0.0019	0.0701	−0.2916	0.5449	1.4856	9.4899
Voyager Token	0.0053	0.0707	−0.2895	0.6041	2.9011	18.7814
Particl	0.0021	0.0707	−0.4289	0.7996	3.1103	33.3640
Fantom	0.0084	0.0739	−0.3774	0.5023	1.2033	6.1742
Filecoin	0.0056	0.0765	−0.3229	0.9446	2.8890	29.3971
SALT	0.0024	0.0768	−0.3322	0.9293	3.5769	32.5609
Oxen	0.0036	0.0794	−0.4812	1.2130	6.4980	85.2633
Propy	0.0058	0.0899	−0.3206	0.9882	4.6737	38.8721

(continued)

Table 5 (continued)

Variable	Mean	Std. Dev.	Minimum	Maximum	Skewness	Kurtosis
Validity	0.0066	0.0923	−0.4903	1.2961	3.2822	40.4403
INO COIN	0.0061	0.0927	−0.7992	2.0449	10.7306	239.1793
PLATINCOIN	0.0026	0.1072	−0.6442	2.1088	8.4404	166.4128
The Midas Touch Gold	0.0051	0.1336	−0.5823	2.7594	11.1308	203.1793
WhiteCoin	0.0138	0.1667	−0.7652	2.3695	5.9748	69.4835
Adshares	0.0127	0.2092	−0.7979	5.8731	21.4706	597.1117
Autonio	0.0365	0.6969	−0.7301	20.7473	26.1230	760.9504

Source of data CoinMarketCap website

Table 6 List of vaccines and producers

Country	Developer	Clinical phase	Efficacy (%)	Doses
China	CanSino	3	64	1
China	Sinopharm	3	78	2
China	Sinovac	3	51–84	2
India	Bharat Biotech	3	78	2
Russia	Gamaleya	3	78	2
United Kingdom, Sweden	Oxford-AstraZeneca	2 and 3	74–100	2
United States, Germany	Pfizer-BioNTech	3	91	2
United States & India	Baylor, Biological E	3	90+	2
United States	Johnson & Johnson	3	64–72	1
United States	Moderna	3	93–98	2
United States	Novavax	3	90	2

Source Council on Foreign Relations (https://www.cfr.org/backgrounder/guide-global-COVID-19-vaccine-efforts) as of 19 July 2022. Efficacy depends on dosage, the severity of the infection and the COVID-19 variant

References

Atalan, A. (2020). Is the lockdown important to prevent the COVID-19 pandemic? Effects on psychology, environment and economy-perspective. *Annals of Medicine and Surgery, 56*, 38–42. https://doi.org/10.1016/j.amsu.2020.06.010

Caferra, R., & Vidal-Tomás, D. (2021). Who raised from the abyss? A comparison between cryptocurrency and stock market dynamics during the COVID-19 pandemic. *Finance Research Letters, 43*, 101954.

Cao, K. H., Woo, C. K., Li, Y., & Liu, Y. (2020). COVID-19's effect on the alpha and beta of a US stock Exchange Traded Fund. *Applied Economics Letters, 29*(2), 123–128. https://doi.org/10.1080/13504851.2020.1859447

Carhart, M. M. (1997). On persistence in mutual fund performance. *Journal of Finance, 52*(1), 57–82.

Cheah, E.-T., Mishra, T., Parhi, M., & Zhang, Z. (2018). Long memory interdependency and inefficiency in bitcoin markets. *Economics Letters, 167*, 18–25. 10.1016/j. Econlet.2018.02.010

Collins, C. (2019). *What is market capitalisation (market cap) and why does it matter?* https://www.bitpanda.com/academy/en/lessons/what-is-market-capitalisation-market-cap-and-why-does-it-matter/. Accessed 25 Jan 2021.

Corbet, S., Larkin, C., & Lucey, B. (2020). The contagion effects of the COVID-19 pandemic: Evidence from gold and cryptocurrencies. *Finance Research Letters, 35*(1), 1–7. https://doi.org/10.1016/j.frl.2020.101554

Cummings, J. R., Wolfson, J. A., & Gearhardt, A. N. (2022). Health-promoting behaviors in the United States during the early stages of the COVID-19 pandemic. *Appetite, 168*, 105659. https://doi.org/10.1016/j.appet.2021.105659

Dai, X. J., Shao, Y., Ren, L., Tao, W., & Wang, Y. (2022). Risk factors of COVID-19 in subjects with and without mental disorders. *Journal of Affective Disorders, 297*, 102–111. https://doi.org/10.1016/j.jad.2021.10.024

Demir, E., Bilgin, M. H., Karabulut, G., & Doker, A. C. (2020). The relationship between cyrptocurrencies and COVID-19 pandemic. *Eurasian Economic Review, 10*, 349–360.

Fama, E. F. (1970). Efficient capital markets: A review of theory and empirical work. *Journal of Finance, 25*(2), 383–417. https://doi.org/10.2307/232548

Fama, E. F., & French, K. R. (1993). Common risk factors in the returns on stocks and bonds. *Journal of Financial Economics, 33*(1), 3–56.

Ftiti, Z., Louhichi, W., & Ameur, B. H. (2021). Cryptocurrency volatility forecasting: What can we learn from the first wave of the COVID-19 outbreak? *Annals of Operations Research*, 1–26.

Herwany, A., Febrian, E., Anwar, M., & Gunardi, A. (2021). The influence of the COVID-19 pandemic on stock market returns in Indonesia stock exchange. *The Journal of Asian Finance, Economics and Business, 8*(3), 39–47. https://doi.org/10.13106/jafeb.2021.vol8.no3.0039

Hossain, M. (2021). The effect of the COVID-19 on sharing economy activities. *Journal of Cleaner Production, 280*, 124782. https://doi.org/10.1016/j.jclepro.2020.124782

Inman, P. (2020). *Christine Lagarde under fire for ECB coronavirus response*. https://www.theguardian.com/world/2020/mar/12/ecb-announces-plan-to-help-eurozone-banks-withstand-coronavirus

Jarboui, A., & Mnif, E. (2021). Cryptocurrency bubble risk and the FOMC announcements during COVID-19 black swan event. *Journal of Investment Compliance, 22*(1), 95–108. https://doi.org/10.1108/JOIC-12-2020-0048

Jayaseelen, R., & Kok, C. (2017). *Bank Negara reins in digital currencies*. Star Online. Retrieved from https://www.thestar.com.my/business-news/2017/11/23/banknegara-reins-in-digital-currencies/

Jia, Z., Wen, S., & Lin, B. (2021). The effects and reacts of COVID-19 pandemic and international oil price on energy, economy, and environment in China. *Applied Energy, 302*, 117612. https://doi.org/10.1016/j.apenergy.2021.117612

Jiang, F., Yang, W. L., Wang, J. W., Zhu, Z., Luo, C., Arendt-Nielsen, L., & Song, X. J. (2021). Pain during and after coronavirus disease 2019: Chinese perspectives. *Pain Reports, 6*(1). https://doi.org/10.1097/PR9.0000000000000931

Khalfaoui, R., Nammouri, H., Labidi, O., & Jabeur, S. B. (2021). Is the COVID-19 vaccine effective on the US financial market? *Public Health, 198*, 177–179. https://doi.org/10.1016/j.puhe.2021.07.026

Khan, K., Zhao, H., Zhang, H., Yang, H., Shah, M. H., & Jahanger, A. (2020). The impact of COVID-19 pandemic on stock markets: An empirical analysis of world major stock indices. *The Journal of Asian Finance, Economics, and Business, 7*(7), 463–474. https://doi.org/10.13106/jafeb.2020.vol7.no7.463

Kim, K., & Lee, M. (2021). The impact of the COVID-19 pandemic on the unpredictable dynamics of the cryptocurrency market. *Entropy, 23*(9), 1234. https://doi.org/10.3390/e23091234

Lahmiri, S., & Bekiros, S. (2020). The impact of COVID-19 pandemic upon stability and sequential irregularity of equity and cryptocurrency markets. *Nonlinear Science, and Nonequilibrium and Complex Phenomena, 138*. https://doi.org/10.1016/j.chaos.2020.109936

Li, X., Li, B., Wei, G., Bai, L., Wei, Y., & Liang, C. (2021). Return connectedness among commodity and financial assets during the COVID-19 pandemic: Evidence from China and the US. *Resources Policy, 73*, 102166. https://doi.org/10.1016/j.resourpol.2021.102166

Mnif, E., & Jarboui, A. (2021). COVID-19, bitcoin market efficiency, herd behavior. *Review of Behavioral Finance, 13*(1), 69–84. https://doi.org/10.1108/RBF-09-2020-0233

Mnif, E., Jarboui, A., & Mouakhar, K. (2020). How the cryptocurrency market has performed during COVID 19? A multifractal analysis. *Finance Research Letters, 36*. https://doi.org/10.1016/j.frl.2020.101647

Nusratullin, I., Mrochkovsk, N., Yarullin, R., Zamyatina, N., & Solntseva, O. (2021). The financial implications of the coronavirus COVID-19 pandemic: A review. *Cuestiones Políticas, 39*(68).

Rouatbi, W., Demir, E., Kizys, R., & Zaremba, A. (2021). Immunising markets against the pandemic: COVID-19 vaccinations and stock volatility around the world. *International Review of Financial Analysis, 77*, 101819. https://doi.org/10.1016/j.irfa.2021.101819

Salisu, A. A., & Ogbonna, A. E. (2021). The return volatility of cryptocurrencies during the COVID-19 pandemic: Assessing the news effect. *Global Finance Journal*, 1–8.

Umar, Z., & Gubareva, M. (2021). The relationship between the COVID-19 media coverage and the environmental, social and governance leader equity volatility: A time-frequency wavelet analysis. *Applied Economics, 53*(27), 3193–3206. https://doi.org/10.1080/00036846.2021.1877252

Umar, Z., Jareño, F., & de la O González, M. (2021a). The impact of COVID-19-related media coverage on the return and volatility connectedness of cryptocurrencies and fiat currencies. *Technological Forecasting and Social Change, 172*, 121025. https://doi.org/10.1016/j.techfore.2021.121025.

Umar, Z., Jareno, F., & Gubareva, M. (2021b). The impact of COVID-19-related media coverage on the return and volatility connectedness of cryptocurrencies and fiat currencies. *Technological Forecasting and Social Change, 172*(1), 1–16. https://doi.org/10.1016/j.techfore.2021.121025

Urquhart, A. (2016). The inefficiency of Bitcoin. *Economics Letters, 148*, 80–82. https://doi.org/10.1016/j.econlet.2016.09.019

Vaz de Melo Mendes, B., & Fluminense Carneiro, A. (2020). A comprehensive statistical analysis of the six major crypto-currencies from August 2015 through June 2020. *Journal of Risk and Financial Management, 13*(9), 192–213. http://dx.doi.org/https://doi.org/10.3390/jrfm13090192.

Vidal-Tomas, D., & Ibanez, A. (2018). Semi-strong efficiency of bitcoin. *Finance Research Letters, 27*(C), 259–265.

Vukovic, D., Maiti, M., Grubisic, Z., Grigorieva, E. M., & Frömmel, M. (2021). COVID-19 pandemic: Is the crypto market a safe haven? The impact of the first wave. *Sustainability, 13*, 8578. https://doi.org/10.3390/su13158578

Wang, J., & Wang, X. (2021). COVID-19 and financial market efficiency: Evidence from an entropy-based analysis. *Finance Research Letters, 42*, 101888. https://doi.org/10.1016/j.frl.2020.101888

Xin, L., & Chong, W. A. (2017). The technology and economic determinants of cryptocurrency exchange rates: The case of Bitcoin. *Decision Support Systems, 95*, 49–60. https://doi.org/10.1016/j.dss.2016.12.001.

Zhu, P., Zhang, X., Wu, Y., Zheng, H., & Zhang, Y. (2021). Investor attention and cryptocurrency: Evidence from the Bitcoin market. *PLoS ONE, 16*(2), e0246331. https://doi.org/10.1371/journal.pone.0246331

Monetary Policy, COVID-19 and Bitcoin: The Tales of 3 Countries

Noor Azryani Auzairy and Ahmad Ibn Ibrahimy

Abstract This chapter focuses on the relationships between Bitcoin price and monetary policy whether the roles of monetary policy still empower the performances of bitcoin or whether bitcoin price, in this digital era, overruns the monetary policy and government control. In the new norms of COVID-19 pandemic, where the electronic transactions and digital transactions and activities turn up to be the necessities, this chapter also explores whether the relationships between monetary policy and Bitcoin could be weaker. The relationships are compared between 8 months before and 8 months during COVID-19 pandemic for the 3 countries: US, China and Malaysia. The authorities are recommended to focus on the acceptance of cryptocurrency or even to establish one nation's digital currency.

Keywords Bitcoin · COVID-19 · Monetary policy · US · China · Malaysia

1 Introduction

It has always been questioned on the roles of monetary policy when the markets started to use cryptocurrencies as medium of exchange instead of government money. There is no government control on the amount of cryptocurrency available to be used in this world. Would there be any relationship between monetary policy and cryptocurrency, or Bitcoin specifically? In addition, COVID-19 pandemic creates new norms in our daily lives. More of electronic and digital transactions and activities are in power due to such new norms. Could COVID-19 significantly able to influence on the use of Bitcoin (BTC)? Should there be any different in the Bitcoin performances

N. A. Auzairy (✉)
Faculty of Economics and Management, Universiti Kebangsaan Malaysia, Bangi, Selangor, Malaysia
e-mail: azryani@ukm.edu.my

A. I. Ibrahimy
Faculty of Business and Economics, Universiti Malaya, Kuala Lumpur, Malaysia

Z. Abdul Karim et al. (eds.), *Contemporary Issues in Finance, Investment and Banking in Malaysia*,
https://doi.org/10.1007/978-981-99-5447-6_7

and the relationships between Bitcoin and monetary policy tools in the periods before and during COVID-19 pandemic?

The monetary policies implemented by the three countries: the US, China and Malaysia are to be looked into in this chapter. Referring to Statista (Buchholz, 2022), the US is the country, which most commonly used crypto among the developed countries. The US investors earned the most from Bitcoin in 2020, which is three times as high as China (McCarthy, 2021). China is the fastest growing emerging country in the use of digital currency. China was also one of the lowest electricity cost in the world, which managed to attract many crypto miners to mine crypto at lower cost. Despite US and China, there is a need to compare those relationships of the two main countries with Malaysia to ensure Malaysia's feasibility or the need to work on cryptocurrency or digital currency before it is too late.

2 Monetary Policy, Covid and Bitcoin

This chapter focuses on the relationships between Bitcoin price and monetary policy of US, China as well as Malaysia in representing emerging economies. Monetary policy is represented by its tools: overnight policy or interbank overnight interest rates and exchange rates (USD/SDR, CNY/USD and MYR/USD). Bitcoin price in USD is to represent cryptocurrency.

Since COVID-19 pandemic has impacted the world significantly on the economy and way of lives, it is an added advantage to know how the period with and without such pandemic could affect the Bitcoin price and its relation with monetary policy. Is monetary policy still relevant? Thus, this chapter is to explore the relationship between monetary policy and Bitcoin, 8 months before and 8 months during COVID-19 pandemic. To find out whether COVID-19 pandemic could affect the relationship between monetary policy and Bitcoin, daily new positive COVID-19 cases and new death COVID-19 cases, are taken into consideration.

3 Bitcoin

Bitcoin is the most prominent and commonly used virtual currency in the world with its market capitalization constituting 66 per cent of total market capitalization of all cryptocurrencies in 2020 (De Best, Statista, 2021). It is a cryptocurrency, created in 2009, that has emerged as a popular medium of exchange and is the first digital currency that has attracted a substantial number of users. However, number of studies have claimed that Bitcoin and other cryptocurrencies are used as a speculative asset rather than as a medium of exchange (Baur & Dimpfl, 2018; Baur et al., 2017; Cermak, 2017; Glaser et al., 2014).

The Bitcoin performance from 2017 to 2022 is shown in terms of its daily price or value in USD in Fig. 1. The time series graph portrays the increasing at increasing rate

Fig. 1 Bitcoin/US Dollar FX spot rate (January 2017–April 2022) (*Source* Datastream)

of Bitcoin price in 2017, from the lowest price at USD777.57 per BTC on 12 January to the highest price at USD19,050 per BTC on 18 December 2017. Then the price has been scattered around USD10,000 or less per BTC till October 2020. Starting from 20 October 2020, Bitcoin price has boosted up 2.5 times from USD11,740 to 40,857 in less than 3 months. 18 days later, Bitcoin drops by 24% before rising up back by 85.6% to USD57,531 on 22 February 2021. Such hike was due to mass interest and demand fueled by Tesla's announcement on its acquirement of USD1.5 billion worth of the digital coin (De Best, Statista, 2021).

Even though other cryptos experienced another hike in April 2021 due to the Initial Public Offering (IPO) of the US biggest crypto exchange, Bitcoin suffered a significant adjustment after speculation on government regulation. Such largest daily drop was also resulting from the power outage in the Chinese region of Xinjiang, which represents nearly ¼ of the global hash rate (De Best, Statista, 2021). After touching USD59,009 on 9 May, Bitcoin dropped by 44.8% in 15 days till the lowest price at USD29,859 on 21 July.

On 10 November 2021, Bitcoin managed to touch the highest price at USD67,709 before plummetted by 47.8% to USD35,379. Such price hike was related to the launch of a Bitcoin ETF in the US. From 2017 till March 2022, the mean for Bitcoin price is USD16,499 per BTC, lower than its standard deviation or volatility of USD17,378. 2020–2021 portrays remarkable high volatility of Bitcoin prices.

In terms of pricing, Bitcoin price follows the fundamental pricing, irrespective of the evolution of the Bitcoin quantity. The block rewards to miners, which are provided as lump-sum payments in the baseline version, are earned through mining effort (Schilling & Uhlig, 2019). As such, new coins will be minted at a fixed rate, that is, the larger the Bitcoin community and the total computational resources devoted to coin generation, the more difficult the computational puzzle would become (Barber et al., 2012). Through the measurement of long-term memory Bariviera et al. (2017) claims that Hurst exponents change significantly during the first years of existence of Bitcoin, tending to stabilize in recent times and Bitcoin presents large volatility that is reducing over time.

More and more governments have given their legal status for the use of Bitcoin in their countries, as compared to earlier years. This is supported by Sahoo (2017) that in the long run, people would have more faith in the cryptocurrency and the blockchain technology and its usability. If Bitcoin is to be stable in the future, then it would be easily accepted worldwide. Thus, it is important to know whether monetary policy tools will still be relevant. Since the world is becoming more dynamic & uncertain, let us have a look at how the period of pre and during COVID-19 pandamic could affect the Bitcoin performance and its relation to monetary policy tools.

4 COVID-19 Pandemic and Bitcoin

Looking at the performances of Bitcoin prices 8 months before and 8 months during COVID-19 pandemic, from May 2019 to August 2020, in Fig. 2, the Bitcoin price has a mean of USD8,955, max USD12,723 on 27 June 2019, before COVID-19 pandemic and minimum price of USD4,896 on 17 March 2020, during COVID-19 pandemic, which is lower than the starting price, 10 months earlier, on 1 May 2019. Its standard deviation of USD1,559 portrays the volatility of the Bitcoin price within those 16 months.

Figure 2 shows how Bitcoin has experienced its crashed price in March 2020 due to the market uncertainty caused by the pandemic (Abraham, 2021). Such clash also hit the global stock markets and economic output too. This sharp losses affect Bitcoin's identity as a safe haven. Can Bitcoin provide shelter from turbulence? The fall was held alongside the stock markets, which would boost the portfolio downside risk (Conlon & McGee, 2020).

Trillions of dollars of stimulus, then, were pumped into the markets to roar back the asset prices, including Bitcoin. Even though COVID-19 devastated the world's economy, mainstream financial market, however, then started taking Bitcoin seriously. COVID-19 pandemic has made Bitcoin wins attention and obtains growing adoption as a hedge, next frontier for savvy investing and fast profits (Keoun, 2020).

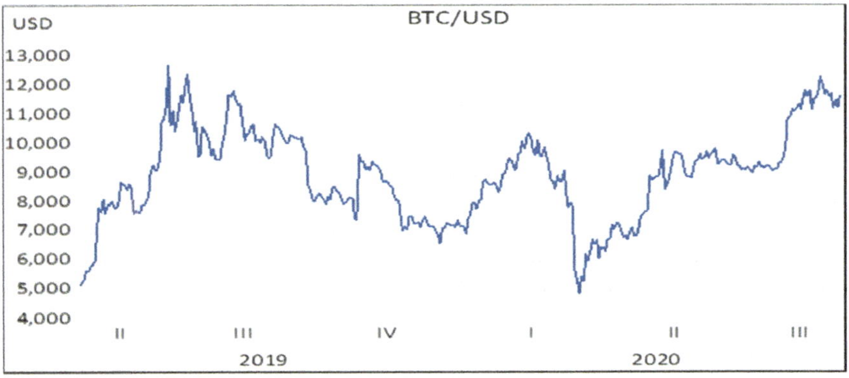

Fig. 2 Bitcoin price (BTC/USD) 8 months before and 8 months during COVID-19 pandemic (May 2019–August 2020) (*Note* Vertical line is the start of COVID-19 positive cases. *Source* Datastream)

Indeed, Sarkodie et al. (2022) claim that COVID-19 shocks induce numbers of cryptocurrencies performance, including Bitcoin by 2.71–3.27%. The higher demand on Bitcoin during this pandemic, has put Bitcoin as risk heaven, while gold was categorized as safe haven during previous crisis (Goodell & Goutte, 2021; Mnif & Jarboui, 2021). Bitcoin is found to be less fractal and more efficient after the outbreak. The pandemic has even reduced the herd bias or bandwagon effect in Bitcoin (Mnif & Jarboui, 2021). According to Wu et al. (2022), during the pandemic, Bitcoin remains efficient and even has smaller extreme values and volatility. They claim that Bitcoin has similar efficiency with spot gold and even better than other cryptocurrencies, such as Ethereum and Binance Coin. Moreover, the pandemic has increased the hedging ability of Bitcoin. Bitcoin futures can hedge the risks in the Bitcoin spot market (Zhang et al., 2021b). Such higher demand in Bitcoin can be seen in the figure above, right after 17 March 2020, that is after the sharp drop of the price from 13 February 2020.

Figure 3 shows the performances of Bitcoin and COVID-19 daily new positive and death cases of the whole globe, China and Malaysia. The daily new positive COVID-19 cases are to represent the increasing or decreasing status of those being infected, rather than the cumulative numbers.

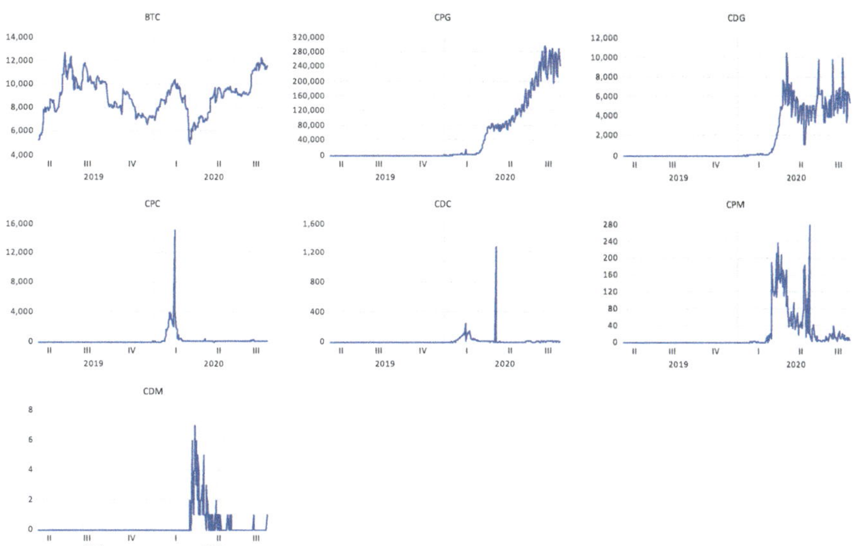

Fig. 3 Performances of Bitcoin price, daily new positive and new death COVID-19 cases of global, China and Malaysia, 8 months before and 8 months during COVID-19 pandemic (*Notes* BTC = Bitcoin/USD, CPG = Global Daily New Positive COVID-19 Cases, CDG = Global Daily New Death COVID-19 Cases, CPC = China Daily New Positive COVID-19 Cases, CDC = China Daily New Death COVID-19 Cases, CPM = Malaysia Daily New Positive COVID-19 Cases, CDM = Malaysia Daily New Death COVID-19 Cases, vertical line = the start of new positive COVID-19 cases. *Source* Datastream)

Generally, Bitcoin has been greatly influenced by its own previous performances. In terms of correlation between Bitcoin prices and each of those COVID-19 cases in the 16 months period of before and during COVID-19 pandemic, each case is significantly correlated with Bitcoin price, except for China COVID-19 new death cases. The correlations are somehow quite weak, especially with China COVID-19 daily new positive cases. Bitcoin and COVID-19 cases are positively correlated except for COVID-19 cases in Malaysia. Throughout those 16 months, the declining movement of COVID-19 cases in Malaysia spurs the increasing movement of Bitcoin prices. Globally, on the other hand, the COVID-19 cases are directly correlated with the Bitcoin prices.

Taking into account the relationships between those COVID-19 cases with other possible factors, and the Bitcoin price, surprisingly, all COVID-19 daily new positive and death cases do not significantly relate with Bitcoin price, except for China's new death cases. The sudden hike of death toll in China, originated country of COVID-19, in mid February 2020, might have awakened the whole world on the seriousness of the virus. Since China's COVID death cases are to be the main concern, it indicates how the initial news on China's high death on COVID is able to influence the Bitcoin investors decision on their investment in Bitcoin. Even though the relationship is quite weak, it still indicates that the higher the number of covid cases, the greater the demand for Bitcoin and thus increase its prices. This could also be due to the first announcement on Wuhan's lockdown, which had triggered people's minds on the need to deal with more online activities and transactions. This matter boosts the need and demand for Bitcoin.

Based on the data obtained from CoinDesk website (Keoun, 2020), Bitcoin prices are rising despite China experiencing a coronavirus crisis. Frost (2020) also claims that the COVID-19 would have a negative impact on the Bitcoin industry in China but the prices of Bitcoin just keep going up. This could be due to the push factors imposed by the government of China on blockchain, even not on Bitcoin, specifically, at the same time when China is distracted by the coronavirus, COVID-19.

5 Monetary Policy and Bitcoin

Monetary policy is under the control of countries' Central Banks, with its goals to stable prices or low inflation rates or stable currency exchange rates, promote maximum employment and moderate long-term interest rates. The implementation of an effective monetary policy, could help maintain stable price level, thus induce for long-term economic growth and maximum employment. Central banks are in the power of managing the size and growth rate of money supply in the economy. Money supply is a powerful tool to regulate macroeconomic variables. The implementation of monetary policies could be done through interest rate adjustment, change in reserve requirements and open market operations, that is the purchase or sale of government securities.

The existence of cryptocurrencies, specifically Bitcoin, other than the government money, as medium of exchange, could affect the power of monetary policy. Having no control on the quantity and value of Bitcoin, and not even the transactions done, could jeopardize the roles of monetary policy. Sahoo (2017) indicates that most of the governments have not given their legal status for the use of Bitcoin in their countries. However, if Bitcoin would be stable in the future, then it is easy to be accepted worldwide. In the long run, people will have greater faith in such cryptocurrency technology and its usability.

When cryptocurrencies, specifically Bitcoin, are inevitable, then what could happen to monetary policy? Could monetary policy affect the performance of Bitcoin or at least somehow associate to the performance of Bitcoin? How relevant the monetary policy is in this era? Could the interest rate adjustment or the change in currency exchange rates and money supply affect the Bitcoin performances?

Vidal-Tomás and Ibañez (2018) find that Bitcoin is not responding to international monetary policy, although it does respond to Bitcoin news. In other words, the digital currency is behaving as a consequence of particular news that is only based on Bitcoin without being affected by the policies of central banks. There is also a claim that Bitcoin connectedness to monetary policy is substantially greater during stress time rather than the normal time. Such relationships could be due to policy shock, political uncertainty and systemic crisis (Aharon et al., 2021).

There are mixed findings on the relationship between Bitcoin and monetary policy implemented by the US versus China. Bitcoin and other 3 major cryptocurrencies have given significant response to China's tightening monetary policy. Those cryptos, including Bitcoin, however, have given no significant response to the US monetary policy (Nguyen et al., 2019). On the other hand, on the day of the US Federal Open Market Committee (FOMC) meeting, Bitcoin prices drop 0.25% upon the unexpected monetary tightening. The cumulative effect, indeed, is much powerful in the next few days following the FOMC meeting. Indeed, during a market boom, the monetary policy surprises could greatly affect Bitcoin prices (Ma et al., 2022).

6 Interest Rate & Bitcoin

Bitcoin is found to be independent of interest rates (Aharon et al., 2021). This indicates Bitcoin's hedging ability to be treated as safe haven or risk haven property. On the other hand, based on dynamic analysis, Bitcoin is found to be highly connected to interest rates during stress time but not during normal time (Aharon et al., 2021). Interest and prices are negatively correlated. The interest in Bitcoin appears to have an asymmetric effect during the bubble formation. During the bubble formation, interest boosts the Bitcoin prices further, and during the bursting, it pushes them lower (Kristoufek, 2015). In terms of cryptocurrency lending, interest rates show high connection with the volatility of Bitcoin price (Zhang et al., 2021a).

Figure 4 supports the findings of Aharon's et al. (2021) static analysis which shows no correlation between Bitcoin price and interest rates for all the 3 countries. In terms

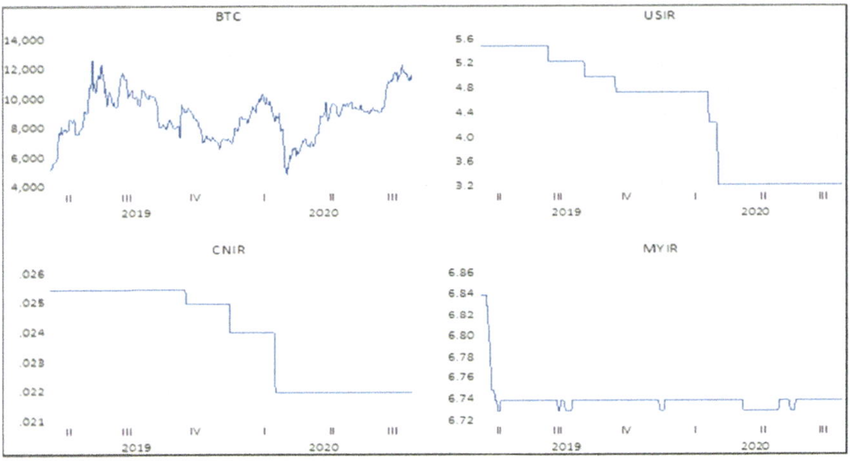

Fig. 4 Performances of Bitcoin price and interest rates of the US, China and Malaysia, 8 months before and 8 months during COVID-19 pandemic (*Notes* BTC = Bitcoin/USD, USIR = The U.S.A. interest rates, CNIR = China interest rates, MYIR = Malaysia interest rates, vertical line = the start of new positive COVID-19 cases. *Source* Datastream)

of correlation between the two, Bitcoin and each interest rates, Malaysia interest rates seem to have significant negative correlation with Bitcoin. The interest rates are no longer significantly related to Bitcoin prices during those 16 months period of before and during COVID-19 pandemic after controlling for stock markets, gold and oil prices. Taking into consideration the impact of daily new positive and death COVID-19 cases, interest rates for all the 3 countries still show no relationship with Bitcoin price. Thus, the interest rates adjustment generally is meant for economic recovery purpose, but not being able to affect the Bitcoin price.

7 Exchange Rates and Bitcoin

Exchange rate, generally, is found to have significant impact on the Bitcoin price. They are positively related to each other, not only to the main safe-haven fiat currencies (Canadian Dollar, Swiss Franc, Euro, Japanese Yen and British Pound Sterling [Aharon et al., 2021]) but also to those currencies of developing countries (Sadraoui et al., 2021).

Figure 5 portrays the movements of Bitcoin prices in comparison with the movements of 3 countries exchange rates: USD per SDR (USD/SDR), CNY per USD (MYR/USD) and MYR per USD (MYR/USD). Generally, we can see that the exchange rates, mainly the USD/SDR, are positively related to Bitcoin during those 16 months period. The greater the appreciation of Special Drawing Rights (SDR), which is the values in USD based on a basket of major currencies (the US dollar,

Euro, Japanese yen, pound sterling and the Chinese renminbi), the greater the appreciation on Bitcoin. In other words, the greater the depreciation of the US dollar, the higher the price of Bitcoin. This is supported by Ciaian et al. (2016), who conclude that an increase in the exchange rate between the euro and the US dollar would lead to a decrease in the amount of US dollars that have to be paid for one Bitcoin, which decreases its price.

There are positive correlations between Bitcoin and USD/SDR, and between Bitcoin and MYR/USD but the correlation with MYR is much weaker, especially before COVID-19 pandemic. CNY, on the other hand, has no significant correlation with Bitcoin. After controlling for stock markets, gold and oil prices, the relationship between USD/SDR and Bitcoin remains significant, especially during COVID-19 pandemic. The relationship becomes stronger when COVID-19 positive and death cases are taken into consideration. This result is consistent with the findings by Aharon et al. (2021) stating that Bitcoin is very much connected to exchange rates during stress or crisis time. Rajput et al. (2020) also claim that Bitcoin and USD are asymmetrically and negatively associated in the short run, but also in the long run.

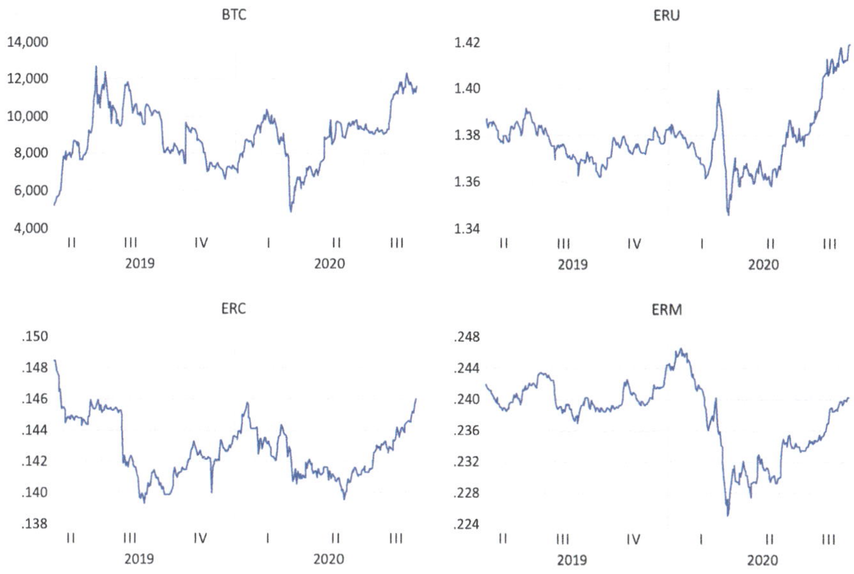

Fig. 5 Performances of Bitcoin price and exchange rates of the US, China and Malaysia, 8 months before and 8 months during COVID-19 pandemic (*Note* BTC = USD per Bitcoin, ERU = The U.S.A. exchange rates [USD per SDR], ERC = China exchange rates [USD per CNY], ERM = Malaysia exchange rates [USD per MYR)], vertical line = the start of new positive COVID-19 cases. *Source* Datastream)

8 Summary and Conclusion

As a conclusion, during the 8 months before and 8 months during COVID-19 pandemic, central banks' monetary policy still plays a role in relation to Bitcoin performance but not powerful enough. The applied interest rates, either in US or in China, does not relate to the movement of the Bitcoin price. Only US dollar exchange rates have significant relationship with Bitcoin. US dollar is negatively related to Bitcoin, which could be due to the use of USD for the buying and selling of Bitcoin for transactions and investment purposes. Thus, the control on USD by the Federal Reserves could somehow influence the demand for Bitcoin, and thus determine the Bitcoin price.

The COVID-19 pandemic does contribute to an acute fall in Bitcoin price but for a very short time. The bear market shows a drop by 53% within 1 month. This indicates the sensitivity of such currency, and thus create an argument on its popularity as safe haven or risk haven. After that 1 falling month, the Bitcoin price manages to climb back to its earlier highest position in August 2020. Indeed, from that moment, Bitcoin continuously soars way up and high. It goes from USD12000/BTC to almost USD60,000 in March 2021. There could be a greater impact of COVID-19 pandemic on Bitcoin price to be seen if such impact is analysed for longer time period, rather than in just 8 months during the pandemic.

It is recommended that the government authorities should act on digital currency in order to maintain the control of the money supply. This would be able to ensure the significant roles of monetary policy.

Acknowledgements Grateful appreciation goes to FEP UKM Research Initiative Grant: EP-2020-054 for the financial support to conduct this research activity.

References

Abraham, M. (2021). An event study analysis of Bitcoin and Altcoins under COVID-19. *African Review of Economics and Finance-AREF, 13*(2), 7–24.

Aharon, D. Y., Umar, Z., & Vo, X. V. (2021). Dynamic spillovers between the term structure of interest rates, bitcoin, and safe-haven currencies. *Financial Innovation, 7*(1), 59.

Barber, S., Boyen, X., Shi, E., & Uzun, E. (2012). *Bitter to better—How to make bitcoin a better currency*. In International Conference on Financial Cryptography and Data Security (pp. 399–414). Springer, Berlin, Heidelberg.

Bariviera, A. F., Basgall, M. J., Hasperué, W., & Naiouf, M. (2017). Some stylized facts of the Bitcoin market. *Physica A: Statistical Mechanics and Its Applications, 484*, 82–90. https://doi.org/10.1016/j.physa.2017.04.159

Baur, D., & Dimpfl, T. (2018). *Excess volatility as an impediment for a digital currency* (Working paper). Perth, Australia: University of Western Australia, Tüebingen, Germany: University of Tüebingen.

Baur, D., Hong, K., & Lee, A. D. (2017). Bitcoin: Medium of exchange or speculative assets? *Journal of International Financial Markets, Institutions, and Money, 54*, 177–189.

De Best, R. (2021). Distribution of the biggest cryptocurrencies from 2015 to 2020, based on market capitalization. Cryptocurrency, *Statista.*

Buchholz, K. (2022). Where cryptocurrency is most heavily used. Cryptocurrency, *Statista.*

Cermak, V. (2017). *Can Bitcoin become a viable alternative to fiat currencies? An empirical analysis of Bitcoin's volatility based on a GARCH model* (Working paper). Saratoga Springs, NY, USA: Skidmore College.

Ciaian, P., Rajcaniova, M., & Kancs, D. A. (2016). The economics of BitCoin price formation. *Applied Economics, 48*(19), 1799–1815.

Conlon, T., & McGee, R. (2020). Safe haven or risky hazard? Bitcoin during the COVID-19 bear market. *Finance Research Letters, 35*, 101607.

Frost, L. (2020). *Why the coronavirus hasn't affected the price of Bitcoin.* Retrieved from decrypt.co. https://decrypt.co/17911/why-the-coronavirus-hasnt-affected-the-price-of-bitcoin

Glaser, F., Zimmermann, K., Haferkorn, M., Weber, M. C., & Siering, S. (2014). *Bitcoin—Asset or currency? Revealing users' hidden intentions* (Working paper). Karlsruhe: Karlsruhe.

Goodell, J. W., & Goutte, S. (2021). Co-movement of COVID-19 and Bitcoin: Evidence from wavelet coherence analysis. *Finance Research Letters, 38*, 101625.

Keoun, B. (2020). *Bitcoin prices in 2020: Here's what happened markets.* CoinDesk. https://www.coindesk.com/markets/2020/12/30/bitcoin-prices-in-2020-heres-what-happened/

Kristoufek, L. (2015). What are the main drivers of the Bitcoin price? Evidence from wavelet coherence analysis. *PLoS ONE, 10*(4), e0123923.

Ma, C., Tian, Y., Hsiao, S., & Deng, L. (2022). Monetary policy shocks and Bitcoin prices. *Research in International Business and Finance, 62*, 101711.

McCarthy, N. (2021). Where Investors earned the most from Bitcoin in 2020. Bitcoin, *Statista.*

Mnif, E., & Jarboui, A. (2021). COVID-19, bitcoin market efficiency, herd behavior. *Review of Behavioral Finance, 13*(1), 69–84.

Nguyen, T. V. H., Nguyen, B. T., Nguyen, K. S., & Pham, H. (2019). Asymmetric monetary policy effects on cryptocurrency markets. *Research in International Business and Finance, 48*, 335–339.

Rajput, S. K. O., Soomro, I. A., & Soomro, N. A. (2020). Bitcoin sentiment index, bitcoin performance and US dollar exchange rate. *Journal of Behavioral Finance, 23*(2), 150–165.

Sadraoui, T., Nasr, A., & Mgadmi, N. (2021). Studding relationship between bitcoin, exchange rate and financial development: A panel data analysis. *International Journal of Managerial and Financial Accounting, 13*(3–4), 232–252.

Sahoo, P. K. (2017). Bitcoin as digital money: Its growth and future sustainability. *Theoretical & Applied Economics, 24*(4), 53–64.

Sarkodie, S. A., Ahmed, M. Y., & Owusu, P. A. (2022). COVID-19 pandemic improves market signals of cryptocurrencies-evidence from Bitcoin, Bitcoin Cash, Ethereum, and Litecoin. *Finance Research Letters, 44*, 102049.

Schilling, L., & Uhlig, H. (2019). Some simple Bitcoin economics. *Journal of Monetary Economics, 106*, 16–26.

Vidal-Tomás, D., & Ibañez, A. (2018). Semi-strong efficiency of Bitcoin. *Finance Research Letters, 27*, 259–265. https://doi.org/10.1016/j.frl.2018.03.013

Wu, X., Wu, L., & Chen, S. J. (2022). Long memory and efficiency of Bitcoin during COVID-19. *Applied Economics, 54*(4), 375–389.

Zhang, S., Hou, X. Y., & Ba, S. S. (2021a). What determines interest rates for bitcoin lending? *Research in International Business and Finance, 58*(C), 101443.

Zhang, Y. P., Zhu, P. P., & Xu, Y. Y. (2021b). Has COVID-19 changed the hedge effectiveness of bitcoin? *Frontiers in Public Health, 9*, 704900.

Fintech, Financial Literacy and Islamic Banks

Nurul Murshida Benjamin, Aisyah Abdul-Rahman, and Syajarul Imna Mohd Amin

Abstract Systematic reviews have been conducted to determine how Fintech and financial literacy influence the adoption of Islamic banking products. Guided by the PRISMA (Preferred Reporting Items for Systematic reviews and Meta-Analyses) method, a systematic review from Scopus, Web of Science, Dimensions and Google Scholar databases has identified 19 related studies. Three main themes have been found: Fintech, Financial Literacy, additional factors and demographic. These four themes further produced a total of 17 sub-themes. Past studies found that fintech and financial literacy have positively influenced the behavioural intention in adopting Islamic banking products. Most researchers investigated how perceived usefulness, perceived ease of use and perceived risk influence the customers' adoption decision. With regard to fintech infrastructure, policymakers and industry players should pay attention to the management of platforms, products and features offered. In terms of Islamic financial literacy, awareness and knowledge of the society can be enhanced via educational and training programs in social media to instill positive attitudes towards Islamic banking products and services. Further, religion, product pricing, cost–benefit analysis, reputation, social influence and government support also play a role in influencing the customers' decision towards the adoption of Islamic banking products and services. Besides, demographic indicators like gender, age, education level and employment status should be appropriately targeted by the relevant authorities when developing strategic programs to boost the adoption level of Islamic banking products and services within the context of fintech and financial literacy.

Keywords Fintech · Financial literacy · Islamic banks · Systematic review literature

N. M. Benjamin
Faculty of Economics and Management, Universiti Kebangsaan Malaysia, Bangi, Selangor, Malaysia

A. Abdul-Rahman (✉) · S. I. M. Amin
Faculty of Economics and Management and Institute of Islam Hadhari, Universiti Kebangsaan Malaysia, Bangi, Selangor, Malaysia
e-mail: eychah@ukm.edu.my

Z. Abdul Karim et al. (eds.), *Contemporary Issues in Finance, Investment and Banking in Malaysia*,
https://doi.org/10.1007/978-981-99-5447-6_8

1 Introduction

This study uses a Systematic Literature Review (SLR) to investigate how financial technology (fintech) and financial literacy affect the adoption of Islamic banking products and services. Fintech refers to technology and innovation in the finance industry that aims to compete with traditional methods in delivering financing services. Meanwhile, financial literacy denotes people's ability to process economic information and make financial decisions such as financial planning, wealth accumulation, debt and pension. It is also known as the knowledge, skills, awareness, attitudes and behaviour required to make appropriate decisions related to financial resources. Focusing on the Islamic perspective, Antara et al. (2016) indicated that Islamic financial literacy (IFL) refers to the degree to which a person has a set of knowledge and skill to understand the importance of Islamic financial services that affect their attitude regarding the intention to use Islamic financing and services.

While studies on fintech are limited (Amin, 2017; Alalwan et al., 2016; Ali et al., 2018; Baber, 2020; Haider et al., 2018; Morgan & Trinh, 2019; Raza et al., 2019), studies on financial literacy-banking adoption relationships are many. Previous studies have outlined the influence of financial literacy on the growth of Islamic banking service quality (Al-Tamimi & Kalli, 2009; Jabnoun & Khalifa, 2005), awareness level (Bley & Kuehn, 2004), religion (Al-Tamimi & Kalli, 2009; Bley & Kuehn, 2004), trust (Jabnoun & Khalifa, 2005), perception (Al-Tamimi & Kalli, 2009; Bley & Kuehn, 2004), marketing (Bley & Kuehn, 2004), customer satisfaction (Al-Tamimi & Kalli, 2009; Jabnoun & Khalifa, 2005) and knowledge (Bley & Kuehn, 2004; Jabnoun & Khalifa, 2005).

The novelty of this research is that it investigates the effect of fintech and financial literacy in the Islamic banking industry. Further, this study fills in the gap in understanding and identifying the characteristics of fintech and financial literacy that impact the intention to adopt Islamic banking products and services. Implementing financial technology is not as easy as it looks. It involves a high initial cost to ensure secure digital access besides improving the banks' service quality, which is a critical factor to sustain in the industry.

This study is derived from the main research question: How do fintech and financial literacy affect the adoption of Islamic banking products and services? Financial literacy influential factors such as demographic, attitudes and religion have significant relationships towards the intention to adopt fintech or mobile banking services that may also influence the decision to adopt Islamic banking products and services. In addition, previous studies also indicate that religiosity, reputation, perception of electronic service, value and efficacy are other factors contributing to shaping the intention of consumers to adopt Islamic banking products and services.

The organisational structure of this chapter is as follows. The next section explains the methodology of systematic review literature using PRISMA Statement (Preferred Reporting Items Systematic Reviews and Meta-Analysis) approach. The following section systematically reviews and synthesises the scientific literature to identify, select and appraise relevant research on fintech and financial literacy in an Islamic bank. The last section identifies future research priorities and agendas.

2 Methodology

The review was guided by the PRISMA Statement (Preferred Reporting Items for Systematic Reviews and Meta-Analyses), as shown in Fig. 1. The PRISMA Statement allows for a rigorous search of terms related to the adoption of Islamic Banking products and services in response to fintech and financial literacy. The study relied on four central journal databases—Scopus, Web of Science (WoS), Dimensions and Google Scholars. Four stages were involved in the systematic review process: identification, screening, eligibility and data analysis. The first phase identified keywords used for the search process. Relying on previous studies and thesaurus, keywords similar and related to fintech, financial literacy and Islamic bank were used (Table 1). At this stage, after careful screening, three duplicated articles were removed.

3 Results and Discussion

Table 2 reveals the thematic analysis findings. This study discovers four main themes from the reviewed articles and a few sub-themes. The first theme is Fintech, and its sub-themes are Platform, Product and Feature. The second theme is Financial Literacy with three sub-themes: Knowledge, Attitude and Adoption of Islamic banking products and services. Also, knowledge can be further divided into two categories: Conventional Financial Knowledge and Islamic Financial Knowledge. The third central theme is Additional Factors that cover Religion, Pricing of Products and Services, Cost–Benefit and Reputation. Finally, Demographics, specifically gender, is another theme that plays a role in influencing the behavioural adoption of Islamic banking products and services.

4 Themes and Sub-Themes

4.1 Fintech Infrastructure

4.1.1 Platform

The platform is one of the web media delivery software company. Fintech can be analysed from the role of financial intermediaries in using information technology platforms to engage banking contracts for both parties, the supply and demand side

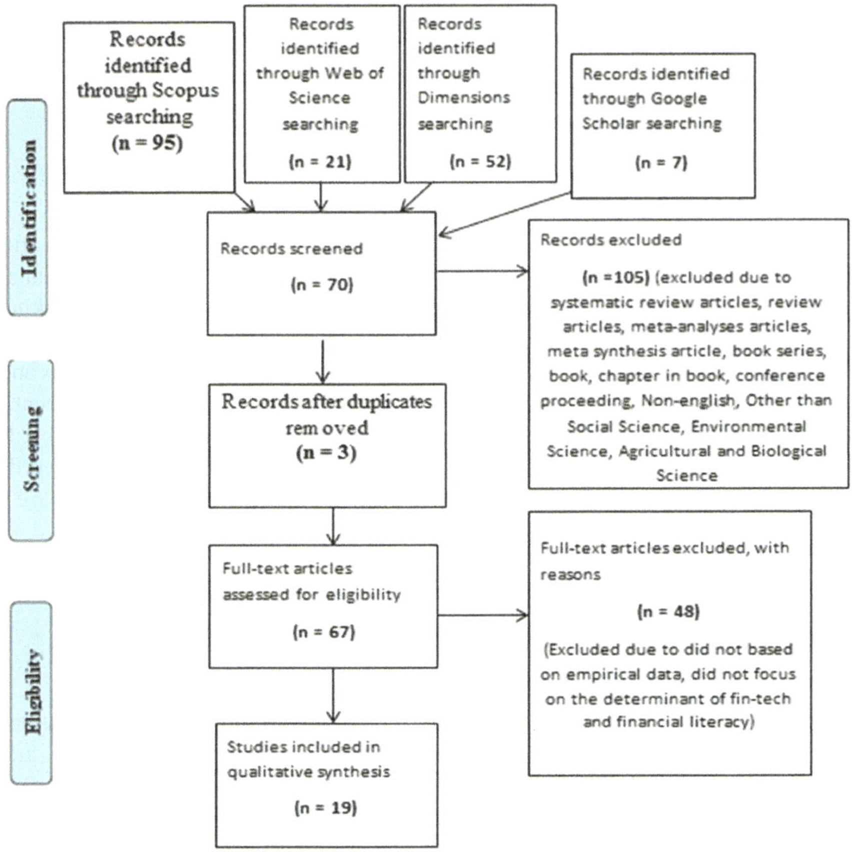

Fig. 1 PRISMA (Preferred Reporting Items for Systematic Reviews and Meta-Analyses)

of the fund. Mobile banking, digital banking and Neo-banking have been adopted as platforms that allow financial technology use in banking institutions (Yu, 2012). Research regarding individual platforms has been conducted in the case of Pakistan (Ali et al., 2018; Haider et al., 2018; Raza et al., 2019), Malaysia (Amin, 2017), Vietnam (Morgan & Trinh, 2019) and Jordan (Alalwan et al., 2016). Meanwhile, Baber (2020) investigated two country platforms for the case of Malaysia and the UAE. Researchers usually look at the Perceived Usefulness, Perceived Ease of Use and Perceived Risk when analysing the fintech platform of a country (Alalwan et al., 2016).

4.1.2 Product

Morgan and Trinh (2019) defined a fintech product as digital financial services transacted through electronic devices, such as savings, credit, insurance and payment

Table 1 Keywords and searching information

Databases	Keywords used
Scopus	TITLE-ABS-KEY ((“Islamic financial literacy” OR “Islamic financial education*” OR “Islamic financial knowledge” OR “Islamic financial proficiency” OR “Islamic financial learning” OR “intention” OR “attention” OR “perceived norms”) OR (“fintech” OR “financial technology” OR “fin-tech” OR “mobile bank*” OR “Islamic mobile bank*” OR “information technolog*” OR “internet bank*” OR “digital financial service” OR “service deliver*” OR “blockchain technolog*” OR “branchless banking” OR “robo-advisory”) AND (“Islamic bank” OR “shariah bank*” OR “Islamic bank*” OR “Islamic institutions” OR “Islamic institut*”) AND (“Islam” OR “m*sl*m*”))
Web of Science	TS = ((“Islamic financial literacy” OR “Islamic financial education*” OR “Islamic financial knowledge” OR “Islamic financial proficiency” OR “Islamic financial learning”) OR (“fintech” OR “financial technology” OR “fin-tech” OR “mobile bank*” OR “islamic mobile bank*” OR “information technolog*” OR “ internet bank*” OR “digital financial service” OR “blockchain technolog*” OR “branchless banking”) AND (“islamic bank” OR “shariah bank*” OR “islamic bank*” OR “Islamic institutions” OR “Islamic institut*”) AND (“Islam” OR “muslim” OR “moslem”))
Dimensions	(“Islamic financial literacy” OR “Islamic financial education*” OR “Islamic financial knowledge” OR “Islamic financial proficiency” OR “Islamic financial learning”) OR (“fintech” OR “financial technology” OR “fin-tech” OR “mobile bank*” OR “Islamic mobile bank*” OR “information technolog*” OR “internet bank*” OR “digital financial service” OR “blockchain technolog*” OR “branchless banking” OR “intention” OR “attention” OR “perceived norms”) AND (“Islamic bank” OR “shariah bank*” OR “islamic bank*” OR “Islamic institutions” OR “Islamic institut*”)
Google Scholars	“Islamic financial literacy” OR “Islamic financial education*” OR “Islamic financial knowledge” OR “Islamic financial proficiency” OR “Islamic financial learning” “fintech” OR “financial technology” OR “fin-tech” OR “mobile bank*” OR “Islamic mobile bank”

facilities. Mobile top-ups and utility bill payments through a formal bank account that is carried out via the internet or cell phones are examples of digital financial activities. Barber (2020) tested the role of fintech in financing to retain Islamic banking customers. Specifically, the fintech application in financing is investigated regarding promoting equity financing, social cohesion, financial inclusion, financing alternatives and low cost of financing. However, he failed to show significant evidence for the relationship between fintech financing and retaining Islamic banking customers in UAE and Malaysia.

4.1.3 Features

While Islamic and conventional banks have different guidelines underpinning their transactions, they have similar features for mobile banking services (Thaker et al., 2019). Features in fintech focus on Cloud Computering, Big data analytics, Robo

Table 2 Thematic analysis

No.	Authors/ Sample country	Journal index	Fintech Infrastructure			Financial literacy				Additional factor					Demography				
						Knowledge		Attitude	Adoption										
			PL	PR	FE	CFK	IFK	AT	IN	RG	PS	CB	RP	SN	GS	GD	AG	EL	ES
1	Kaakeh et al. (2018)/Spain	WoS (Q4)				/		/	/	/	/								
2	Ali et al. (2018)/ Pakistan	Dimension	/	/	/	/		/											
3	Albaity and Rahman (2019)/UAE	WoS (Q3)				/	/		/			/	/						
4	Alam et al. (2010)/Sudan	Scopus				/		/				/							
5	Haider et al. (2018)/ Pakistan	Google scholar	/					/	/					/		/			
6	Lajuni et al. (2017)/ Malaysia	Google scholar						/	/	/	/			/	/				
7	Thaker et al. (2019)/ Malaysia	WoS (ESCI)							/			/		/					
8	Oseni et al. (2018)/ Malaysia	WoS (ESCI)						/	/					/					

(continued)

Table 2 (continued)

No.	Authors/ Sample country	Journal index	Fintech Infrastructure			Financial literacy				Additional factor					Demography				
						Knowledge		Attitude	Adoption										
			PL	PR	FE	CFK	IFK	AT	IN	RG	PS	CB	RP	SN	GS	GD	AG	EL	ES
9	Raza et al. (2019)/ Pakistan	Google scholar	/					/	/*					/					
10	Morgan and Trinh (2019)/ Vietnam	Google scholar	/			/		/	/										
11	Abou-Youssef et al. (2015)/ Egypt	WoS (Q2)						/	/#	/						/			
12	Ayyub et al. (2020)/ Pakistan	WoS (Q4)						/	/					/					
13	Warsame and Ireri (2018)/ UAE						/		/#	/			/			/	/	/	/
14	Souiden and Rani (2015)/ Tunisia	Scopus						/	/	/									

(continued)

Table 2 (continued)

No.	Authors/ Sample country	Journal index	Fintech Infrastructure			Financial literacy				Additional factor						Demography			
						Knowledge		Attitude	Adoption										
			PL	PR	FE	CFK	IFK	AT	IN	RG	PS	CB	RP	SN	GS	GD	AG	EL	ES
15	Amin (2017)/ Malaysia	Scopus	/					/	/										
16	Han et al. (2018)/ Western China	Google scholar						/	/	/				/					
17	Amin et al. (2011)/ Malaysia	WoS (ESCI)						/	/	/	/			/	/				
18	Alalwan et al. (2016)/Jordan	WoS (Q2)	/					/	/										
19	Baber (2020)/ Malaysia and UAE	Scopus	/	/	/				/#										
	TOTAL		7	2	2	5	2	15	14	7	3	3	2	8	2	3	1	1	1

(continued)

Table 2 (continued)

Fintech	Knowledge	Attitude	Adoption of Islamic bank	Additional Factor		Demography
PL = Platform PR = Product FE = Feature	CFK = Conventional Financial Knowledge IFK = Islamic Financial Knowledge	AT = Attitude	IN = Intention	RG = Religion PS = Pricing of Product and Services CB = Cost Benefit RP = Reputation	SN = Social Norms GS = Government Support	GD = gender AG = Age EL = Education level ES = Employment status

Note: /*—study both behavioral intention and adoption while /#—study adoption of Islamic banking product advisor, Artificial intelligence and Internet of Things (IoT). Baber (2020) explored the unique characteristics of fintech in terms of payments, advisory services, compliance and crowdfunding for customer's retention. The application of fintech in payments is cashless payments, e-payment process, the blockchain, payment convenience, security, traceability and easy access. Meanwhile, the application of fintech in advisory services includes investment advices, asset management consultation, insurance service, customer support and management decisions. For the case of compliance, the fintech application is in terms of compliance with abiding regulations, regulatory technology (RegTech), policies, standards and laws and compliance with shariah rules. Finally, the crowdfunding mechanism is also analysed according to its type: donation-based, reward-based, lending-based and equity-based. The empirical finding showed that all four fintech features play a significant positive role in retaining Islamic banks' clients, with the largest magnitude for crowdfunding, followed by compliance, payments and advisory services.

4.2 Financial Literacy

4.2.1 Knowledge

This study finds knowledge as a central sub-theme under financial literacy along with Attitude and Adoption. Knowledge can further be divided into Conventional Financial Knowledge and Islamic Financial Knowledge. Most of the previous study shows knowledge has a significant relationship with behavioural intention and adoption. Financial knowledge influences customers' decisions to use Islamic banking products and services.

4.2.2 Conventional Financial Knowledge

Conventional Financial knowledge refers to general financial ability based on the various aspect of financial behaviour, including saving, use of credit, preparation for retirement and awareness and adoption of various financial services. It is not based on the Shariah principle. Researchers have conducted various studies and found significant positive financial literacy-adoption relationships in the case of Spain (Kaakeh et al., 2018), Pakistan (Ali et al., 2018), UAE (Albaity & Rahman, 2019), Sudan (Alam et al., 2010) and Vietnam (Morgan & Trinh, 2019).

4.2.3 Islamic Financial Knowledge

Islamic Financial Knowledge is based on the Shariah principle. Specifically, Islamic Financial Knowledge refers to the level of individuals' possession pertaining knowledge and skills in understanding Islamic contracts, which finally affect their attitude regarding the intention to use Islamic financing (Antara et al., 2016). Meanwhile, Rahim et al. (2016) defined Islamic Financial Knowledge in a broader context, covering an individual's ability, skill and attitude to understand and analyse financial information offered by Islamic financial institutions. Empirical evidence on the impact of Islamic Financial Literacy on behavioural intention to adopt Islamic banking products and services has been found in UAE (Albaity & Rahman, 2019; Warsame & Ireri, 2018).

4.2.4 Attitude

Attitude is the most significant factor influencing the behavioural intention of customers to use Islamic banking products and services (Amin et al., 2013). Besides, financial knowledge and marketing have been the antecedence of attitude in attracting Muslims and non-Muslims to choose Islamic banking products and services (Lajuni et al., 2017). Also, some researchers discovered that awareness influences an individual's attitude towards the intention to use Islamic Banking products (Barreda et al., 2015).

4.3 Adoption of Islamic Banking Products and Services

Empirical research in Pakistan has shown that behavioural intention precedes adopting Islamic banking products and services (Raza et al., 2019). In addition, most studies in other fields also found a positive association between intention and adoption (Bassir et al., 2014; Chaouch, 2017; Kaabachi & Obeid, 2016; Md Husin & Ab Rahman, 2016). Besides, some researchers argued that intention and adoption should only be tested in longitudinal studies as it takes time for the behavioural intention to materialise. The behavioural intention has been tested in Spain (Kaakeh et al., 2018), UAE (Albaity & Rahman, 2019), Pakistan (Ayyub et al., 2020; Haider et al., 2018), Malaysia (Amin, 2017; Amin et al., 2011; Lajuni et al., 2017; Oseni et al., 2018; Thaker et al., 2019), Vietnam (Morgan & Trinh, 2019), Tunisia (Souiden & Rani, 2015), Western China (Han et al., 2018) and Jordan (Alalwan et al., 2016). Meanwhile, the adoption of Islamic banking studies has been investigated in the case of Malaysia and UAE (Baber, 2020), UAE (Warsame & Ireri, 2018) and Eygpt (Abou-Youssef et al., 2015).

4.4 Additional Factors

4.4.1 Religion

Religion is defined as a social-cultural system of designated behaviours and practices, morals, worldviews, texts, sanctified places, prophecies, ethics or organisations that relates humanity to supernatural, transcendental or spiritual elements (McDaniel & Zeithaml, 1984). In short, it is a belief in God and a commitment to follow principles set by God. Religion contributes to the base of knowledge that justifies and controls the attitude and behaviour of an individual (Foxall & Goldsmith, 1994). Research on Muslims in Spain (Kaakeh et al., 2018), Malaysia (Lajuni et al., 2017), Eygpt (Abou-Youssef et al., 2015) and Tunisia (Souiden & Rani, 2015) showed a significant direct effect of religious awareness and motivation towards adoption of Islamic banking products. Nonetheless, Warsame and Ireri (2018) discovered that although religiosity influences the banks' reputation, it does not significantly impact the decision of customers in the UAE to adopt Islamic banking products. Similarly, Amin et al. (2011) and Lajuni et al. (2017) revealed that religious obligation does not significantly impact the intention to adopt Islamic banking products in Malaysia.

4.4.2 Pricing of Products and Services

Technology has grown rapidly and is a necessity for every household. So, financial institutions take the advantage to promote their products and services through fintech and at the same time increase competition (Royne Stafford, 1996). During the intense competition, pricing is an essential factor that can affect one's decision regarding which bank to utilise and which banking services to give their patronage. Amin et al. (2011) found that the product's pricing has an inverse relationship with the intention to adopt personal financing for three central Islamic banks in Malaysia, while Lajuni et al. (2017) found insignificant findings for the case of Malaysian conventional banks' customers. In support of Lajuni et al. (2017), Kaakeh et al. (2018) indicated that product pricing does not play a significant role in determining Muslims' intention for Islamic banking adoption by Spain.

4.4.3 Cost–Benefit Analysis

Theoretically, customers' attitude towards choosing banks is mainly concerned with the cost–benefit analysis since they allocate significant weight to the availability of cost-effective financial solutions (Awan et al., 2011). Thus, cost–benefit analysis should also be essential for customers' intention to use Islamic banking products and services (Dusuki & Abdullah, 2007). This hypothesis has been empirically supported by Alam et al. (2010), who found outweighing benefit over cost positively encourage customers to adopt Islamic banking product and services in Sudan. For the Malaysian case, Albaity and Rahman (2019) showed that cost–benefit analysis does not directly affect Islamic banking adoption, but significantly influences adoption mediated by attitude. In another study, Thaker et al. (2019) found that cost–benefit (measured by risk and perceived usefulness) are significant factors influencing the Malaysian intention to adopt Islamic mobile banking services among the existing users.

4.4.4 Reputation

A good reputation is essential in ensuring the banking system's sustainability. Researchers hypothesised that the higher the bank's reputation, the more likely the customers will select the bank. Empirical findings in Malaysia showed that reputation has a significant positive relationship with attitude and behavioural intention to adopt Islamic banking products and services (Albaity & Rahman, 2019). For the case of UAE, Warsame and Ireri (2018) revealed that awareness (of Islamic banking products and services, financial services marketing and level of Islamic financial literacy) and religion positively affect banks' reputation, which finally influences the customers' decision to adopt Islamic banking products and services. In addition, they also found that demographic factors (gender, age, type of bank account, level of education and employment status) to some extent moderated the reputation-adoption relationships in UAE.

4.4.5 Social Norms

Social norms or subjective norms refer to individuals' behaviour influenced by people close to us such as friends, families and relatives. In modern days, social norms can be vastly influenced by the activities like group works on IT, online communication via email, online gaming, internet banking and mobile banking adoption (Chan & Lu, 2004; Riquelme & Rios, 2010; Schepers & Wetzel, 2007). A few previous studies stated social norm shows a positive relationship with adopting Islamic banking in Pakistan (Haider et al., 2018) and Malaysia (Lajuni et al., 2017). Even though social norms are not significant for the intention to use Islamic mobile banking in Malaysia (Thaker et al., 2019) and Pakistan (Raza et al., 2019), it is positively significant to influence the intention to use online dispute resolution mechanism in Malaysia (Oseni et al., 2018).

4.4.6 Government Support

Government support refers to governmental action that affects the behaviour and decision of households, institutions and companies (Amin et al., 2011). Government support significantly impacts and strongly influences the demand for Islamic banking products. As an international Islamic financial centre, Malaysia has full government support to strengthen the dual banking systems where Islamic banking is practiced hand in hand with the conventional banking system (Amin et al., 2011). The positive relationship between Malaysian government support and intention to adopt Islamic banking products and services has been empirically proven by Lajuni et al. (2017).

4.4.7 Demographic

Demographic may strengthen or weaken the relationships between two factors. Warsame and Ireri (2018) showed that gender (female customers) plays a significant role in moderating the relationship between awareness of Islamic Financial Services Marketing and bank reputation in the UAE, leading to adoption. Furthermore, they also discovered that age, level of education and employment status had moderated the impact of Islamic financial literacy and awareness of Islamic banking products on bank reputation, which then affected customers' adoption decisions. Using a separate dataset for males and females, Haider et al. (2018) revealed that Pakistani males are more task-driven and desire personality, values and status, so their intention to adopt Islamic banking is significantly influenced by perceived usefulness and perceived self-expressiveness. In contrast, females have found a lack of IT knowledge and trust; thus, perceived credibility affects their behavioural intention substantially. In another study, Abou-Youssef et al. (2015) found that different level of religiosity produces different attitudes towards Islamic banks in Egypt that may affect future intention and behaviour.

5 Summary and Conclusion

This objective of this study is to provide a systematic review of literature regarding the effect of fintech and financial literacy on the behavioural intention to adopt Islamic banking products and services. Research has shown that, to some extent, fintech and financial literacy have positively impacted the intention to adopt Islamic banking products. Most researchers examined how perceived usefulness, perceived ease of use and perceived risk influence the customers' adoption decision. For fintech infrastructure, policymakers and industry players should pay attention to the platforms, products and features offered. Regarding financial literacy, the regulatory bodies should strategise to improve awareness and knowledge of the society via training and educational programs in social media to inculcate positive attitudes towards Islamic banking products. In addition, religion, product pricing, cost–benefit analysis, reputation, social influence and government support also play a role in influencing the customers' decision towards the adoption of Islamic banking products and services. Besides, demographic factors such as gender, age, education level and employment status may be appropriately targeted by the relevant authorities in maximising the result of any strategic programs being offered.

Acknowledgements This research was supported by the Fundamental Research Grant Scheme, Ministry of Higher Education, Malaysia [grant number: FRGS/1/2019/SS01/UKM/02/3] and YTI-UKM [EP-2020-003].

References

Abou-Youssef, M. M. H., Kortam, W., Abou-Aish, E., & El-Bassiouny, N. (2015). Effects of religiosity on consumer attitudes toward Islamic banking in Egypt. *International Journal of Bank Marketing, 33*(6), 786–807.

Alalwan, A. A., Dwivedi, Y. K., Rana, N. P., & Williams, M. D. (2016). Consumer adoption of mobile banking in Jordan: Examining the role of usefulness, ease of use, perceived risk and self-efficacy. *Journal of Enterprise Information Management, 29*(1), 118–139.

Alam, N., Magboul, I. H. M., & Raman, M. (2010). Challenges faced by Sudanese banks in implementing online banking: Bankers' perception. *Journal of Internet Banking and Commerce, 15*(2), 1–9.

Ali, H., Zain, M. Z., Hashmi, H. S., Abbas, M. H., Shahid, M. W., & Tariq, U. (2018). Awareness and knowledge of fintech among Islamic banking and finance students in Pakistan. *Islamic Banking and Finance Review, 5*, 02–22.

Albaity, M., & Rahman, M. (2019). The intention to use Islamic banking: An exploratory study to measure Islamic financial literacy. *International Journal of Emerging Markets, 14*(5), 988–1012.

Al-Tamimi, H. H. A., & Kalli, A. (2009). Financial literacy and investment decisions of UAE investors. *The Journal of Risk Finance, 10*(5), 500–516.

Amin, H. (2017). Consumer behaviour of Islamic home financing: Investigating its Determinants from the theory of Islamic consumer behaviour. *Humanomics, 33*(4), 517–548.

Amin, H., Rahman, A. R. A., Sondoh, S. L., & Hwa, A. M. C. (2011). Determinants of customers' intention to use Islamic personal financing: The case of Malaysian Islamic banks. *Journal of Islamic Accounting and Business Research, 2*(1), 22–42.

Amin, H., Abdul Rahman, A. R., & Abdul Razak, D. (2013). An integrative approach for understanding Islamic home financing adoption in Malaysia. *International Journal of Bank Marketing, 31*(7), 544–573.

Antara, P. M., Musa, R., & Hassan, F. (2016). Bridging Islamic financial literacy and halal literacy: The way forward in halal ecosystem. *Procedia Economics and Finance, 37*(16), 196–202.

Awan, H. M., Bukhari, K. S., & Iqbal, A. (2011). Service quality and customer satisfaction in the banking sector: A comparative study of conventional and Islamic banks in Pakistan. *Journal of Islamic Marketing, 2*(3), 203–224.

Ayyub, S., Xuhui, W., Asif, M., & Ayyub, R. M. (2020). Determinants of intention to use Islamic banking: A comparative analysis of users and non-users of Islamic banking: Evidence from Pakistan. *International Journal of Islamic and Middle Eastern Finance and Management, 13*(1), 147–163.

Baber, H. (2020). FinTech, crowdfunding and customer retention in Islamic banks. *Vision, 24*(3), 260–268.

Barreda, A. A., Bilgihan, A., Nusair, K., & Okumus, F. (2015). Generating brand awareness in online social networks. *Computers in Human Behavior, 50*(9), 600–609.

Bassir, N. F., Zakaria, Z., Hasan, H. A., & Alfan, E. (2014). Factors influencing the adoption of Islamic home financing in Malaysia. *Transformations in Business & Economics, 13*(1), 155–174.

Bley, J., & Kuehn, K. (2004). Conventional versus Islamic finance: Student knowledge and perception in the United Arab Emirates. *International Journal of Islamic Financial Services, 5*(4), 17–30.

Chan, S. C., & Lu, M. T. (2004). Understanding internet banking adoption and use behaviour: A Hong Kong perspective. *Journal of Global Information Management, 12*(3), 21–43.

Chaouch, N. (2017). An exploratory study of Tunisian customers' awareness and perception of Islamic banks. *International Journal of Islamic Economics and Finance Studies, 3*(2), 1–26.

Dusuki, A. W., & Abdullah, N. (2007). Why do Malaysian customers patronise Islamic banks? *International Journal of Bank Marketing, 25*(3), 142–160.

Foxall, G. R., & Goldsmith, R. E. (1994). *Consumer psychology for marketing.* Routledge.

Haider, M. J., Changchun, G., Akram, T., & Hussain, S. T. (2018). Does gender differences play any role in intention to adopt Islamic mobile banking in Pakistan? An empirical study. *Journal of Islamic Marketing, 9*(2), 439–460.

Han, Z., Yeoh, E. K., & Wan Marhaini, W. A. (2018). Does religious obligation of Muslims in western China influence their intention to adopt Islamic banking? *Contemporary Chinese Political Economy and Strategic Relations: An International Journal, 4*(3), 1207–1244.

Jabnoun, N., & Khalifa, A. (2005). A customised measure of service quality in the UAE. *Managing Service Quality: An International Journal, 15*(4), 374–388.

Kaakeh, A., Hassan, M. K., & Van Hemmen Almazor, S. F. (2018). Attitude of Muslim minority in Spain towards Islamic finance. *International Journal of Islamic and Middle Eastern Finance and Management, 11*(2), 213–230.

Kaabachi, S., & Obeid, H. (2016). Determinants of Islamic banking adoption in Tunisia: Empirical analysis. *International Journal of Bank Marketing, 34*(7), 1069–1091.

Lajuni, N., Wong, W. P. M., Yacob, Y., Ting, H., & Jausin, A. (2017). Intention to use Islamic banking products and its determinants. *International Journal of Economics and Financial Issues, 7*(1), 329–333.

McDaniel, S. W., & Zeithaml, V. A. (1984). The effect of fear on purchase intentions. *Psychology & Marketing (pre-1986), 1*(3–4), 73–82.

Md Husin, M., & Ab Rahman, A. (2016). Do Muslims intend to participate in Islamic insurance? Analysis from theory of planned behaviour. *Journal of Islamic Accounting and Business Research, 7*(1), 42–58.

Morgan, P. J., & Trinh, L. Q. (2019). *Fintech and financial literacy in the Lao PDR* (ADBI Working Paper 933). Tokyo: Asian Development Bank Institute. https://www.adb.org/publications/fintech-and-financial-literacy-lao-pdr

Oseni, U. A., Adewale, A. A., & Omoola, S. O. (2018). The feasibility of online dispute resolution in the Islamic banking industry in Malaysia: An empirical legal analysis. *International Journal of Law and Management, 60*(1), 34–54.

Rahim, S. H. A., Rashid, R. A., & Hamed, A. B. (2016). Islamic financial literacy and its determinants among university students: An exploratory factor analysis. *International Journal of Economics and Financial Issues, 6*(7), 32–35.

Raza, S. A., Shah, N., & Ali, M. (2019). Acceptance of mobile banking in Islamic banks: Evidence from modified UTAUT model. *Journal of Islamic Marketing, 10*(1), 357–376.

Riquelme, H., & Rios, R. E. (2010). The moderating effect of gender in the adoption of mobile banking. *International Journal of Bank Marketing, 28*(5), 328–341.

Royne Stafford, M. (1996). Demographic discriminators of service quality in the banking industry. *Journal of Services Marketing, 10*(4), 6–22.

Schepers, J., & Wetzel, M. (2007). A Meta-analysis of the technology acceptance model: Investigating subjective norm and moderation effects. *Information and Management, 44*(1), 90–103.

Souiden, N., & Rani, M. (2015). Consumer attitudes and purchase intentions toward Islamic banks: The influence of religiosity. *International Journal of Bank Marketing, 33*(2), 143–161.

Thaker, M. A. B. M. T., Pitchay, A. B. A., Thaker, H. B. M. T., & Amin, M. F. B. (2019). Factors influencing consumers' adoption of Islamic mobile banking services in Malaysia: An approach of partial least squares (PLS). *Journal of Islamic Marketing, 10*(4), 1037–1056.

Warsame, M. H., & Ireri, E. M. (2018). Moderation effect on Islamic banking preferences in UAE. *International Journal of Bank Marketing, 36*(1), 41–67.

Yu, C. S. (2012). Factors affecting individuals to adopt mobile banking: Empirical evidence from the UTAUT model. *Journal of Electronic Commerce Research, 13*(2), 104–121.

Factors Influencing Online Investment Adoption: A Systematic Review

Siti Aisyah Shari, Aisyah Abdul-Rahman, and Syajarul Imna Mohd Amin

Abstract This study reviews the factors influencing the adoption of online investment. Guided by PRISMA (Preferred Reporting Items for Systematic Reviews and Meta-Analyses) review method, we identified 16 related studies using Web of Science and Scopus databases. In depth review of these articles have brought us to five main themes—attitude, subjective norms, perceived behavioural control and others. These five main themes have been further narrowed down into 29 sub-themes. There are few recommendations discussed in this study for future researchers' references.

Keywords Systematic review · Adoption online investment · Stock trading · Fintech · Behaviour

1 Introduction

Financial technology or also known as "Fintech" is driving significant growth of adoption rates in recent years. Although, earlier noticeable as a complicated way of managing finance is currently in hype by millions of people around the world due to increasing of online financial platforms such as online banking, online investment, e-wallet and others. Fintech is combination of two words which are finance and technology. Fintech defined as technologically empowered financial innovation that could affect in new business models, processes, products, or application with related material result on financial institutions and market and the provision of financial services (FSB, 2017). According to EY Global Fintech Adoption Index 2019, the adoption has arisen significantly from 2015 the introduction year of fintech adoption

S. A. Shari (✉) · S. I. M. Amin
Faculty of Economics and Management, Universiti Kebangsaan Malaysia, Bangi, Selangor, Malaysia
e-mail: eychah@ukm.edu.my

A. Abdul-Rahman
Faculty of Economics and Management and Institute of Islam Hadhari, Universiti Kebangsaan Malaysia, Bangi, Selangor, Malaysia

Z. Abdul Karim et al. (eds.), *Contemporary Issues in Finance, Investment and Banking in Malaysia*,
https://doi.org/10.1007/978-981-99-5447-6_9

index with 16% to 33% in 2017 and 64% in 2019. Additionally, the index also found that 96% of the 27,000 consumers acknowledged of fintech payment or transfer service. There are few categories of fintech services including money transfers and payments, financial planning and budgeting, savings and investments, borrowing and insurance stated in Ernst & Young Global Fintech Adoption Index 2019. In this study, the authors focused fintech in investment services. Even though there are quiet numbers of fintech services in investments including lending on peer-to-peer platforms, investment via crowdfunding platforms, online investment advice and investment management, online stock broking and online spread betting, there is still

The history of the financial technology (fintech) industry in Malaysia started in 2001. The early incentive that Malaysia took towards fintech in that year, when every Malaysian holds an innovative national identity card referred to as MyKad. This card could be used as an ATM card, an e-wallet and a transit card all in one which lead Malaysia one of the first countries to establish itself in the fintech industry. During 2015, Bank Negara Malaysia (BNM) which is the central bank, made Malaysia the first country in Southeast Asia to propose and introduce a regulatory framework that aids fintech companies manage their operations in innovation while still retaining their financial stability and securing customer rights. The fintech sector in Malaysia has expanded dramatically due to numerous of advantages that not only build a base of customers and offer an environment for doing business but also boost the economy and develop more employment opportunities. In Malaysia, internet penetration is quiet high which is 85.7% and online banking penetration is 85.1%, there is high chances in fintech industries as high demand and penetration but only 41% of Malaysian has savings (Global Findex Report, 2018). Based on the statistics above, it is important Malaysian to improve their financial planning including investment for future needs to improve their financial well-being and economic inequality. Therefore, it is necessary to understand what factors influence their investment intentions in financial markets.

Systematic Literature Review (SLR) is one of methods to review existing literature in more systematic ways. Based on Dewey and Drahota (2016), systematic literature review is a process of identify, selects and critically appraisal the prior research to answers formulated questions. While traditional literature review has few issues of rarely comprehensive, highly disposed to reviewer bias and rarely take into account differences in the quality of studies (Robinson & Lowe, 2015). Moreover, SLR implements a rigorous methodology in an attempt to limit bias with the aim to produce a scientific summary of evidence in any field. According to Higgins (2016), SLR comprehensively synthesised related researches using systematic and transparent procedures throughout the process. Therefore, this can produce quality evidence with more significant results (Mallet et al., 2012). This study attempt to contribute to the existing body of knowledge by developing systematic literature review on factors influencing of online investment.

Based on prior research, there has been quiet numbers research on adoption of online investment (Loh et al., 1998; Volpe et al., 2002; Lee-Partridge & Ho, 2003; Teo et al., 2004; Gopi & Ramayah, 2007; Ramayah et al., 2009; Lee, 2009; Singh et al.,

2010; Abroud et al., 2015; Ramayah et al., 2014; Gazali et al., 2016; Afif et al., 2018; Abdullah et al., 2008; Akhtar & Das, 2019; Khan et al., 2020a; Khan et al., 2020b). There are few theories supported the prior research on factors influencing adoption of online investment including Technology Acceptance Model (TAM) (Loh et al., 1998; Singh et al., 2010, Gazali et al., 2016), Decomposed Theory of Planned Behaviour (Lee-Partridge & Ho, 2003), Transaction Cost Theory (Teo et al., 2004; Abroud et al., 2015), Theory of Planned Behaviour (Gopi & Ramayah, 2007; Akhtar & Das, 2019), Decomposed Theory of Reasoned Action (Ramayah et al., 2009), Integrated Theory of Planned Behaviour (Lee, 2009; Afif et al., 2018), Decomposed of Technology Acceptance Model (Abroud et al., 2015), Integrated Decomposed Theory of Planned Behaviour (Ramayah et al., 2009), Unified Theory of Acceptance and Use of Technology (Abdullah et al., 2008), Perceived Risk Theory (Khan et al., 2020a, 2020b) and Social Cognitive Theory (Khan et al., 2020a, 2020b).

However, there were still insufficient studies that reviewed systematically the existing studies. Therefore, it is vital to find out the answers to the question – what factors influencing adoption of online investment? Based on the research question stated, this study aims to systematically review the existing literature on the factors influencing of adoption in online investment. This study more focusing on behavioural intention and behavioural usage or adoption of online investment. This study organized into few sections as mentioned follows: section 2 details out the method implemented; section 3 explained the findings of systematic literature review including descriptive analysis and thematic analysis; section 4 discussion of the topic; section 5 provides recommendation for future studies and section 6 concludes all the study.

2 Methodology

This section highlighted the method applied to retrieve prior articles of factors influencing adoption of online investment. The first sub-section explained about Preferred Reporting Items for Systematic Reviews and Meta-Analyses Approach and also known as PRISMA. The next sub-section focused on the main resources applied in this study and followed by the systematic review process that including identification, screening and eligibility of articles from resources. Quality appraisal and data abstraction analysis also been discussed in this section.

2.1 PRISMA

PRISMA (Preferred Reporting Items for Systematic Reviews and Meta-Analyses) approach has been implemented in this study. To make this approach unbiased and transparent, PRISMA statement consists of 27 items checklist to facilitate this study of their robustness evaluation on systematic review (Moher, et al., 2009). However, consistent with this nature of study, not all items are competent to be implemented in this study as PRISMA is usually used by medical research areas. PRISMA attempts to screen large database of scientific literature in a defined time which allows for rigorous search of terms that relevant to the factors influencing adoption of online investment.

2.2 Resources

This study relied on two main indexed databases which are Web of Science and Scopus. Both databases are related to current nature of study as both databases are the leading indexing systems for citations and has wide coverage. Web of science is a trusted and reliable citation database and powerful research engine that can be access via institutional library subscription. The database for web of science consists of more than 159 million records, 1.7 billion cited references and over 9,000 leading institutions including academic, corporate and government. Meanwhile, Scopus is one of the largest and trusted citations and abstracts databases that consists of journals, books and conference proceedings. This database is also can be assessed by institutional library subscription but has some free features from Scopus Preview for non-subscriber. The databases for Scopus consist of 75 million records 1.4 billion cited references and over 70,000 institutional subscribers.

2.3 Systematic Review Process

Systematic Review consists of 3 processes including selecting articles which are identifications, screening and eligibility.

2.3.1 Identification

The first process or step in systematic review is identification of information such as keywords for searching purposes. The identification started from identify the main keywords for this study which are fintech, investment and adoption. Afterward, the process continued by determine the synonym, related and suggested terms from dictionary, thesaurus, keywords from prior researchers and suggested keywords from Scopus search engine. Next, search strings from Web of Science and Scopus are developed and tested (refer Table 1). This process retrieved 142 articles from Web of Science and 276 articles from Scopus databases.

Table 1 The search string

Database	Search string
Web of Science	TS = ((“internet stock trading” OR “internet-based stock trading” OR “online stock trading” OR “electronic stock trading” OR “internet share trading” OR “online share trading” OR “electronic share trading” OR “fintech” OR “financial technology” OR “fin-tech” OR “e-financ*” OR “efinanc*” OR “digital financ*” OR “electron* financ*” OR “online investment” OR “online financial application” OR “online investor” OR “online trading system” OR “online trading system”) AND (“invest” OR “investing” OR “investment” OR “stock*” OR “Mutual fund*” OR “portfolio” OR “unit trust*” OR “sukuk” OR “capital market” OR “money market” OR “non-banking invest*”) AND (“factor” OR “adoption” OR “impact” OR “determinant” OR “acceptance” or “intention” or “influence”))
Scopus	TITLE-ABS-KEY ((“internet stock trading” OR “internet-based stock trading” OR “online stock trading” OR “electronic stock trading” OR “internet share trading” OR “online share trading” OR “electronic share trading” OR “fintech” OR “financial technology” OR “fin-tech” OR “e-financ*” OR “efinanc*” OR “digital financ*” OR “electron* financ*” OR “online investment” OR “online financial application” OR “online investor” OR “online trading system” OR “online trading system”) AND (“invest” OR “investing” OR “investment” OR “stock*” OR “Mutual fund*” OR “portfolio” OR “unit trust*” OR “sukuk” OR “capital market” OR “money market” OR “non-banking invest*”) AND (“factor” OR “adoption” OR “impact” OR “determinant” OR “acceptance” OR “intention” OR “influence” OR “literacy”))

2.3.2 Screening

Screening is a process of exclude and include articles based on criteria chose by the authors with help of specific databases. In the process of screening, eligibility including the inclusion and exclusion criterion were set up to find suitable articles with the research topic to be either included or excluded. The first criterion of screening is document types, only research articles with empirical data were selected. While others document types are excluded such as systematic review, review, meta-analysis, meta-synthesis, book, chapter in book and conference proceeding as the documents are not considered as primary sources. The second criterion on the review was language. All non-English and non-Malay papers were excluded to avoid difficulties in translations in proper word and confusion of the word usage. After the identification process, out of 418 articles, 160 papers are been excluded in the process of screening as the papers did not fit the inclusion criteria. Moreover, to make sure the quality of the paper, only articles with empirical data and published in indexed journal are selected. In addition, only studies published in English are included in the review to avoid mistranslation and confusion in understanding. 13 duplicated papers were removed and the remaining 258 papers were processed in the next step which is eligibility (Table 2).

Table 2 The inclusion and exclusion criteria

Criterion	Inclusion	Exclusion
Document type	Journal (research articles)	Systematic review, review, meta-analysis, meta-synthesis, book, chapter in book, conference proceeding
Language	English and Malay	Non-English, non-Malay

Note The time period of the search string is February 2020

2.3.3 Eligibility

Next process is eligibility where the authors manually checked the retrieved papers to make sure all the remaining articles are followed with the criteria listed. This process includes reading the articles' title and abstract. Eligibility process excluded 228 articles because the articles focus on traditional-based investment instead of adoption of online investment, focus on impact of online investment not factors influencing, focus on online banking not focusing about online investment, focus on challenges, definition and products, methodology and finding is not clearly discussed, and published in the form of chapter in book. After all the eligibility process, there were 16 articles selected in the review.

2.3.4 Quality Appraisal

For qualifying the quality of the articles' content, the articles selected were presented to two experts for quality assessment. The experts should rank the selected articles into three categories of quality including high, moderate and low. The experts focused on the methodology and supported theories to determine the rank of the quality. So as to achieve the articles that can be included in this study, both authors must agree with each other and after discussion, the authors decided to accept the paper that the quality at least at moderate level. Any different in idea were discussed between the authors before the exclusion and inclusion of articles for review. This process had ranked all the papers with moderate to high quality. Therefore, all the remaining articles were accepted for the review.

2.3.5 Data Abstraction and Analysis

This study depends on integrative review. The integrative review accepted qualitative, quantitative and mixed method designs to be included in the review. Referred to Whittemore and Knafl (2006), the ideal way to synthesis a mix research design in the review is by performing a mixed method or qualitative techniques that validate the researcher to perform iterative comparisons across the primary data sources. With the purpose to answer the research question, the authors read all the main

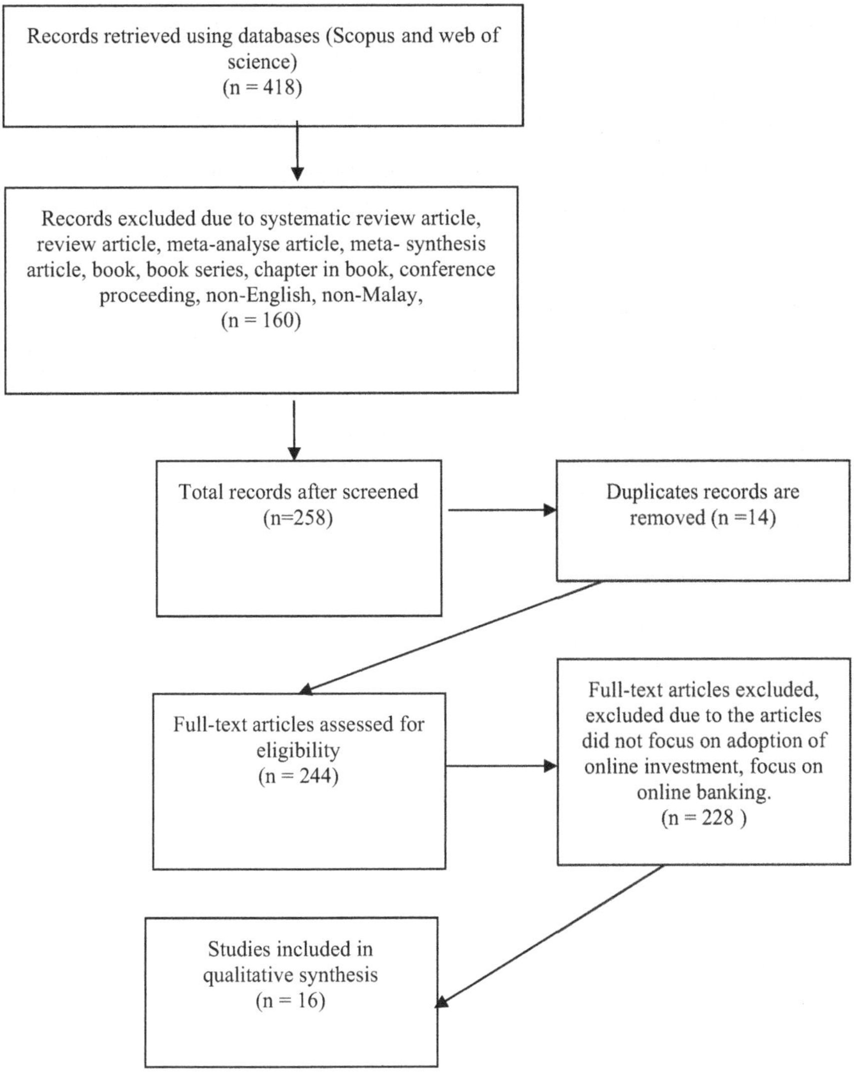

Fig. 1 The flow diagram of the study

contents of all 16 articles. The data from the reviewed articles that are able to answer the research questions are abstracted and built in a table. Next, the authors conduct thematic analysis that recognized themes and sub-themes (2019). Along with creating themes, the authors tried to recognize the patterns that appeared among abstracted data of all reviewed articles. Any similar or related abstracted data are pooled in a group and then a total of four main groups were generated from the reviewed articles. The authors then rechecked the four groups of data and found other 29 sub-groups.

3 Results

3.1 Descriptive Analysis

The review managed to select 16 related articles. Four themes have been built on the basis of thematic analysis which are attitude, subjective norms, perceived behavioural control and other factors. Further analysis of the themes has resulted in 29 sub-themes. The review and 29 sub-themes created on prior research trends and patterns in adoption of online investment researches resulted in four themes. The four main themes are attitude (10 sub-themes), subjective norms (3 sub-themes), perceived behavioural control (9 sub-themes) and others factor (7 sub-themes). With a total 16 research studies, the results constructed a comprehensive analysis of trends and pattern in adoption of online investment (Table 3).

All of prior studies focused on quantitative methods in their studies. While in respect of published years, one article was published 1998, one in 2002, one in 2003, one in 2004, one in 2005, one in 2007, three in 2009, two in 2010, one in 2013, one in 2014, one in 2016, one in 2017, two in 2018, one in 2019, and two articles published in 2020. Figure 2 categorizes articles according to their indexed impact in WOS and Scopus database that reflects the journal's quality. The number of articles indexed in WOS exceeds SCOPUS between year 1998 to 2020. There are articles published in Q1, Q2, Q3, Q4 and Emerging Sources Citation Index (ESCI) analysed in this review.

Out of 16 articles, five studies were conducted in Malaysia, three studies were conducted in Singapore, two studies were conducted in India, Iran, Indonesia and United States, one study was conducted in these countries namely China, UAE, Taiwan and Pakistan (Fig. 3).

3.2 Themes and sub-themes

3.2.1 Attitude

Attitude is one of factor that influencing the adoption of online investment. Attitude can be defined as the scale of a person negative and positive feeling to the specific object or intention of fulfilling a particular behaviour. In the scope of online investment, the more positive the attitude of a person to the object and behaviour, the stronger her or his intention to utilize it and performed it well (Ramayah et al., 2014). Many researchers found significant impact of attitude on intention to use (Loh & Ong, 1998; Lee-Partridge & Ho, 2003; Teo et al., 2004; Gopi & Ramayah, 2007; Ramayah et al., 2009; Lee, 2009; Singh et al., 2010; Abroud et al., 2015; Ramayah et al., 2014; Gazali, Adeyemi & Alhabshi, 2016; Afif, Handayani & Pinem, 2018; Abdullah et al., 2008, Akhtar & Das, 2019; Khan, 2020). There are 14 prior studies that focused on attitude, particularly in the adoption of online investment. There are few

Table 3 Table of findings

Authors	Region	Attitude											Subjective Norms			
		AT	PU	PE	PR	PB	EV	TR	SQ	IE	NH	FK	SN	IN	DN	SF
Loh and Ong (1998)	Singapore		/	/					/							
Volpe et al. (2002)	United States															
Lee-Partridge and Ho (2003)	Singapore		/	/					/	/	/					/
Teo et al. (2004)	Singapore						/									
Gopi and Ramayah (2007)	Malaysia	/											/			
Ramayah et al. (2009)	Malaysia		/	/										/	/	
Lee (2009)	Taiwan		/	/	/	/		/					/			
Singh and Kundu (2014)	India			/												
Abroud et al. (2015)	Iran		/	/			/	/								
Ramayah et al. (2014)	Malaysia		/	/	/									/	/	
Gazali et al. (2016)	Malaysia			/												
Afif, et al. (2018)	Indonesia		/	/				/					/			
Abdullah et al. (2008)	Malaysia		/	/												/
Akhtar and Das (2019)	India	/										/	/			
Khan et al. (2020a, 2020b)	Pakistan				/			/				/				
Khan et al. (2021)	China															
Total number of documents		2	8	10	2	1	2	4	2	1	1	2	4	2	2	2

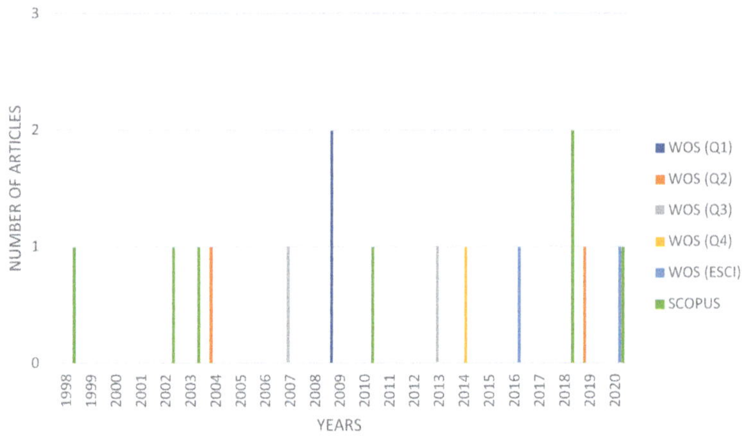

Fig. 2 Distribution of documents and indexed categories per years

Fig. 3 Country where studies on adoption of online investment were conducted

factors that affecting attitude which are perceived usefulness or relative advantage, perceived ease of use or complexity, perceived risk, perceived benefits, economic value, trust, lifestyle, system quality, internet experience, needs for human interaction and financial knowledge. There are 11 sub-themes under this theme, included perceived usefulness or also known as relative advantage (8 studies), perceived ease of use or complexity (10 studies), perceived risk (3 studies), perceived benefits (1 study), economic value (2 studies), trust (4 studies), lifestyle (1 study), system quality (2 studies), internet experience (1 study), needs for human interaction (1 study) and financial knowledge (1 study).

Perceived Usefulness

In the circumstance of online investment, perceived usefulness shows degree of person views on online investment as offering advantages over previous ways of performing stock trading transaction. As online investment has 24 hours access to investment report and advice, it makes the instrument is more convenient and relative advantage compared to previous traditional stock trading. The advantages of online investment will affect the attitude of an individual and will influence his or her intention to perform online investment. Many studies found that perceived usefulness is affecting individual's attitude to use (Loh & Ong, 1998; Ramayah et al., 2014; Lee-Partridge & Ho, 2003; Gazali et al., 2016; Lee, 2009; Afif et al., 2018; Ramayah et al., 2009; Abroud et al., 2015; Abdullah, E.M.E et al., 2008; Singh et al., 2010).

Perceived Ease of Use

While perceive of ease of use, shows degree of online investment would be perceived as easy to understand, learn and use. Some research found that perceived ease of use is affecting attitude (Ramayah et al., 2014; Ramayah et al., 2009; Lee, 2009, Afif et al., 2018; Abroud et al., 2015; Abdullah et al., 2008). Low complexity in operating a system can lead a person's attitude to use it (Ramayah et al., 2014). A study found that investors' concerns, expectations, perceived ease of use and the real value-added system and trading behaviour are important factors to ultimate adoption of online investment (Loh & Ong, 1998). When investors feel the online investment is easy to use, themore benefits they can get from the system (Afif et al., 2018). There is also relationship between perceived ease of use and perceived usefulness as the less effort or less complex will directly support to increase the level of performance (Afif et al., 2018). There is a study found that there is negative effect of PEOU to attitude towards adoption of online investment (Lee-Partridge & Ho, 2003). This happened because during 2003, online investment is still at infancy stage where most of them were new to investment or non-adopters that makes them unable to assess perception of the system complexity precisely.

Perceived Risk

Perceived risk is also one of the factors that influencing the attitude to intention to use. In the scope of internet stock trading or online investment, a person who acknowledges the internet to be safe and trustworthy will lead the attitude to use the internet stock trading. A study from Taiwan found that many investors believe that they are unsafe and exposed to fraud and identity theft while using online investment (Lee, 2009). Because of the risk concern, adoption of online investment in Taiwan is still low. A study found that, inverse relationship between perceived risk and attitude (Ramayah et al., 2014) while another study found that perceived risk has a positive effect on attitude and intention to trade online (Lee, 2009). Khan et al. found that there are negative and adverse relationship between time, financial, privacy, performance, social, opportunity cost risk on Pakistani users' intention to use online investment (2020a, 2020b). This result indicates that if investors experience monetary loss because of uncertain technology, hacking and fraud in online investment, they will lose social status (Khan et al., 2020a, 2020b). Not just that, they also feel that they will lose social status as involved in religiously illegitimate activities because there is a study stated that stock investing is religiously illegitimate activity (Ali et al., 2012).

Moreover, chances of fraud occur in online investment and lack of formal proceeding and receipts in Pakistan makes users unable to claim compensation if mistakes occurred in transaction (Khan et al., 2020a, 2020b). The investor also worried about the possible technology malfunction that might be occurred during online stock trading such as low internet speed or disconnection and server breakdown that may cause loses (Khan et al., 2020a, 2020b). Next, investors concerned about misuse of sensitive private information by hackers or stockbrokerages. Lastly, investor concerned about time consume because they need time to analyse the stocks before trade and also need to learn of using online investment (Khan et al., 2020a, 2020b).

Perceived Benefits

Perceived benefits defined as benefits that customers and bank gained from electronic platform (Gazali et al., 2016). Customers gained benefits which are cost saving, earned more return than offline trading and convenience which made them more intend to use online investment platform (Gazali et al., 2016). A study named perceived benefits as perceived financial return as the online investor gained more return financially compared to offline investor (Gazali et al., 2016). Some studies found that perceived benefits influence user to adopt online investment positively (Lee, 2009; Gazali et al., 2016).

System Quality

System Quality refers to degree of how well an investor perceives the performance of particular system (Loh & Ong, 1998). Lee-Partridge & Ho (2003) found that system quality has insignificant effect on attitude towards online investment. The investors may think system quality is not affected their adoption of online investment because the system did not charge high tax as low of demand in orders. Moreover, the brokerage also provides high maintenance for the system and makes the system rarely having a breakdown (Lee-Partridge & Ho, 2003). In contrast with another study found that system quality has positive relationship with behavioural usage of online investment (Loh & Ong, 1998). By having a system that user-friendly, make the system easily accepted by users and fulfil users' needs (Loh & Ong, 1998).

Internet Experience

Past computer experience influenced individuals to use computer technology especially internet. Internet has increasing individual's job performance thus, the individual is more comfortable and confident in performing the activities such as online investment (Lee-Partridge & Ho, 2003). There is a study found that internet experience has positive relationship towards attitude and perceived behavioural control (Lee-Partridge & Ho, 2003). Investors who has internet savvy may have already developed adequate experiences in online information search and able to solve minor problems while retrieving investment related information from particular online brokerage website (Lee-Partridge & Ho, 2003). Investor who has internet savvy is confident to the system will lead to good control in online trading (Lee-Partridge & Ho, 2003).

Needs for Human Interaction

Need for human interaction is defined as investors depends or preferred helps from stockbrokers to update the market development. But a study found that needs for human interaction has negative relationship towards behavioural intention (Lee-Partridge & Ho, 2003). This is because there is robo-advisor in the system that will suggest investor about investment portfolio or market development.

Financial Knowledge

Awareness defined as users and their knowledge towards the availability of online investment services, its advantages and the use of online investment. Before adopting or using a product, user experience process of knowledge, influence, decision and confirmation. Users accept or reject of a product or services based on their awareness of the products and services. Intention to use online investment is significant and positive affected by awareness and knowledge (Khan et al., 2020a, 2020b).

Economic Value

Economic value in online investment referred to degree of cost reduction and time saving (Abroud et al., 2015). Abroud et al. found that there is significant effect between cost reduction on investors' attitude towards online investment (Abroud et al., 2015; Teo et al., 2004). While, time saving is having insignificant effect towards attitude of investors towards online investment (Abroud et al., 2015). Time saving act as insignificant as the study focused on young investor and most of the respondents are inexperience in online investment as they experienced online investment less than a year. Consequently, the investors could not compare their experience with traditional trading investment and online investment (Abroud et al., 2015). Nevertheless, due to lesser transaction cost, online investment offers cost effective platform that can influence investors' attitude towards online investment (Abroud et al., 2015).

3.2.2 Subjective Norms

Next, social environment or social pressure is also a factor that influencing the adoption of online investment. Based on prior research, non-user of online investment could be influenced to use online investment by those who important to them which means social pressure makes an individual performs the behaviour even though he or she not in favour to do so (Ramayah et al., 2014). Although information about online investment is available, there are some information that missing such as the security, privacy and others, the individual would refer to referent group or individuals with trusted information sources about online inevstement (Gopi & Ramayah, 2007). Thus, the influence of people surrounding has impacted the individuals to adopt online investment. Studies found that subjective norm is affecting the intention to use (Gopi & Ramayah, 2007; Ramayah et al., 2014; Ramayah et al., 2009; Lee, 2009; Akhtar & Das, 2019; Abdullah et al., 2008). The higher level of investor confidence in online investment will motivate the investor to influence the family or people around them (Afif et al., 2018). Under this theme, there are 3 sub-themes were developed.

Injunctive Norms

Injunctive norms defined as perceived belief involve perceptions of which behaviours is approved or disapproved. Ramayah et al., (2009; 2014) found that there is positive relationship between injunctive norms towards subjective norms.

Descriptive Norms

Descriptive norms defined as normative influence in which behaviour performed by social sanctions or social pressure. Ramayah et al. (2009; 2014) found that there is positive relationship between descriptive norms and subjective norms. The study also discovered, based on the result even though there is only 35% are internet stock trader, the non-users could be influenced by people that they considered important to adopt online investment.

Social Factors

Social factors refer to individuals are affected by the referent group they know or mingle such as friends, colleagues and family in influencing them towards adopting of online investment. A study found that there is significant and positive relationship between social factors and behavioural intention to adopt online investment (Lee-Partridge & Ho, 2003).

3.2.3 Perceived Behavioural Control

Under this theme, this review obtained 10 sub-themes. Perceived Behavioural Control is based on prior experience and second-hand information from family and friends (Ramayah et al., 2014). Past researchers found that PBC is affecting intention to use positively (Ramayah et al., 2014; Lee-Partridge & Ho, 2003; Gopi & Ramayah, 2007; Lee, 2009; Abdullah et al., 2008, Afif et al., 2018). PBC is a function of facilitating conditions in the environment and perceived self- efficacy. The level of investor confidence in the online investment affects the adoption as when there are enough resources available such as funds and internet networks (Afif et al., 2018). The higher level of investor confidence in online investment, the better investor will control the use of online investment according to enough resources. For example, when investor has high confidence on online investment, they will invest most of their money through online investment (Afif et al., 2018).

Facilitating Condition

Facilitating conditions refer to external components in an individual environment which make a particular behaviour easy or difficult to perform. There are two components in facilitating condition which are resource factors such as time and money and technological capacity. Technological advanced system and greater resources (time and money) influence their PBC and intention to use online investment. The organizational effort of providing training and support for online investment would improve their self confidence in using online investment.

Computer Self-efficacy

Furthermore, another factor that influencing PCB towards intention to use is computer self-efficacy. Computer self-efficacy is individual's ability to use computer to complete a task. In this context, investors with computer self-efficacy will perceived that they have the ability to perform stock transaction through internet because they are well versed in internet and computer which make them more receptive (Ramayah et al., 2014; Lee-Partridge & Ho, 2003).

Government Support

Another factor that influencing PCB towards intention to use is government support. Government support in this context prescribed as involvement of government in promoting online financial services from traditional banking transaction influenced to adopt the online stock trading. According to Ramayah et al., (2014) currently Bank Negara Malaysia took less action towards regulation of price for internet stock trading transaction which make it as a constraint to a person acceptance of internet stock trading. While in Singapore, government has taken a lot of effort in promoting online platform but investors do not feel the effort was targeted them and enhancing the online investment (Lee-Partridge & Ho, 2003). Few studies found that government support has insignificant impact towards PCB (Ramayah et al., 2014; Lee-Partridge & Ho, 2003).

Training and Provision Support

Next, a study found that there is positive relationship between training and provision support and PBC (Ramayah et al., 2014). Due to the result, the organizational effort of giving training and support can enhance or improved individuals' self confidence in operating online investment.

Resource Support

Resource support defined as adequacy of resources support provided by organization will enhance or refuse the user to adopt a system. For example, if Organization A did not have enough resources support, the users tend to deem the systems as complex and lead to low usage of the system. A study found that there is positive but insignificant effect of resource support and PBC (Lee-Partridge, 2003). With bigger prospects base, more stockbrokerages are using online investment, giving investors with lots of opportunities to try others alternative mode of online investment. In Singapore, there are companies that giving a free initial entrance fee for opening internet trading account to enhance investors to trade online. Some also set up cyber cafes for society to make online trading. (Lee-Partridge & Ho, 2003). In contrast, Ramayah et al. found that there is positive relationship between resources and PBC as having greater resources including time and money influence PBC (2014). When there is enough time and money to invest in online investment, individual is confident to adopt online investment.

Security/Perceived Technology Uncertainty

Security defined as protection of data and system from all illegal interruption and losses. Security constructs based on privacy and secureness of stock trading system (Loh & Ong, 1998). There are few studies found that security is significant factors that influencing the adoption of online investment (Loh & Ong, 1998; Lee-Partridge & Ho, 2003; Gazali et al., 2016; Singh et al., 2010, Khan et al., 2020a, 2020b; Teo et al., 2004). Individuals concerned the security level, their confidential information, privacy level of platform; thus, they tend to be very careful in exposing sensitive, private information in online. Individual only performed an action if the individual reached certain level of trust. Thus, a system with higher level of security is important to encourage investors to use online investment frequently. Security also closely related to trust because the users need to trust the system before they use it (Teo et al., 2004).

Technology Facilitating Condition

Technology facilitating condition also has direct and positive relationship with PBC (Ramayah et al., 2014). Having technologically advanced system increased their confidence towards online investment.

Information Quality

Information quality has positive and significant relationship between attitude and perceived behavioural control towards adopting online investment (Lee-Patridge & Ho, 2003). Information quality improves perceived usefulness which can enhance investor perceptions on online investment. For example, an investor invests in online stock trading for making his or her money to grow, thus investor favour a system that provides them accurate and timely information that helps them trade more profitability and effectively. Moreover, in perceived behavioural control, high information quality is making the investor confidence and not confuse. Investor confidence to trading online because trust and can rely on relevant and up to date information for investment decisions (Lee-Partridge & Ho, 2003).

Financial Self-efficacy

Financial self-efficacy influence risk taking by affecting an individual's insight about opportunities and threats. A study found that financial self-efficacy mediating the personality traits on individual's investment intention and also has direct and significant relationship towards investment intention (Akhtar & Das, 2019). With financial self-efficacy, investor is still having interest in online investment even under uncertain situation (Akhtar & Das, 2019).

Trust

Trust is considered as factor that encourage individual confidence online investment. This shows when investors trust the honest act of stockbrokers, they tend to increase their usage of electronic stock trading. Trust in electronic stock trading nurtured by their activeness and experience in stock trading (Khan et al., 2020a, 2020b). There a few studies found that trust is important in adopting online investment (Khan et al., 2020a; Lee, 2009; Khan et al., 2020b, Abroud et al., 2015; Afif et al., 2018). Stock exchange created marketing and promotional campaigns about online investment's benefits and advantages that could improve awareness of online investment and create positive attitude towards online investment, indirectly will improve trust on this platform (Abroud et al., 2015).

3.2.4 Others Factor

There are few others factor that influencing the adoption of online investment which are investor personality traits, demographic, Islamic worldview, perceived religion, perceived regulatory uncertainty, perceived information asymmetry and perceived service intangibility.

Investor Personality Traits

Personality traits in a study focused on financial behaviour of investor to adopt in online investment or financial decision making (Akhtar & Das, 2019). There are two personality traits that present in investor which are risk taking propensity and preference for innovation. Akhtar and Das, found that personality traits preference for innovation and risk-taking propensity have positive and significant towards investment intention mediated by financial self-efficacy, indicating that individual who is risk taker and innovator has a greater tendency towards investment intention (2019).

Demographic

Inexperienced, young and non-businessman investors were more tend to utilize online investment compared to experienced, aged people and businessman (Singh et al., 2010). Aged people were expected more experienced in any profession and they value the information in internet less than younger one who has less experience. Older people had come to near to retirement thus less time to utilize the benefits of their investments while younger people are more exposed to internet, more dependent to internet and made them more confident in internet's abilities to benefit them. Education level and income of investor are not influencing a user to adopt online investment (Singh et al., 2010). Older user, male, higher education level is more interesting and knowledgably about online investment compared to younger user, female and college education or high school diploma (Volpe et al., 2002). While another study found that male, higher income, experienced and stock trading frequency are affecting intention to adopt online investment compared to female, lower income, inexperienced and infrequent in stock trading (Teo et al., 2004). These happened because male is more interested in online investment or fintech than female, but there is significant increase in adoption because increasing in internet usage (Teo et al., 2004). While income factors came from the result of most of Singapore internet stock trading brokerages require deposit of initial investment of $1000 and the system is still new, only people with higher income may try the new services and take risk (Teo et al., 2004). Experienced people that considered more than 1-year experience stock trading is more tend to do online investment and people who frequently invest in stock trading is more likely to invest in online investment (Teo et al., 2004).

Islamic Worldview

Islamic worldview is not the core view of physical world neither man's historical, culture, social and political involvement but covered both al-dunya (worldly) and al-akhirah (hereafter) (Gazali et al., 2016). A study found that Islamic worldview affecting individual to adopt online investment (Gazali et al., 2016). By the reason of all muslims are responsible for their actions in the hereafter as the living in the world is temporary and not their final destination. Thus, the muslims must ensure their actions and activities are comply with Islamic rules and shariah.

Perceived Religion

Religiosity defined as practises and teachings amongst faith community. Religiosity is the key dimension of muslim personality between muamalat and ritual aspects (Gazali et al., 2016). There is a study found that perceived religion is an important factor that influence a person to use online investment (Gazali et al., 2016). Those who have strong religious belief would practice religious principles as a guide and advices others that involve immoral behaviour (Gazali et al., 2016).

Perceived Regulatory Uncertainty

Perceived regulatory uncertainty refers to investors' perception towards instability and uncertainty in regulatory system (Khan et al., 2020a, 2020b). Uncertain and fake government regulation towards internet stock trading make investors unwilling to adopt online investment. Khan et al., found that there is significance relationship between perceived regulatory uncertainty and internet stock trading as perceived regulatory plays important role on investor's intention to adopt internet stock trading (2020a, 2020b). From the study, the authors found that it is important to develop comprehensive, clear legal regulations and standards for all stakeholders involved entire system in order to make investors more willingness to adopt online investment.

Perceived Service Intangibility

Perceived Service Intangibility defined as investors' perceptions of difficulty in conceptualizing the services in representation mentally, describing or defining internet stock trading (Khan et al., 2020a, 2020b). A study found that there is insignificant relationship between perceived service intangibility and internet stock trading as traditional telephonic method of stock trading is also intangible, thus intangibility of internet stock trading did not affect the intention to adopt internet stock trading (Khan et al., 2020a, 2020b). Next, online investment is much more useful than traditional method as online investment has benefited the investors on saving time, cost and effort.

Perceived Information Asymmetry

Perceived Information Asymmetry defined as investors' perceptions that the stockbrokers have better information about the stock market products than investors (Khan et al., 2020a, 2020b). Examples of information are internet stock trading service's functions, privacy protection, account security, charges, and others information. The stockbrokers may misuse the private information of users or disclose their account details, such as passwords, which inhibits investors acceptance of online investment. A study found that perceived information asymmetry is negatively and significantly associated with the investors' intention to adopt internet stock trading (Khan et al., 2020a, 2020b).

4 Discussions

Four themes were developed and 29 sub-themes in the thematic analyses. Further discussions of developed themes presented in this section. Based on the findings, Figure 4 was developed in this study to present all factors that influencing adoption of online investment with theories adopted by prior 16 reviewed articles. There are 6 theories found in 16 reviewed articles including technology acceptance model (4 papers), theory of planned behaviour (2 papers), theory of reasoned action, perceived risk theory (1 paper), social cognitive theory (1 paper) and transaction cost theory (2 papers).

There are also some theories that has been decomposed and integrated such as decomposed theory of planned behaviour (1 paper), decomposed theory reasoned action (1 paper), integrated theory of planned behaviour (2 papers), decomposed technology acceptance model (1 paper), integrated decomposed theory of planned behaviour (1 paper) and unified theory acceptance of use technology (1 paper). These theories will be supporting the themes and sub-themes in this review.

In this section, further discussion on importance of themes and sub-themes developed will be presented. Firstly, attitude has positive relationship between

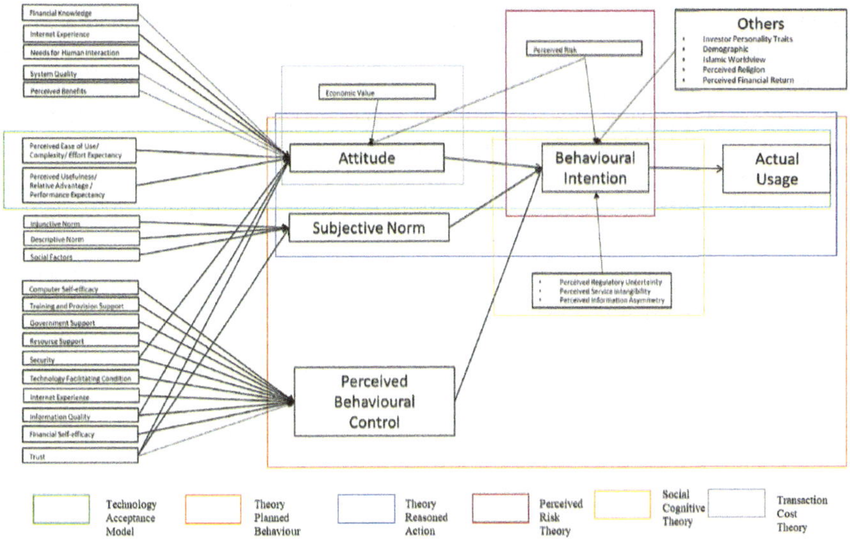

Fig. 4 Summary of factors influencing adoption of online investment categorized by theories adopted in the research

behavioural intention towards online investment, this result aligned with theory of planned behaviour, theory reasoned action and technology acceptance model. E-stockbrokerage could provide all related information towards enhancing positive attitude. Organizations can emphasis on advantages of adopting online investment such as easy to access to perform online transaction, low fees, up-to date market reports such as trends of markets and stocks and 24-hours accessibility to encourage societies to trade online. Moreover, with easy accessibility and user-friendly system and effective, it could enhance favourableness in attitude towards online investment (Gopi & Ramayah, 2007). There is positive relationship between perceived ease of use and attitude aligned with theory of technology acceptance model. When investors are disclosed to unfamiliar system, the system should require least learning effort that could lead higher motivation for investors to explore more. If difficulties of adopt online investment could not be solve, investors would not explore more even the system can perform a beneficial task. This will affect user's satisfaction that can influence the user's perceptions and adoption (Loh & Ong, 1998).

Secondly, subjective norms also known as social pressure and social factors, has positive relationship with behavioural intention towards online investment, this finding aligned with theory of reasoned action, unified theory of acceptance and use technology and theory of planned behaviour. Online investment could increase if the users perceive that most of people who are important to them encourage them to invest online. Despite information about online investment is accessible, the information is still incomplete as the information available is not including the security and privacy which the most concern factors among online investor. Thus, with the incomplete information potential investors would tend to trust on information given by referent group or trusted and resourceful person about online investment. The potential investor will influence to adopt online investment with positive information and social pressure given by referent group and individuals that trusted and resourceful (Gopi & Ramayah, 2007). Furthermore, organizations could provide incentive programs to online investor in introducing online investment to potential investor such as some amount of free transactions, free in opening secondary account and upgraded credit limit that could encourage the investor to introduce and invest online. Social pressure and with help of incentives could influence intention in adopting of online investment.

Thirdly, according theory of planned behaviour, there is positive relationship between perceived behavioural control and behavioural intention towards online investment. In Malaysia, most investors have some experiences on online platform such as online banking, latest stock information, online bill payment, online purchasing, foreign stock market and Malaysia market condition information (Gopi & Ramayah, 2007). Thus, with the experience gained will increase the confidence on adoption of online investment. E-stockbrokerage can implement marketing efforts and training to increase the level of perceived behavioural control to encourage the adoption of online investment.

Fourthly, perceived risk has negative affect towards intention to adopt online investments which not aligned with the theory of perceived risk. This shows the essential for effective risk-reducing strategies to promote online investment adoption (Khan et al., 2020a, 2020b). Implementing the latest user-friendly technology of online investment also can encourage potential investor to adopt online investment. The size of user of online investment correlates to the confidence of potential investor to invest on the system. The impact of risk also can be reduced by hiring technical staff that can help investors in solving their problems in real time. With good services and user-friendly of the systems and helps from the technical staff would encourage potential user to adopt online investment

5 Future Direction

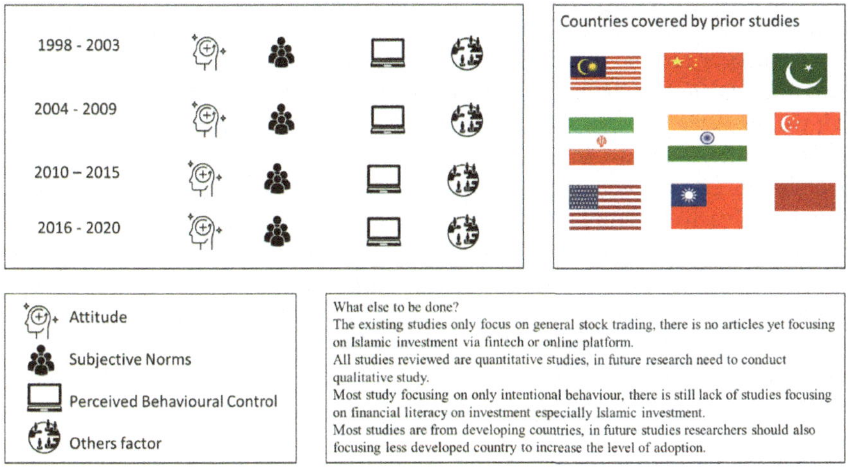

This review suggested few recommendations for future direction that might be useful to future researchers. First, more studies needed to review adoption of online investment especially in qualitative studies as all the studies reviewed were quantitative method of research approach. As qualitative method explains in-depth of a topic and has detailed explanations compared to quantitative method. Next, the existing studies only focus on general stock trading, there is no article yet focusing on Islamic online investment. Most studies focusing on only behavioural intention, there is still lack of study focusing on financial literacy on online investment. Lastly, most of studies are from developing countries, in future research study should also focusing on less developed country to increase the level of awareness and adoption of online investment.

There are some limitations in this review that may be considered to be improved for future studies. This systematic review process of two online databases. Therefore, it may overlook contributions from other databases. Next, the limitation of language as the authors only literate with English and Malay language. However, there is no article published in Malay retrieved from two databases. This study also overlooked contributions from book, systematic review, reviews. In addition, the findings need to be supported with empirical study to come up with suitable models. Thus, future researchers could examine the adoption of online investment in empirical framework.

6 Conclusion

This systematic literature review emphasizes the factors influencing adoption of online investment. By creating theme and sub-themes through analysis constructed from related articles, it can be seen more clearly that the sub-themes either influence the adoption or not and the factors that influencing can be focused to provide new ideas to create more awareness to online investment. Online investment is important as it will improve financial well-being for individuals for future needs and decrease the economic inequality. In fact, there is still lack of research related to adoption of online investment compared to online banking. There are 4 themes which are attitude, subjective norms, perceived behavioural control and others factors that influencing the adoption of online investment. There are 29 sub-theme that influencing the adoption of online investment which are perceived ease of use, perceived usefulness, perceived risk, perceived security, financial knowledge, internet experience, needs for human interactions, system quality, perceived benefits, economic value, injunctive norms, descriptive norms, social factors, computer-self efficacy, training and provision support, government support, security, technology facilitating condition, information quality, financial self-efficacy, trust, investor personality traits, demographic, Islamic worldview, perceived religion, perceived financial return and perceived uncertainties that influence the adoption of online investment.

This study provides some recommendations for future studies. First, the existing studies only focus on general stock trading, there is no articles yet focusing on Islamic investment via fintech or online platform. Second, need to conduct qualitative study as qualitative study is more in-depth and detailed explanation than quantitative study because all reviewed studies are quantitative studies. Thirdly, needs of study focused on undeveloped countries.

Acknowledgements This research was supported by the Fundamental Research Grant Scheme, Ministry of Higher Education, Malaysia [grant number: FRGS/1/2019/SS01/UKM/02/3].

References

Abdullah, E. M. E., Rahman, A. A., & Rahim, R. A. (2008). Adoption of financial technology (Fintech) in mutual fund/unit trust investment among Malaysians: Unified theory of acceptance and use of technology (UTAUT). *International Journal of Engineering and Technology, 7*(2), 29.

Abroud, A., Choong, Y. V., Muthaiyah, S., & Fie, D. Y. G. (2015). Adopting e-finance: Decomposing the technology acceptance model for investors. *Service Business, 9*(1), 161–182.

Afif, F. P., Handayani, P. W., & Pinem, A. A. (2018). Determinant factors of new investor intention for using online trading system. In *Third International Conference on Informatics and Computing (ICIC)* (pp. 1–6). IEEE.

Akhtar, F., & Das, N. (2019). Predictors of investment intention in Indian stock markets. *International Journal of Bank Marketing*,.

Dewey, A., & Drahota, A. (2016). *Introduction of systematic reviews: Online learning module*. Cochrane Training.

EY Global Financial Services. (2019). Global Fintech Adoption Index 2019. https://assets.ey.com/content/dam/ey-sites/ey-com/en_gl/topics/financial-services/ey-global-fintech-adoption-index-2019.pdf?download

Financial Stability Board. (2017). Financial stability implications from FinTech. http://www.fsb.org/2017/06/financial-stability-implications-from-fintech/

Gazali, H. M., Adeyemi, A. A., & Alhabshi, S. M. S. J. (2016). Exploring the influential factors on online investment platform. In *6th International Conference on Information and Communication Technology for The Muslim World (ICT4M)* (pp. 166–170). IEEE.

Gopi, M., & Ramayah, T. (2007). Applicability of theory of planned behaviour in predicting intention to trade online. *International Journal of Emerging Markets,*.

Higgins, S. (2016). Meta-synthesis and comparative meta-analysis of education research findings: Some risks and benefits. *Review of Education, 4*(1), 31–53.

Khan, S. U., Liu, X., Khan, I. U., Liu, C., & Rasheed, M. I. (2020a). Assessing the investors' acceptance of electronic stock trading in a developing country: The mediating role of perceived risk dimensions. *Information Resources Management Journal (IRMJ), 33*(1), 59–82.

Khan, S. U., Liu, X. D., Liu, C., Khan, I. U., & Hameed, Z. (2020b). Understanding uncertainty dimensions and Internet stock trading service in China from a social cognitive perspective. *Information Technology & People.*

Lee, M. C. (2009). Predicting and explaining the adoption of online trading: An empirical study in Taiwan. *Decision Support Systems, 47*(2), 133–142.

Lee-Partridge, J. E., & Pei, S. H. (2003). A retail investor's perspective on the acceptance of Internet stock trading. In *36th Annual Hawaii International Conference on System Sciences* (p. 11). IEEE.

Loh, L., & Ong, Y. S. (1998). The adoption of Internet-based stock trading: A conceptual framework and empirical results. *Journal of Information Technology, 13*(2), 81–94.

Mallett, R., Hagen-Zanker, J., Slater, R., & Duvendack, M. (2012). The benefits and challenges of using systematic reviews in international development research. *Journal of Development Effectiveness, 4*(3), 445–455.

Ramayah, T., Rouibah, K., Gopi, M., & Rangel, G. J. (2009). A decomposed theory of reasoned action to explain intention to use Internet stock trading among Malaysian investors. *Computers in Human Behavior, 25*(6), 1222–1230.

Ramayah, T., Soto-Acosta, P., Colomo-Palacios, R., Gopi, M., & Popa, S. (2014). Explaining the adoption of Internet stock trading in Malaysia: Comparing models. *Asian Journal of Technology Innovation, 22*(1), 131–151.

Robinson, P., & Lowe, J. (2015). Literature reviews vs systematic reviews. *Australian and New Zealand Journal of Public Health, 39*(2), 103. https://doi.org/10.1111/1753-6405.12393

Singh, A., & Kundu, S. C. (2014). Investors' adoption of internet stock trading: A study. *The Journal of Internet Banking and Commerce, 15*(1), 1–21.

Teo, T. S., Tan, M., & Peck, S. N. (2004). Adopters and non-adopters of internet stock trading in Singapore. *Behaviour & Information Technology, 23*(3), 211–223.

Volpe, R. P., Kotel, J. E., & Chen, H. (2002). A survey of investment literacy among online investors. *Journal of Financial Counselling and Planning, 13*(1), 1.

Whittemore, R. & Knafl, K. 2006. The integrative review: update methodology. *Journal of Advanced Nursing, 52*(5), 546–553.

World Bank Global Findex Report. (2018). Malaysia Fintech Report 2018. https://openknowledge.worldbank.org/bitstream/handle/10986/29510/9781464812590.pdf

Millennials and Gen-Z Ethical Banking Behaviour in Malaysia

Siti Aisyah Zahari, Shahida Shahimi, Suhaili Alma'amun, and Mohd Mursyid Arshad

Abstract Millennials (born between 1981 and 1996) and generation Z (born between 1997 and 2012, also known as Gen-Z) make up more than half the world's population (Deloitte, 2020). Together they form the largest demographic globally. Both generations are categorised as being technology savvy, well educated and entrepreneurial (DeVaney, 2015), accounting for most of the global workforce with the former at their prime earning years. According to Morgan Stanley report in 2019, 95% of millennials are interested in sustainable investing or want to tailor their investments to their values. Another survey in 2018 indicated that 87% of high net worth (HNW) millennials considered a company's ethical, sustainable and governance (ESG) track record as an essential investment decision consideration. The inclination of these generations towards sustainable and ethical investing is very much understandable as millennials and Gen-Z are tackling their concerns by taking socially conscious actions to protect the planet and shine a spotlight on societal issues. Millennials said protecting the environment was their top concern, followed by health care and disease prevention, unemployment and income inequality/distribution of wealth (Deloitte, 2020). Preference towards ethical banking reflects a desire for their money not just to earn a return but to align with their values and contribute to the social good. Therefore, instead of being conceptualised as a niche market, Millennials and Gen-Z should be treated as submarkets that differ in their levels of awareness of ethical issues, consider discrete motives when making financial decisions and are willing to engage in cause-related banking to varying degrees. Connecting with these customers with different banking behaviour and preference is a critical part of any bank's entry-point marketing strategy. In doing so, it is important to understand factors influencing ethical banking behaviour among millennials and Gen-Z. Following the ethical decision-making model by Bayer et al. (Journal of Business Economics 89:655–697, 2019) and Rest (Moral development: advances

S. A. Zahari · S. Shahimi (✉) · S. Alma'amun
Faculty of Economics and Management, Universiti Kebangsaan Malaysia, Bangi, Selangor, Malaysia
e-mail: shahida@ukm.edu.my

M. M. Arshad
Faculty of Educational Studies, Universiti Putra Malaysia, Serdang, Selangor, Malaysia

Z. Abdul Karim et al. (eds.), *Contemporary Issues in Finance, Investment and Banking in Malaysia*,
https://doi.org/10.1007/978-981-99-5447-6_10

in research and theory, Praeger, 1986), this study incorporated constructs, namely, religious value, technology-related factors and ethical obligations. This study frames its analysis based on a sample of 500 millennials and Gen-Z banking customers to provide evidence for Malaysian market. The expected findings suggest that millennials and Gen-Z in Malaysia felt that their intentions to engage in ethical banking are motivated by the perceptions of their own capabilities, attitudes and perceptions of other people close to them. Based on these findings, it is recommended that banks should refocus their attention on the banking needs of these generations of customers to gain a better understanding of what influences their behaviours. Retail banking executives and marketers need to adjust their approaches, products and messaging to keep pace with unique behaviour of these generations. Banks can make use of the findings to improve their marketing strategies for customised ethical products and services offered to leverage on this significant segment of populations, thus increasing profitability.

Keywords Digital-savvy · Green banking · Social banking · Value-based banking (VBB) · Value-based intermediation (VBI)

1 Introduction

Millennials and Gen-Z form more than half of the world's population (Deloitte, 2020). Together they form the largest demographic globally. According to the Department of Statistics Malaysia (DOSM), in 2021, there are approximately 17.1 million millennials and Gen-Z or 52.5% of the Malaysian population. Both generations are categorised as being technology savvy, well educated and entrepreneurial (DeVaney, 2015), and have shifted their concern towards sustainable, green, social, valuable and ethical products that could promote good causes in the future (ICMR, 2021). According to Morgan Stanley report in 2019, 95% of millennials are interested in sustainable investing or want to tailor their investments to their values. Another survey in 2018 indicated that 87% of high net worth (HNW) millennials considered a company's ethical, sustainable and governance (ESG) track record as an essential investment decision consideration. The consideration of these generations towards ethical and sustainable financing reflects the passion for their money not only to earn a return but also to align with their values and contribute to the social good. Therefore, instead of being conceptualised as a niche market, millennials and Gen-Z should be treated as submarkets that differ in their levels of awareness of ethical issues, consider discrete motives when making financial decisions and are willing to engage in cause-related banking to varying degrees. Connecting with these customers with different banking behaviour and preference is critical to any bank's entry-point marketing strategy. The ethical banking behaviour among both generations could be the central reference point and foundation for developing ethical banking in Malaysia's banking institutions.

Ethical banking has proven to be extremely robust to the financial crisis and may prove to be a viable alternative to the current traditional banking. The recent pandemic COVID-19 created not only health risks but also economic, social, psychological, political and ethical consequences, which have impacted the financial and banking system. In turn, consumers are no longer drawn only by the financial return but also by ethical considerations. Connecting with these customers with different banking behaviour and preference is a critical part of any bank's entry-point marketing strategy. Thus, this chapter will discuss millennials and Gen-Z ethical banking behaviour as well as an overview of ethical banking in Malaysia. Banks can make use of the findings to improve their marketing strategies for customised ethical products and services offered to leverage on this significant segment of populations, thus increasing profitability. The remainder of the chapter is organised as follows: In Sect. 2, the overview of millennials and Gen-Z are described. Section 3 discussed ethical banking followed by literature on ethical banking in Malaysia. In Sect. 5, we discussed ethical banking behaviour. In the next section, we present the factors influencing ethical banking behaviour among millennials and Gen-Z in Malaysia, followed by the discussion on several implications pertaining to ethical banking behaviour among millennials and Gen-Z. The last section concludes the paper.

2 Millennials and Gen-Z

Following Generational Theory, millennials (roughly born between 1981 and 1995) current age is 27–41 years old. Whereas Gen-Z is those born between 1996 and 2012 (currently aged between 10 and 26 years old). However, there is no specific start and end dates for both generational cohorts as they vary by source. There are also a few other names that refer to millennials and Gen-Z cohorts. For instance, some people call millennials Gen-Y, iGeneration, Net Generation, while Gen-Z is known as Post millennials, Gen Tech, Post Generation and Digital Natives. According to McQueen (2010), Generation Y born between the early 1980s and the late 1990s has certainly caused a stir in recent years and is facing the challenge of understanding and engaging a generation who have essentially grown up in a new era. Indeed, other terms of millennials and Gen-Z reflect their characteristics which were born in the era of technological diversity. Therefore, millennials have become the largest generational cohort in the workplace with more personal time off and looking for remote working opportunities (Farhan & Serpa, 2021).

Millennials and Gen-Z had diverse behaviour as compared with previous generations. According to Galdames and Guihen (2022), millennials are the largest segment in the workforce which has different levels of commitment ranging from professional-level commitments to low-level commitments in the workplace. Meanwhile, most of the Gen-Z are students either they are college students or high school students. The oldest of the Gen-Z are just entering the workforce as employees or entrepreneurs. Both generations are highly educated, responsible and tech-savvy compared to the previous generations. Millennials and Gen-Z share a few characteristics regarding their concern for sustainable and ethical products. As information is at their fingertips, they tend to weigh the pros and cons of every product and service, and compare extensively before making the final purchase decision. For instance, they will prefer sustainable retail practices during shopping as it will help preserve nature and enhance well-being (Mishra et al., 2022).

In the context of the banking sector, millennials in India recognise that their banking behaviour directly impacts the environment and often use digital banking to support environmental protection strategies (Tiwari, 2023). Millennials are more likely to invest in products and services that could bring positive outcomes which go beyond profit (Ed Grattan, 2019). At the same time, Gen-Z were also interested in practicing socially responsible investment (SRI) because they wanted to promote sustainable practices and values through a choice of financial instruments (Chen et al., 2019). The younger generation, aged 27 years old, considered in the millennials and Gen-Z cohorts, were considering the use of ethical banking in their new phase of life after university (Bayer et al., 2019). Their consideration of ethical banking are driven by their aims to help lift people out of poverty and protect the environment.

3 Ethical Banking

Ethical banking is a new form of financial business that goes beyond the economic return of traditional banking. Ethical banking has no uniform concept as it varies widely between nations and sources. Instead, social, ethical, green, environmental, ecological, alternative, sustainable development and solidarity banking and finance were arbitrarily employed in past studies to refer to the same reality (Chew et al., 2016; DeClerck, 2009). Ethical banking refers to the bank or financial institution that embeds economic, social and environmental in its business model. In this view, ethical banking is a type of financial intermediation that creates new economic ties based on social solidarity and environmental protection (Martínez et al., 2021). In short, ethical banking refers to a decision made by banks to provide products and services to customers who consider the environmental and social impact in addition to the financial return of their actions.

The first incarnation of the establishment of an ethical bank was started in 1986 where Adriaan Deking Dura, Dieter Brüll, Lex Bos and Rudolf Mees started researching on sustainability (Triodos Bank, n.d.). The first ethical bank known as Triodos Bank was established in the Netherlands in 1980. Triodos Bank aims to help savers who want a more compassionate and sustainable society fund social, environmental and cultural groups (Climent, 2018). As for now, Triodos Bank has actively implemented in six European countries with over EURO 15 billions of assets (Triodos Bank, n.d.). Figure 1 illustrates the history of Triodos Bank since inception until 2013.

Indeed, ethical banks are independent banks such as Triodos Bank, GLS Bank, ShoreBank, Cooperative Bank and Charity Bank. Nowadays, banking institutions around the globe have adopted ethical banking in their business model. For instance,

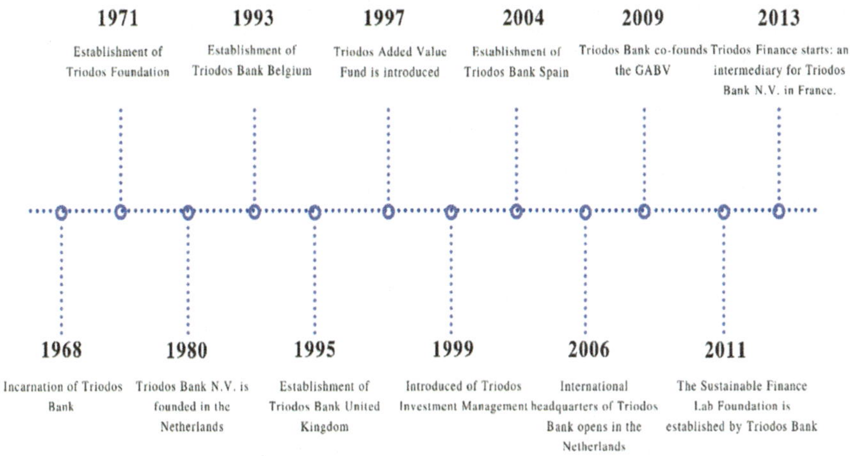

Fig. 1 The development of Triodos Bank (*Source* Adapted from Triodos Bank [n.d.])

banks in Pakistan practice green banking to reduce the impact of the carbon footprint on the environment by enhancing the adoption of online banking (Rehman et al., 2021).

ASEAN countries are also implementing ethical banking practices in their business model. For example, Bank Indonesia is scaling up the utilisation of Sustainable Financing Instrument in their business model to preserve the environment and enhance the society. The development of an ethical bank aiming to have a fairer financial system led to the establishment of the Global Alliance for Banking on Value (GABV) in 2009. The members of GABV operate their business model based on Principle of Value-Based Banking (see Fig. 2) to make sure the banking systems are transparent and support the economic, social and environmental sustainability (GABV, n.d.).

3.1 Ethical Banking in Malaysia

As for the Malaysian banking industry, ethical banking practices have been implemented by a wide range of products and services either in conventional or Islamic banking practices. Maybank Berhad has been recognised as the first sustainable bank in Malaysia, emphasising the 3Ps (Planet, People and Profit) in their business model. They also committed to a sustainable agenda by integrating it into their risk management, investment and philanthropy (Tan et al., 2017). In 2020, over RM69 billion was contributed by Maybank under their sustainability plan to uplift the community during the COVID-19 pandemic (Maybank, 2020). As part of the M25 sustainability plan (see Fig. 3), Maybank Berhad committed to uplifting their sustainability plan by emphasising four ESG commitments (see Fig. 4).

Fig. 2 Overview of principle of value based-banking (*Source* Adapted from Global Alliances for Banking on Values [n.d.])

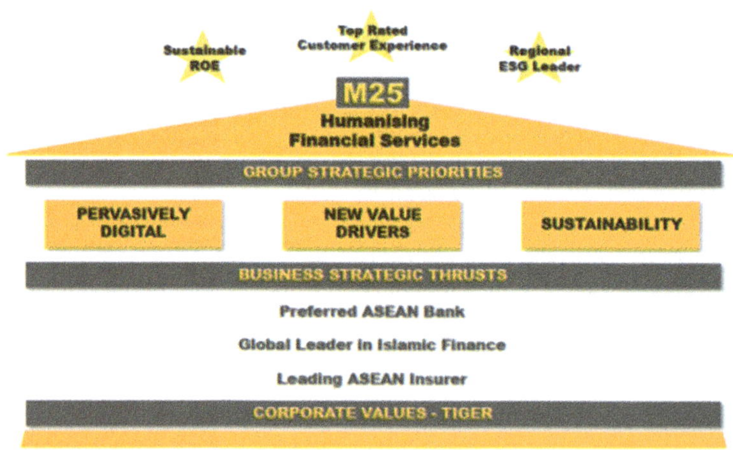

Fig. 3 Overview of Maybank M25 strategy plan (*Source* Maybank Press Release [2021])

In addition, Bank Islam Malaysia Berhad (BIMB) introduced BangKIT Microfinance to provide proprietary microfinance to less capable segments of society that aim to grow their business (BIMB, 2020). CIMB Islamic Bank also offered products to serve less capable segments, e.g., iTekad for micro-entrepreneurs among B40 and asnaf to help them generate sustainable income (CIMB, 2020). Besides, HSBC Islamic Bank launched their first ESG Islamic Structured Product in the Malaysian market, in line with Bank Negara Malaysia's (BNM) Value-Based Intermediation (VBI) initiative.

VBI initiative is a guidance document introduced by BNM to strengthen the roles and impact of Islamic finance in their current corporate environment (Ismail

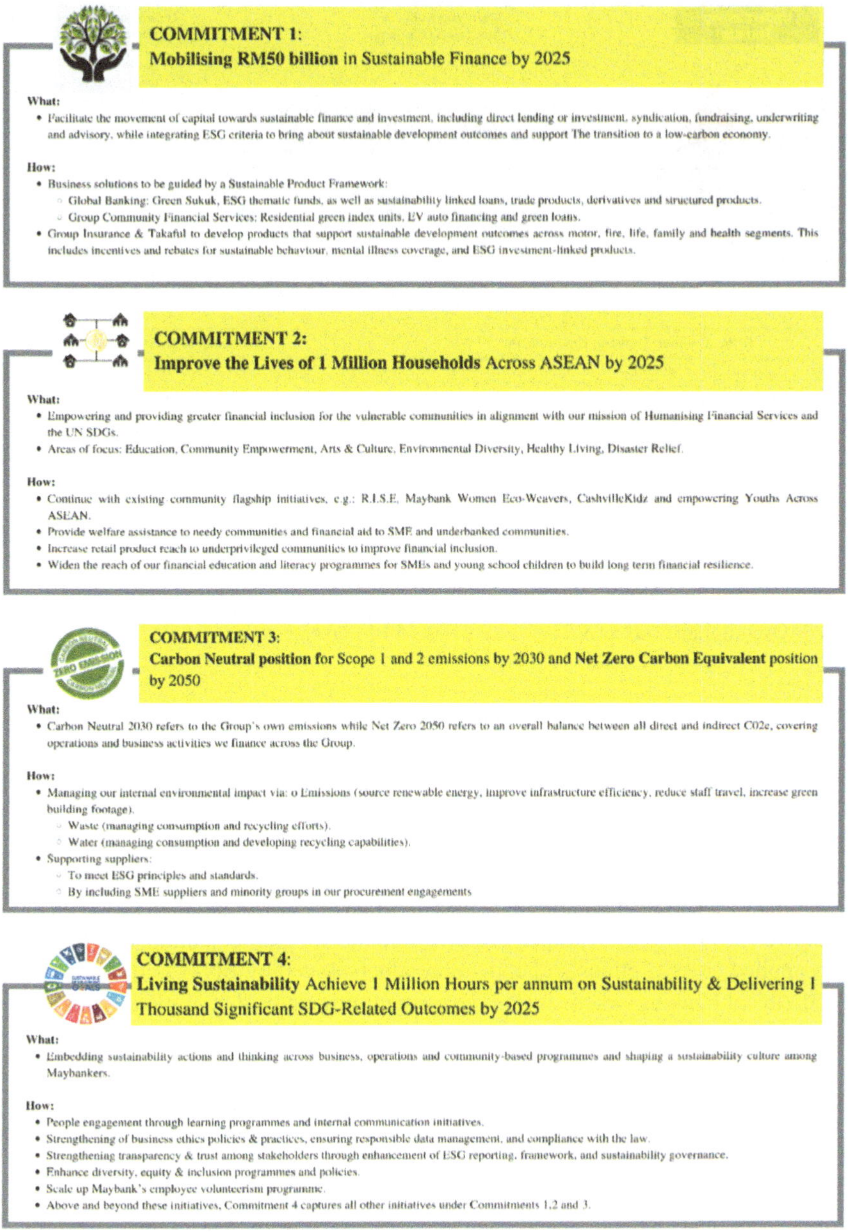

Fig. 4 Maybank ESG commitments (*Source* Adapted from Maybank Group Investor Day; Sustainability [2021])

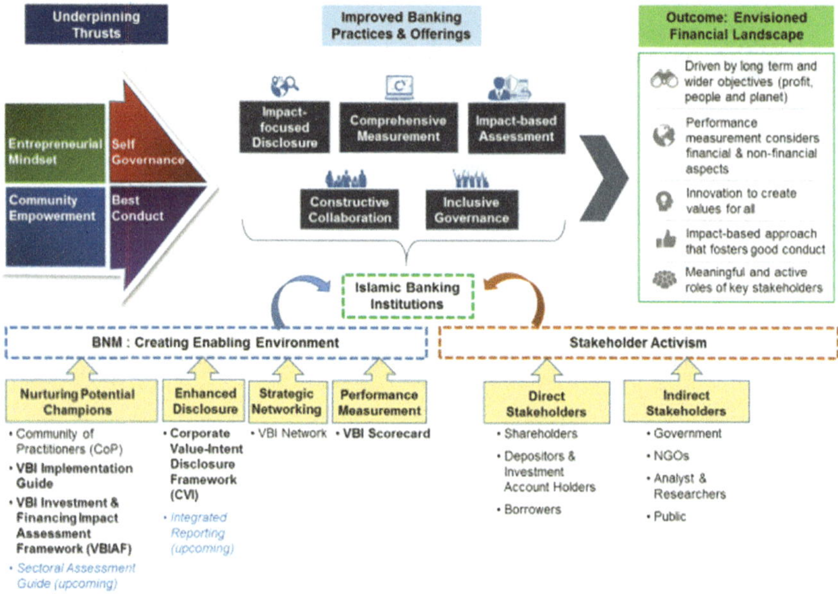

Fig. 5 Overall framework of VBI (*Source* BNM's VBI Implementation Guide [2018])

et al., 2020). Currently, 15 Community of Practitioners (CoPs) have implemented the VBI framework (see Fig. 5) in their business model. From 2017 to 2020, Islamic banks disbursed a total of RM94.2 billion towards VBI financing (AIBIM, 2020). This shows that the VBI framework has become eminent in connecting banking business processes with ethical standards. Thus, the wider adoption of VBI among financial institutions will enhance more ethical and responsible finance (BNM, 2022). Other than VBI, ethical banking practices in Malaysia are undertaken based on bank initiatives as there is no proper policy guideline for implementing it. The banks also applied code of ethics and code of conducts issued by BNM in order to set up good ethical banking practices and have sound principles that guide all employees (Maybank, n.d.).

4 Ethical Banking Behaviour

Ethical banking behaviour is demonstrated if people become a customer of an ethical bank. In a study in India, the attitude had been found to be the most significant factor influencing customers to adopt sustainable banking (Taneja & Ali, 2021). Moreover, Bryson et al. (2016) had highlighted a positive relationship between collectivism, environmental concern, perceived consumer integrity and attitude towards customer intention to use green banking. In another study, Bayer et al. (2019) examined the younger generation's ethical banking intention using the EDM model and confirmed that concern and a low level of scepticism encourage the customer to switch to ethical banking products and services in the future.

The intention is always debated as the best predictor of behaviour among customers. Bayer et al. (2019) further indicate that the relationship between intention and ethical banking behaviour is vital for the EDM model. Customers, especially millennials and Gen-Z, engage in ethical banking will drive future customer sentiments and preferences over the next decade. Therefore, it is important to understand these cohorts' ethical banking behaviour and preference so that the banks could provide better products and services for customers.

5 Factors Influencing Ethical Banking Behaviour Among Millennials and Gen-Z in Malaysia

This study extended the Ethical Decision Making (EDM) model (see Fig. 6) developed by Bayer et al. (2019) and Rest (1986) by additionally including essential factors. Rest's model consists of awareness, judgement, intention and behaviour which will be the main chain process for the EDM model. Meanwhile, Bayer's model consists of perceived consumer effectiveness (PCE), concern, scepticism, information, moral intensity, social context, neutralisation, reputation, service quality, convenience and economic benefit. Motivated by millennials and Gen-Z uniqueness as well as customers' preferences towards banking services in Malaysia, technology-related factors, religious values and ethical obligations were envisaged throughout this study. Figure 6 presents the modified ethical banking framework developed in this study.

The result from the structural model assessment discovered that concern, information, scepticism, ethical banking awareness, ethical banking judgement, service

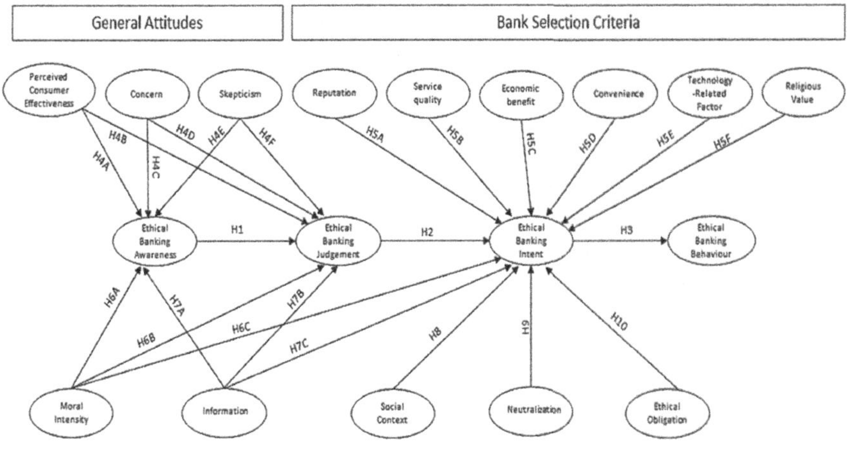

Fig. 6 Modified ethical banking framework (*Source* Zahari et al. [2022])

quality, convenience, religious value, social context, ethical obligation and ethical banking intention significantly and positively influence different stages of the EDM process to involve in ethical banking (see Table 1). However, PCE, reputation, economic benefit, technology-related factors, moral intensity and neutralisation provide insignificant relationship with the EDM process.

In the first stage of making an ethical decision concern, information and scepticism were found to have a significant positive relationship. Knowledge regarding the topic will help customers better understand the products, which may lead to a high level of awareness (Sulaiman et al., 2022). Customers among millennials and Gen-Z who receive sufficient and reliable information will be more concerned about the impact of their decision to participate in ethical banking products and services. Thus, it will lead to the enhancement of ethical banking awareness among both generations.

Interestingly, it was discovered that scepticism had a noteworthy and positive influence on the level of awareness regarding ethical banking among the millennial and Gen-Z. The discovery of this phenomenon was surprising, given previous research had emphasised a negative correlation between scepticism and awareness. This might be explained by the high level of interest that millennials and Gen-Z exhibit (Goldgehn, 2004) and their passion of learning new things (Vieira et al., 2020). The younger generations exhibit a notable degree of scepticism regarding ethical banking, which tends to heighten their understanding once they have comprehended the underlying business model of ethical banking.

Meanwhile, in the second stage of the EDM model, only awareness and concern significantly affect the ethical banking judgement. A possible explanation for this might be that nowadays, recognising ethical issues among both generations improves their ability to judge the advantage and disadvantages of their decision-making to be involved in ethical banking.

In the second stage of the EDM model, judgement, service quality, convenience, social context, religious value and ethical obligation had highlighted the significant and positive influence on ethical banking intention. The positive relationship between judgement and intention may be due to relativism and idealism (Arli et al., 2014) that develops from the awareness of millennials and Gen-Z. Secondly, service quality tends to be the most prominent aspect of the bank selection criteria for any service industry's success. This is due to the provision of efficient products, customer relations, communication techniques and bank record transactions. In contrast, in terms of convenience, various ethical banking products and services, time of services and the incorporation of technology in the ethical banking business model attract customers to adopt ethical banking behaviour in the future.

Concerning the religious value, in Malaysia, Islamic banking conforms to the ethical banking criteria, which solely focus on profit-maximisation (Musa et al., 2020) to enhance sustainable development goals (SDGs). This relationship indicates that customers of both generations with solid religious values were more confident about the advantage of ethical banking and would consider practicing it in the future. Millennials and Gen-Z are optimistic that obeying God's rules will bring positive outcomes to the society and environment.

Table 1 Summary of significant and positive factors of the EDM model

Factors	Explanation	Supporting literature
Ethical banking Awareness		
Concern	Concern refers to the level of interest and ethical/ sustainable/social/green consciousness	De Pelsmacker and Janssens (2007), Yadav and Pathak (2017), and Ye et al. (2020)
Scepticism	Customer's distrust of the ethical value delivered by the ethical bank	–
Information	Information comprises the category of knowledge, quantity and quality of the information or knowledge, and ethical cognitive effort	Papaoikonomou et al. (2011) and Bayer et al. (2019)
Ethical Banking Judgment		
Awareness	Person's recognition of ethical aspects in ethical banks	Rest (1986), Deng (2015), Martinez and Jaeger (2016)
Concern	Concern refers to the level of interest and ethical/ sustainable/social/green consciousness	De Pelsmacker and Janssens (2007) and Bayer et al. (2019)
Ethical Banking Intent		
Judgment	Individual assessment of ethical or unethical actions or behaviours	Rest (1986), Agag (2019), and Bayer et al. (2019)
Service Quality	Service quality include the degree of responsiveness of their services, the competence of employees as well as reliability of the services	Lymperopoulos et al. (2012), Khan et al. (2015), and Nisha (2016)
Convenience	Convenience comprises the aspect that makes customers comfortable and easier to access with banking institutions	Khare et al. (2012), Patterson and McEachern (2018), and Iqbal et al. (2018)
Religious Value	The role of religion in influencing individual's decision and activities	Bukhari et al. (2019), Alsaad et al. (2020), and Janah et al. (2020)
Social Context	People's/organization influence on the customer to decide whether they approve/disapprove to use the specific product	Iqbal et al. (2018), Bayer et al. (2019), and Taneja and Ali (2021)
Ethical Obligation	Individual's internalised ethical rules, which reflect personal beliefs about appropriate behaviour (S	Shaw and Shiu (2002), Haines et al. (2008), and Tullani et al. (2018)
Ethical Banking Behaviour		
Intention	The intention of millennials and Gen-Z to engage with ethical banking in banking institutions	Rest (1986), Djafarova and Foots (2022), and Kashif et al. (2021)

Source Authors' own compilation (2022)

Regarding social context, the suggestions and opinion of the reference group, especially family members, close friends, co-workers, neighbours, colleagues and promotion by the bank and the government influence their decision whether to adopt ethical banking or not in the future. A significant positive social influence aided by word-of-mouth will increase customers' awareness of ethical banking and enhance their intention to engage in ethical banking in the future. On the ethical obligation, a strong ethical obligation from customers' social and environmental values guides them in their decision to be involved in ethical banking, which brings to the enchantment of the ethical banking intention (Tullani et al., 2018).

Lastly, the ethical banking intent was found to influence ethical banking behaviour among millennials and Gen-Z. These generation cohorts would shift from traditional banking to ethical banking if they feel the products bring positive outcomes in the future. Millennials in Malaysia intend to shift their current purchasing behaviour to ethical products after exploring the motivation and advantages (Hasbullah et al., 2022). This research has confirmed that ethical banking intention has been marked as a highly significant antecedent of ethical banking behaviour among millennials and Gen-Z in Malaysia. Hence, with regard to the main objective of this study, it can be concluded that concern, information, scepticism, ethical banking awareness, ethical banking judgement, service quality, convenience, religious value, social context, ethical obligation and ethical banking intention were the contributing factors that influence millennials and Gen-Z to engage in ethical banking behaviour in Malaysia.

6 The Implication of Ethical Banking Behaviour Among Millennials and Gen-Z

Information and concern influence ethical banking awareness. Thus, banks need to focus on increasing information and marketing campaigns to promote the use of ethical banking, especially among potential customers. Therefore, consumer education programs are critical to raising their knowledge of ethical banking's particular traits and the wide variety of financial products. While we are in the era of technological diversity, banks and policymakers need to utilise social media to broaden the awareness of ethical banking. The provision of transparent, sufficient, and reliable information pertaining to ethical banking would significantly reduce the prevailing skepticism among millennials and Gen-Z on this practice.

Additionally, banks must manage their target customers through their service quality and convenience of ethical banking services. The variation of products, high responsiveness, reliability, good communication skill and ease of use was the prominent factors that promote the service quality and the convenience of ethical banking to build a firm intention of ethical banking behaviour among customers. Banks should focus on providing the ease of use of products and services in the Malaysian context to meet customers' specific needs, especially among millennials and Gen-Z. In short, ethical banks should offer excellent service quality and provide convenient banking services to enhance ethical banking intent and satisfy the needs of their clients.

On the other side, religious values have significant effects on ethical banking as well, which suggests that millennials and Gen-Z are more confident in their commitment to ethical banking as a result of religious values. The concept of ethical banking has always been closely associated with Islamic banking. The preservation of the economy, society, and nature is a central objective of ethical banking, as emphasised in the maqasid shariah framework. This framework is rooted in the principle of conserving life, intellect, posterity, and wealth. Thus, the business model of ethical banking needs to comply with Shariah and provides tools and services that reinforce religious values. In order to enhance ethical obligation among millennials and Gen-Z, the banking sector must embrace the ethical aspects in every part of their future direction and business model to attract both generations to be involved in the products and services provided by the banks.

By understanding millennials' and Gen-Z ethical banking behaviour, banking institutions can develop ethical banking products and services that meet both generations' preferences, which may help them increase their market share of ethical banking. In addition, at the regulatory level, a national regulatory framework by Bank Negara Malaysia (BNM) is crucial to driving the implementation of ethical financing standards to make a significant difference in serving the banking industry.

7 Conclusion and Policy Implication

The Millennials and Gen-Z ethical banking behaviour have highlighted a significant impact on the banking sectors, enhancing them to adopt ethical banking in their products and practices in the future. This chapter provides an overview of factors influencing ethical banking behaviour among millennials and Gen-Z in Malaysia. It supports the effectiveness of Rest's EDM model in explaining millennials and Gen-Z behaviour towards ethical banking in Malaysia and thus, has contributed theoretically to the literature. Furthermore, Bayer's holistic EDM model and additional variables included by the authors (religious value, ethical obligation and technology-related factors) were also envisaged. The result of the analysis had identified concern, scepticism, information, service quality, convenience, religious value, social context, ethical obligation, ethical banking awareness, ethical banking judgement and ethical banking intent as the factors influencing ethical banking behaviour among millennials and Gen-Z in Malaysia.

Hence, by understanding a broader spectrum of the millennials and Gen-Z ethical banking behaviour, banks can adjust their marketing approaches, products and services to keep pace with these generation preferences. Given that both generations will drive the banking industry in the next era, thus, this information will help the policymakers and industry players to draft a more holistic approach for the development of ethical banking in Malaysia and remain relevant among target customers. Consequently, developing ethical banking practices in Malaysian banking services will help promote sustainability and contribute to a prosperous, inclusive, and sustainable Malaysia.

Acknowledgements We want to thank the Faculty of Economics and Management (FEP), Universiti Kebangsaan Malaysia (UKM), for the research grant EP-2021-009 (Conceptualising and Profiling Ethical Banking Behaviour among Millennials and Gen-Z in Malaysia).

References

Agag, G. (2019). Understanding the determinants of guests' behaviour to use green P2P accommodation. *International Journal of Contemporary Hospitality Management, 31*(9), 3417–3446.

Association of Islamic Banking and Financial Institutions Malaysia (AIBIM). (2020). *Value-based intermediation preview report 2017–2020*. https://aibim.com/contents/upload/Inaugural-Islamic-Banking-Industry-Value-based-Intermediation-Preview-Report-2017-2020.pdf

Alsaad, A., Saif-Alyousfi, A. Y. H., & Elrehail, H. (2020). Religiosity, idealism, and ethical consumption: The mediating effect of perceived customer effectiveness and moral obligation. *Journal of Social Marketing, 11*(1), 25–43.

Arli, D., Tjiptono, F., & Winit, W. (2014). Consumer ethics among young consumers in developing countries: A cross-national study. *Social Responsibility Journal, 11*(3), 449–466.

Bank Islam Malaysia Berhad (BIMB). (2020). *BangKIT eBrochures*. https://www.bankislam.com/wp-content/uploads/BangKit-eBrochure-24.11.pdf

Bank Negara Malaysia (BNM). (2018). *Implementation guide for value-based intermediation*. https://www.bnm.gov.my/documents/20124/761682/Implementation+Guide+for+Value-based+Intermediation.pdf

Bank Negara Malaysia (BNM). (2022). *Financial sector blueprint 2022–2026*. https://www.bnm.gov.my/documents/20124/5915429/fsb3_en_book.pdf

Bayer, S., Gimpel, H., & Sarikaya, S. (2019). Bank customers' decision-making process in choosing between ethical and conventional banking: A survey-based examination. *Journal of Business Economics, 89*(6), 655–697.

Bryson, D., Atwal, G., & Dave, K. (2016). Antecedents of intention to use green banking strategic change: Briefings in entrepreneurial. *Finance, 25*(5), 551–567.

Bukhari, S. A. A., Hashim, F., & Amran, A. (2019). Determinants of green banking adoption: A theoretical framework. *KnE Social Sciences*, 1–14.

Chen, M. H., Chen, B. H., & Chi, C. G. (2019). Socially responsible investment by Gen-Z: A cross-cultural study of Taiwanese and American investors. *Journal of Hospitality Marketing & Management, 28*(3), 334–350.

Chew, B. C., Tan, L. H., & Hamid, S. R. (2016). Ethical banking in practice: A closer look at the Cooperative Bank UK PLC. *Qualitative Research in Financial Markets, 8*(1), 70–91.

CIMB Islamic Bank. (2020). *Itekad 2.0 introduced to extend support for the Asnaf and B40 communities*. https://www.cimbislamic.com/en/newsroom/2021/itekad-2-0-introduced-to-extend-support-for-the-asnaf-and-b40-communities.html

Climent, F. (2018). Ethical versus conventional banking: A case study. *Sustainability, 10*(7), 2152.

DeClerck. (2009). Ethical banking. In *Ethical prospects: Economic, society and environment* (pp. 209–228). Springer.

Deloitte. (2020). *The Deloitte Global Millennial Survey 2020*. Deloitte Global. https://www2.deloitte.com/content/dam/Deloitte/global/Documents/About-Deloitte/deloitte-2020-millennial-survey.pdf

Deng, X. (2015). Understanding Chinese consumers' ethical purchasing decision-making process: A combination of qualitative and quantitative study. *Geoforum, 67*, 204–213.

Department of Statistics Malaysia (DOSM). (2021). *Current population estimates Malaysia*. https://newss.statistics.gov.my/newss-portalx/ep/epDataRequestForm.seam

DeVaney, S. A. (2015). Understanding the millennial generation. *Journal of Financial Service Professionals*, *69*(6), 11–145.

De Pelsmacker, P., & Janssens, W. A. (2007). Model for fair trade buying behaviour: The role of perceived quantity and quality of information and of product-specific attitudes. *Journal of Business Ethics*, *75*(2), 361–380. https://doi.org/10.1007/s10551-006-9259-2

Djafarova, E., & Foots, S. (2022). Exploring ethical consumption of generation Z: Theory of planned behaviour. *Young Consumers, 23*(3), 413–431.

Ed Grattan. (2019). *Who are the 'ethical natives', and how will they change the world?* Triodos Bank. https://www.triodos.co.uk/articles/2018/who-are-the-ethical-natives-and-how-will-they-change-the-world

Farhan, B. Y., & Serpa, S. (2021). Customising leadership practices for the millennial workforce: A conceptual framework. *Cogent Social Sciences, 7*, 1. https://doi.org/10.1080/23311886.2021.1930865

Galdames, S., & Guihen, L. (2022) Millennials and leadership: A systematic literature review. *Total Quality Management & Business Excellence, 33*(1–2), 146–162. https://doi.org/10.1080/14783363.2020.1812380

Global Alliances for Banking on Value (GABV). (n.d.). *Meets the global alliances for banking on values*. https://www.gabv.org/about-us/

Goldgehn, L. A. (2004). Generation who, what, Y? What you need to know about Generation Y. *International Journal of Educational Advancement, 5*(1), 24–34.

Haines, R. P., Street, M. D., & Haines, D. (2008). The influence of perceived importance of an ethical issue on moral judgment, moral obligation, and moral intent. *Journal of Business Ethics, 81*, 387–399.

Hasbullah, N. N., Sulaiman, Z., Mas'od, A., & Ahmad Sugiran, H. S. (2022). Drivers of sustainable apparel purchase intention: An empirical study of Malaysian millennial consumers. *Sustainability, 14*(4), 1945.

Institute for Capital Market Research Malaysia (ICMR). (2021). *The rise of Millennial & Gen Z Investors: Trends, opportunities, and challenges for Malaysia*. https://www.icmr.my/wp-content/uploads/2021/10/FINAL-VERSION-The-Rise-of-Millennial-and-Gen-Z-Investors.pdf

Iqbal, M., Nisha, N., Rifat, A., & Panda, P. (2018). Exploring client perceptions and intentions in emerging economies: The case of green banking technology. *International Journal of Asian Business and Information Management (IJABIM), 9*(3), 14–34.

Ismail, A. Y., Hameed, L. B. M., Suhaimi, A. F. M., Jamaludin, N. I., & Shahimi, S. (2020). Value based intermediation and interconnection of sustainable development goals in Islamic banking framework. *International Journal of Islamic Economics and Finance Research, 3*(1), 45–56.

Janah, N., Medias, F., & Pratiwi, E. K. (2020). The intention of religious leaders to use Islamic banking services: The case of Indonesia. *Journal of Islamic Marketing, 12*(9), 1786–1800.

Kashif, U., Hong, C., Naseem, S., Khan, W. A., Akram, M. W., Rehman, K. U., & Andleeb, S. (2021). Assessment of millennial organic food consumption and moderating role of food neophobia in Pakistan. *Current Psychology, 42*(1), 1504–1515.

Khan, Z., Ferguson, D., & Pérez, A. (2015). Customer responses to CSR in the Pakistani banking industry. *International Journal of Bank Marketing, 33*(4), 471–493.

Khare, A., Mishra, A., & Singh, A. B. (2012). Indian customers' attitude towards trust and convenience dimensions of internet banking. *International Journal of Services and Operations Management, 11*(1), 107–122.

Lymperopoulos, C., Chaniotakis, I. E., & Soureli, M. (2012). A model of green bank marketing. *Journal of Financial Services Marketing, 17*(2), 177–186.

Martinez, L. F., & Jaeger, D. S. (2016). Ethical decision making in counterfeit purchase situations: The influence of moral awareness and moral emotions on moral judgment and purchase intentions. *Journal of Consumer Marketing, 33*(3), 213–223.

Martínez, M. D. C., Martín-Cervantes, P. A., & Peña Rodríguez, S. (2021). Ethical banking and poverty alleviation banking: The two sides of the same solidary coin. *Sustainability (Switzerland), 13*(21), 11977.
Maybank Press Release. (2021). *Maybank outlines sustainability commitments to spur growth and drive change for better future.* https://www.maybank.com/iwov-resources/corporate_new/document/my/en/pdf/corporate-news-release/2021/press_release_maybank_outlines_sustainability_commitments.pdf
Maybank. (2020). *Maybank sustainability report 2020.* https://www.maybank.com/iwov-resources/corporate_new/document/my/en/pdf/annual-report/2021/Maybank_Sustainability_Report_2020.pdf
Maybank. (2021). *Maybank group investor day: Sustainability.* https://www.maybank.com/iwov-resources/corporate_new/document/my/en/pdf/presentations-and-webcasts/2021/Maybank_Investor_Day-Sustainability_v2.pdf
Maybank. (n.d.). *Maybank group code of ethics & conduct.* https://www.maybank.com/iwov-resources/corporate_new/document/my/en/pdf/Maybank-Group-Code-of-Ethics-Conduct.pdf
McQueen, M. (2010). *The new rules of engagement: A guide to understanding & connecting with Generation Y.* Morgan James Publishing.
Mishra, S., Shukla, Y., Malhotra, G., Chatterjee, R., & Rana, J. (2022, February). Millennials' self-identity and intention to purchase sustainable products. *Australasian Marketing Journal.* https://doi.org/10.1177/18393349221075026
Morgan Stanley. (2019). *Morgan Stanley survey finds investor enthusiasm for sustainable investing at an all-time high.* https://www.morganstanley.com/press-releases/morgan-stanley-survey-finds-investor-enthusiasm-for-sustainable
Musa, M. A., Sukor, M. E. A., Ismail, M. N., & Elias, M. R. F. (2020). Islamic business ethics and practices of Islamic banks: Perceptions of Islamic bank employees in Gulf cooperation countries and Malaysia. *Journal of Islamic Accounting and Business Research, 11*(5), 1009–1031.
Nisha, N. (2016). Exploring the dimensions of mobile banking service quality: Implications for the banking sector. *International Journal of Business Analytics (IJBAN), IGI Global, 3*(3), 60–76.
Papaoikonomou, E., Ryan, G., & Ginieis, M. (2011). Towards a holistic approach of the attitude-behaviour gap in ethical consumer behaviours: Empirical evidence from Spain. *International Advance in Economic Research, 17*(1), 77–88.
Patterson, Z., & McEachern, M. G. (2018). Financial service providers: Does it matter if banks don't behave ethically? *International Journal of Consumer Studies, 42*(5), 1–12.
Rehman, A., Ullah, I., Afridi, F.-A., Ullah, Z., Zeeshan, M., Hussain, A., & Rahman, H. U. (2021). Adoption of green banking practices and environmental performance in Pakistan: A demonstration of structural equation modelling. *Environment, Development and Sustainability, 23*(9), 13200–13220.
Rest, J. R. (1986). *Moral development: Advances in research and theory.* Praeger.
Shaw, D., & Shiu, E. (2002). An assessment of ethical obligation and self-identity in ethical consumer decision-making: A structural equation modelling approach. *International Journal of Consumer Studies, 26*(4), 286–293.
Sulaiman, Z., Ahmad Sugiran, H. S., Hasbullah, N. N., Mas'od, A., Hashim, S., & Bradley, D. A. (2022). Public awareness of consumer products containing radioactive materials: Empirical evidence from Malaysia. *International Journal of Environmental Research and Public Health, 19*(4), 2326.
Tan, L. H., Chew, B. C., & Hamid, S. R. (2017). Service innovation in Malaysian banking industry towards sustainable competitive advantage through environmentally and socially practices. *Procedia—Social and Behavioral Sciences, 9*(4), 359–381.
Taneja, S., & Ali, L. (2021). Determinants of customers' intentions towards environmentally sustainable banking: Testing the structural model. *Journal of Retailing and Consumer Services, 59*(March), 102418.
Tiwari, P. (2023). Influence of the green brand image on the green word of mouth of millennials: A mediation study on banks. *Public Organization Review, 23*, 59–78

Triodos Bank. (n.d.). *About us*. https://www.triodos.com/about-us

Tullani, H., Saha, R., & Dahiya, R. (2018). Green innovation and ethical responsibility: Do they improve customer's green purchase intentions? *International Journal of Sustainable Entrepreneurship and Corporate Social Responsibility, 3*(1), 35–52.

Vieira, J., Frade, R., Ascenso, R., Prates, I., & Martinho, F. (2020). Generation Z and key-factors on e-commerce: A study on the Portuguese tourism sector. *Administrative Sciences, 10*(103), 1–17.

Yadav, R., & Pathak, G. S. (2017). Determinants of consumers' green purchase behaviour in a developing nation: Applying and extending the theory of planned behaviour. *Ecological Economics, 134*, 114–122.

Ye, Y., Lu, X., & Lu. T. (2020). Examining the spillover effect of sustainable consumption on microloan repayment: A big data-based research. *Information & Management, 59*(5), 103288.

Zahari, S. A., Shahimi, S., & Alma'amun, S. (2022). *Factors influencing ethical banking behaviour among millennials and Gen-Z in Malaysia* (Unpublished). Research paper, Master of Islamic Economics, Faculty of Economics and Management, Universiti Kebangsaan Malaysia.

SPRINGER NATURE

GPSR Compliance

The European Union's (EU) General Product Safety Regulation (GPSR) is a set of rules that requires consumer products to be safe and our obligations to ensure this.

If you have any concerns about our products, you can contact us on ProductSafety@springernature.com

In case Publisher is established outside the EU, the EU authorized representative is:

Springer Nature Customer Service Center GmbH
Europaplatz 3
69115 Heidelberg, Germany

The manufacturer's authorised representative in the EU is Springer Nature Customer Service Centre GmbH, Europaplatz 3, 69115 Heidelberg, Germany. If you have any concerns regarding our products, please contact ProductSafety@springernature.com

Printed and bound by CPI Group (UK) Ltd, Croydon, CR0 4YY
30/09/2026
02225324-0001